Eva Cristina Hoffman Jedruch was born in the city of Lwów, Poland, months before the outbreak of the Second World War. After the war she lived in England, Argentina, and since 1969 in the USA. She is a chemical engineer by profession, graduate of the state university of Buenos Aires. She married Dr Jacek Jedruch, nuclear physicist and a Renaissance man, a parliamentary historian. Since 1986, Eva has lived close to New York and worked for the German chemical company, BASF, as an international marketing manager. Widowed, after retirement she enrolled at Drew University in Madison, New Jersey, in the Arts & Letters program, earning a D.Litt. (Doctor of Letters) degree in medieval studies. Eva speaks five languages. She is a board member of the International Commission for the History of Representative and Parliamentary Institutions (ICHRPI). Her two cats, Fritz and Janey, make wonderful companions.

To my mother, Zofia Hoffman, my soulmate, who taught me the meaning of honour and compassion.

Eva Cristina Hoffman Jedruch

CROSSING THE BRIDGES

FROM LVOV ACROSS THE STEPPES OF ASIA
TO LONDON'S DOODLEBUGS: ONE WOMAN'S
WARTIME ODYSSEY

AUSTIN MACAULEY PUBLISHERS™

LONDON * CAMBRIDGE * NEW YORK * SHARJAH

A CIP catalogue record for this title is available from the British Library.

ISBN 9781528985604 (Paperback)
ISBN 9781528985611 (Hardback)
ISBN 9781528985628 (ePub e-book)

www.austinmacauley.com

First Published (2021)
Austin Macauley Publishers Ltd
25 Canada Square
Canary Wharf
London
E14 5LQ

After the Polish edition of my mother's wartime story was published in Poland in 2012, several English and American acquaintances voiced their frustration about the inability to read it and suggested that I translate it. However, attempts at literal translation proved futile. Certain aspects of this story, abundantly clear to the Polish readership because of our shared history, would have been mystifying to many non-Poles. Also, the Polish version contains a number of regional expressions, for a touch of local colour, that would be untranslatable into English. As a result, I opted to write the story from scratch and from a different perspective, and so a new book was born. My thanks go to many people, friends and colleagues, who not only encouraged me to keep writing but gave their time to read the finished manuscript and offered helpful comments.

As for encouragement, none was more persistent than my wonderful friend, Brigitte Sczerbak, who was always there when my optimism flagged. My ICHRPI colleagues, Dr Alastair Mann (University of Stirling) and Dr Gerald Kohl (University of Vienna), were more than generous with their time, reviewing the text thoroughly with academic precision. Sir John Kingman read the manuscript and offered insightful observations. Dr Marion Berghahn shared with me invaluable technical pointers. And then there were my friends from the Summit College Club who were first to ask for a visual presentation of my mother's story; Molly Ball and Leslie Carson, who consistently bucked me up ever since. To all of them go my heartfelt thanks.

My deepest sense of gratitude is for those who are no longer with me: my husband, Jacek, who for many years urged me to write the memoir, even while he cheerfully consumed canned dinners. And my uncle, Dr Zbigniew Neuhoff, whose prodigious memory at the age of ninety-five contributed hundreds of hours of conversation, in spite of considerable physical and emotional stress this entailed, resulting in reams of notes that form the basis for some parts of this memoir.

Don't search for answers that no book can supply.
Memory sleeps, when it must, memory does not die.

– Jan Rostworowski

Chapter I
The Visitor. Bytom, Silesia, 1946

It was the beginning of March. The day was as dreary as only a day could be in a city filled with coke and smoke. The walls of the house across the street were smeared with coal dust and patches of dirty snow covered the pavement. On the street below, loaded carts brimming with coal scattered chunks of black crystals along the way, as their wheels rumbled on the cobblestones. Once the carts passed, old women and young children gathered cracked bits of coal into baskets. I asked Aunt Hania once why they were doing this. *"To keep warm,"* she muttered.

    This greyness and the bleakness streaked with soot were making me feel despondent. Above all, everything felt unbearably dull since my return from prison and back to my old self and real name. That particular day Aunt Hania went grocery shopping and left me with Mrs B., our neighbour across the landing. Her flat and ours were the only two on this floor. Mrs B., seated at the table under a single anaemic light bulb, was wrapped in a grey knit woollen shawl, dozing on and off over her game of patience. Every few minutes her head covered with strands of thinning white hair fastened with hairpins drooped, the shawl slipped off her shoulders and her spectacles slid down to the tip of her nose. But in the end, nothing ever happened because she jerked her head up just in time, pushed back the spectacles, rearranged her shawl, reached for another card in the pack, and dropped off again. So regular, like the little cuckoo bird in our clock that popped in and out every hour on the hour. Meanwhile, I was bored as I camped out on the worn-out leather sofa by the window with my doll, my legs tucked under me, waiting and waiting for Mrs B's shawl to slide to the floor, or the spectacles to fall off, or for my aunt to return with the groceries, none of which was happening soon enough.

In this sad and drowsy atmosphere, I thought of our house and the last summer spent in my native Lwów that now seemed like a faded dream. The garden around the villa, the orchard in the back with the single apple tree, its branches bent to the ground under the weight of golden reinettes, cherry trees loaded with fruit, bunches of red currants and translucent gooseberries shot through with sunrays, blue and yellow iris lined the path all the way from the garden gate to the door, and thick bushes of purple and white lilacs along the fence shielded the house from the street. I often stood on tiptoe at the balcony railing and looked over the canopy of green treetops stretching far into the distance, with roofs scattered among them, some as green as the trees themselves. That balcony was no longer there since it was blown away by two Soviet bombs that night as we huddled in the cellar. Red geraniums that bloomed on the balcony all summer long in wooden boxes, they too were gone. My uncle's black grand piano was spread across the lawn, its shattered legs pointing at the sky, crushing a small rosebush by the debris, and next to it the portrait of the canon in a lavender scarf that hung over the sitting room sofa. Now it all seemed so unreal and so very long ago.

After I returned home from prison Uncle Zbyszek forbade me to talk of my adventure. *"Just remember, not a word to anybody,"* he kept repeating, looking very stern. Such a shame, so many lovely new words that I picked up that had to go to waste. The *green border* that wasn't really green at all, just a wooden bridge covered with dirty snow, the *agent* in a felt brown hat who followed us all the way from the bridge to the railway station. And not a word about the cell where the Czech police locked me and Zofia up. Since I got back Aunt Hania had been hugging me more than ever and crying a lot, who knows why, since in the end nothing bad really happened. Except, of course, that we never made it where we were supposed to go. All this crying made me feel squeamish, I wasn't a small child any longer, I was turning eight in October. Still, she was happy when I gave her back the lovely silk scarf that she had tied around my neck before I left. She wore this scarf only for special occasions. Back in Těšín every night as I fell asleep, I squeezed it in my hand, it felt good and it still smelled of auntie's perfume. But I kept for myself the small rosary of red and white beads from the nuns. Aunt Hania kept repeating how brave I was, so it had to be true, but she got impatient with me whenever we were out in the street and I hung onto her arm and kept looking behind me. It annoyed her greatly. *"Stop turning around all the time,"* she said, *"and stop pulling my arm."* Clearly, she had no idea that the town was packed with secret agents in trench coats and brown felt hats, even in Bytom. It was bad enough that Russian soldiers with red stars on their *shapkas* roamed our streets and toted machine guns and pistols. And then there was that scary communist police, that uncle called UB,[1] eavesdropping on everybody.

Three weeks dragged by since my return from my escape "to the West" that ended in the cell in Těšín, and still no word from my mother. One day uncle said to Aunt Hania that she, my mother, would have been waiting for us where Polish troops were stationed. Well, we never got there. After all that excitement, the sight of Mrs B. snoozing over her cards was deeply unsatisfying. So here I was, curled up on the couch, waiting for my aunt to return and rescue me from the gloomy afternoon and an endless round of patience.

Suddenly, to my great relief, I heard someone knocking on the door of our flat across the landing. I sprung off the couch and rushed to peek outside before Mrs B. could shake off her drowsiness. She picked herself up from her chair slowly, untangled her shawl, and shuffled after me. I opened the door a crack. A woman in a beige coat and a brown woollen cap was standing outside. She had a travelling bag with her that I noticed right away because it was small and shiny, different from our scratched, beat-up suitcases. As I opened the door a little wider the hinges squeaked and she turned around.

"Is this Dr Neuhoff's apartment?" She asked. Forgetting the rule that I was not to speak to strangers, I blurted out: *"Yes, but auntie is out shopping, and Uncle Zbyszek is in Katowice."*

She looked at me for a brief moment biting her lip, as if undecided, then turned to Mrs B. who stood right behind me and said that she was travelling all the way from Kraków, and could she wait for them. *"On a very important matter,"* she added quickly, as she firmly picked up her travelling bag and took a step towards the door. Mrs B. hesitated, because in these times, as she was saying to Aunt Hania only the other day, you never knew who or what. Somewhat reluctantly, she stepped aside and invited her in. Back in the room, Mrs B. settled into her chair and suggested to the lady that she might take off her coat.

The woman shook her head. *"No, thank you, I'm chilled to the bone, I'd rather keep it on,"* she said, wrapping it tighter around her knees. She sat down on the couch next to me, slipping off the brown woollen cap and sweeping her

---

[1] UB: Urząd Bezpieczeństwa: Polish communist secret police, from 1945 under Jakub Berman of the Soviet Politburo.

hand across her short hair which scattered around her face. *"Very pretty,"* she nodded at my rag doll. *"What's her name?"*

"Zosia, like my mummy's."

Her eyes narrowed, as if she were straining to see something far away, although, there was nothing to see except Mrs B. and the wall behind her. I noticed that her eyes were bloodshot, like uncle's every time he returned from his trips to Katowice, except hers were green. I had never seen green eyes.

"So, you must be Ayka," she said, unexpectedly. The question threw me off, but my freshly acquired prison smarts made me wary.

"How do you know my name, ma'am?" I shot back, not very politely. She smiled.

"I am an old friend of your mummy."

With that, she turned back to Mrs B. and paid no more attention to me or to my shabby doll. I watched her from the corner of my eye and wondered whether she was another one of those people from London who visited us on and off. Uncle Zbyszek called them "occasions". Back in January, one day when he was in a meeting at the conservatory where he was offered the post of music director, a young woman popped her head into the conference room and glancing around said in a loud voice:

"I'm looking for Dr Neuhoff."

"Yes, that's me," Uncle Zbyszek answered.

"Sir, I have a message for you from your sister in London."

"Sorry, Miss, this must be a mistake. I don't have a sister in London, or anywhere else for that matter." She stared at him briefly, then silently withdrew and did not return.

"I almost gagged," Uncle Zbyszek told Aunt Hania that evening, *"after she left, there was dead silence in the room. If she was another 'occasion', she was a very stupid one. Or else perhaps she was just a plant?"*

I had no idea what a plant was, but I knew one was not supposed to say that mummy lived in London.

It was different when *pan* Adam and *pani* Zofia showed up a couple of weeks later. We just sat down to supper when we heard a soft knock on the door. That was always scary. Uncle got up to open, but waited for a moment before turning the lock. It was a habit of his. We watched him, Aunt Hania swallowing hard as her hand tightened on the edge of the table. We heard a man's voice asking for Dr Neuhoff. Then a woman's voice pitched in and after a short, muttered exchange they came into the room and introduced themselves as Adam Dydyński and Zofia Mścichowska, mummy's friends from the army they said. Aunt Hania invited them to join us for supper, they were very hungry. It was hard to believe as they sat there with us at the table that just a few days earlier they had been with my mother. I stared at them mouth wide open until uncle told me to close it. I wanted to touch them.

While they were eating, they told us why they came to Poland; he for something personal, he said, she to see her dying mother. But they intended to go back west, and I knew that meant England. After we finished eating, Aunt Hania cleared the table and Zofia stayed with her in the kitchen, while *pan* Adam remained with my uncle. As I hung around the room, I overheard him quietly saying that my mother wanted us to join her in London. They were returning the way they came, across the *green border*, he said, whatever that meant. I let out a little yelp of joy, although I was not supposed to listen to grown-up conversations. Not, when they whispered. Uncle Zbyszek threw me a warning glance, but kept talking and I heard him say that crossing the border with the child would be madness. Another occasion gone. My heart slumped into my stomach, as the lovely image that had popped up before my eyes disappeared in a puff of smoke from my uncle's cigarette. Adam murmured that if he and my aunt were not willing to come…and I didn't hear the rest. But there was a long silence, at that point Aunt Hania ordered me to bed.

"I'm not sure Zosia really meant it, but what can I do?" I heard Uncle Zbyszek say to my aunt that night. He sounded hoarse and spoke so low that I barely heard him through the crack in the door, though I normally heard everything. *"On the other hand, if indeed her mother insists that they take her…"* His voice trailed off, he did not finish the sentence and I heard no more.

Our visitors returned a few more times until one day Uncle Zbyszek told me that I would be going with *pan Adam* and *pani Zofia* to join my mother. This news was exciting beyond words, but what I didn't realise at the time was that I would be parted from him and my aunt. Over the following two weeks, Zofia drilled me into my new identity, who I was supposed to be and what my new name was. In the meantime, Aunt Hania, tight-lipped and with puffy red eyes, scurried around to equip me for the trip, which was no easy matter in those days. Somehow, she got her hands on a pair of pretty white felt boots with red leather trim. On the day of departure, I wore my grey winter coat, a thick woollen muffler around my throat over Aunt Hania's silk scarf, the one she treasured throughout all the war years, mittens, a woollen cap with a pompon, and my precious felt boots. Overnight I became Ewa Dydyńska, Adam's daughter and Zofia's niece, whose mother died during the Warsaw Uprising two years earlier.

On a frosty January morning, my uncle and aunt took me to the train station where Adam and Zofia were waiting. Aunt Hania hugged me and kissed me again and again, then turned away, and Uncle Zbyszek lifted me into the carriage. *"You must be very brave, Ayusia,"* he whispered. As I sat on the hard-wooden bench pressing my nose against the window, it finally hit me that I was leaving them. I stared at Aunt Hania, whiter than snow, and Uncle Zbyszek with his hat pulled low over his eyes and my throat got so tight I could barely swallow. The stationmaster's shrill whistle sent shivers down my spine as it pierced the air, the locomotive heaved, the train jerked with a clang, billows of steam speckled with golden sparks rushed past the window, and then my uncle and aunt became two indistinct forlorn figures on an empty platform.

It was still daylight when we reached Cieszyn. We walked from the train to the bridge on the Olza River that served as the border crossing between the Polish Cieszyn and the Czech Těšín. The border guard seemed bored and indifferent as he checked our documents and waved us on to cross the bridge to the Czech side. At the other end, we were also cleared without much fuss. Going to visit a sick relative in Těšín, Adam told the guard. He looked over our papers and nodded. He too seemed bored. Then, without any detours, we headed for the railroad station, Adam carrying one large suitcase, Zofia a small one with my things.

The cavernous hall was busy at that hour. Adam stopped at the entrance, scanned the area, then dropped the suitcase by the wall and told me to sit on it. *"Don't move from here,"* he said, *"your aunt and I will go to buy the tickets, we'll be right back."* I watched them head towards the ticket booth, then melt into the crowd and disappear from sight. As I sat on the beat-up suitcase in my grey coat and white felt boots, people hurrying by turned to look at me, some smiled, some frowned, an elderly man stared, grimaced, shook his head and made me feel like some ugly bug. As minutes ticked away and Zofia and Adam were nowhere to be seen, I began to panic. The strange world was closing in on me and grew menacing. What if they didn't come back? What if they got lost? What if they couldn't find me? What if… I looked around frantically and then I saw them coming towards me, but as they got closer, I noticed that somebody else was walking alongside them, a man in a trench coat that flapped open with his every step, a brown felt hat slightly tipped backward on his head. I slipped

15

off the suitcase as Adam came up to me and picked it up. He leaned over trying to whisper, but the man waved at us impatiently and let out a sharp whistle, *"Let's go."*

A short distance up the street we came to a police station and entered through a side door into a small basement room. Two uniformed gendarmes were playing chequers at a table by the window, a bed in the corner with a rumpled blanket half thrown back looked as if somebody had just slept in it. The policemen, intent on their game, never spared us a glance, the air was stuffy and reeked of cigarette smoke and coffee. The agent left, then came back and brought us through a short hallway into a cubicle, with a table and a couple of chairs. There he took our documents, asked Adam and Zofia several questions, and made notes. Finally, a policewoman, bosomy and angular, came in and took charge of Zofia and me, while Adam was led away by another policeman. Our suitcases remained behind in the cubicle.

We followed the jail warden down a long corridor lit by a row of single light bulbs strung from the low ceiling. The walls were steely grey, a row of locked metal doors, each with a small shuttered window and a metal bolt across the middle ran on one side of the passage. The opposite wall was blank. Some women were mopping the floor on their knees and without looking at us moved aside to let us pass. Midway down the corridor the stocky guard stopped, took a bunch of keys hanging at her belt, unlocked the door, and pushed it open. She motioned us into the cell with a jerk of her head. There were two plank beds against the walls, between them a small table with a basin and a water jug, and high up, across from the door, a narrow rectangular barred window which let in some daylight. As we entered, a coarse-looking woman got off one bed. The warden pointed to the other bed: *"For you and the child,"* she said curtly to Zofia, then without another word she turned on her heel and left. The door slammed shut with the grating sound of a key turned in the lock and the clang of the metal bar. Immediately the woman in the cell turned on Zofia: *"This cell is clean, you must keep it clean,"* she said gruffly in Czech, waving her hand at a broom in the corner. Zofia nodded mutely, and then slowly sank down onto the edge of our bed. As I slipped next to her, she passed her arm around me, I pressed my face against her shoulder and we stayed that way for a long time without uttering a word. Outside it was dark by now and a bare light bulb clicked on. All the while, our sullen companion sat with her back to us, mending a drab housecoat.

Finally, I whispered to Zofia that I need to pee. She looked around the cell then turned to the woman: *"The child needs to go to the bathroom."* The other one threw me a hostile glance, shrugged her shoulders, but motioned with her head towards the door. It took some time before the warden's scowling face appeared in the little window. *"What?"*

"The child needs to go to the bathroom," Zofia repeated. Eyes bored into me through the bars, as if doubting the truth of my need, but she opened the door. *"It's not the right time,"* she barked, leading us down the passage toward the W.C. As we followed her, Zofia leaned over me: *"Remember, say nothing,"* she whispered hurriedly.

The plank bed in our cell was so narrow that we settled on it for the night lying sideways. I was very tired but I couldn't fall asleep. With my face to the wall, I began to cry silently, squeezing Aunt Hania's silk scarf in my clenched fist. For the first time since leaving home, I felt scared and lonely.

On the fourth day, the door opened at an unusual hour and a young policeman came in with the guard. He said something to Zofia that I did not understand, but though she looked distraught she just nodded, hugged me, gathered a few items of my clothing, and handed him the bundle. Up to that moment, apart from short trips to the bathroom, we had not left the cell, and stepping out into the street I felt overwhelmed by the light, the open space, the sudden surge of fresh air after the stuffiness of the cell, even by the sight of naked branches that appeared menacing in their starkness as they jabbed the winter sky. I felt terribly small.

We did not walk far. My guard rang a doorbell and a nun opened. She nodded, took me by the hand, took my bundle from him, and closed the door. The sisters may have had some qualms about taking in a youthful jailbird foisted on them by the police and, possibly, they were concerned that unwanted little critters may have tagged along with me or on me. A round metal tub with warm water was set up on the kitchen table and I was soaped and scrubbed vigorously from the tip of my head to my smallest toe. The soap was stinging my eyes and getting into my nose, but I didn't dare to complain. When the ordeal was over, I was wrapped in a white towel and entrusted to a young nun, while my clothes went to the laundry. I was given a bowl of oatmeal and a glass of warm milk, and when I finished, my new guardian took me to bed made up in a small room. Even though I was alone in the dark, it felt good. Never again would I so enjoy the touch of pristine crisp sheets as those, after the coarse blanket on the prison bed. In the morning the nuns gave me a pretty coloured cardboard windmill to play with, though I hardly knew what to do with it.

The following day, another policeman showed up. My bundle of freshly cleaned things was brought out and handed to him and the nuns crowded around me. One of them, probably the mother superior, slipped a small rosary of white and red glass beads into my hand. *"This is for you,"* she said in broken Polish, placing her hand on my head, *"It will help you."* She made a sign of the cross on my forehead[2]

Again, we walked on foot, this time clear across town, the policeman holding me tightly by the hand as if afraid I might bolt. We reached a small house on the outskirts, with a low fence and a tiny garden in front of it. As the policeman pushed open the gate, a short, dark-haired woman came out. She smiled at me, took me by the hand, accepted my bundle, they nodded to each other and he was gone.

I retained a hazy memory of the fortnight that followed, of the house and of the family. Father, mother, a teenage son, and a daughter, Jindrka, a couple of years older than me, who shared with me her room where there were two beds. When she was in school, I sat in the kitchen with her mother. I knew I was prone to talk in my sleep, Uncle Zbyszek joked about it. *"You chatter even when you're fast asleep,"* he would say. Now, afraid that I might let slip something that I shouldn't, I panicked. As I sat at the kitchen table with Jindrka's mother, I spun ludicrous tales of family history, confusing stories of an uncle and aunt who died in an air raid, of a mother who went away and never came back. Hard to tell how transparent I was, quite a bit I suspect, but this good woman listened patiently to my prattle as she peeled the potatoes and shelled the peas, never attempting to pry. Maybe she simply didn't care, maybe she was sorry for me.

On days when Jindrka was not in school, she devoted herself to me with a dedication worthy of an older sister. The house stood at the top of a steep and narrow muddy street, covered with enough snow to let us ride on sleighs, which we did, squealing as we slid to the foot of the hill, where it ended among bushes and fences. At other times we went to visit relatives. Once to her aunt's house on the edge of a small moat, where a footbridge led to the door and beyond into an empty room and then straight into the kitchen. The floors were spotless,

---

[2] Years later I realised that the Czech sisters knew by then that my Polish world, taken over by the Russians, had been shattered to smithereens, but may not have yet suspected that their own would shortly follow suit.

wooden boards scrubbed to near whiteness, but the air had a sweetish smell which I found so sickening that I dashed out onto the little bridge and leaned over the railing, gulping and gagging. Ashamed to admit that I found the air nauseating, I mumbled tearfully about feeling sick in tramcars. These people were kind and never mentioned that I was not on a tram, just at auntie's who kept a pigsty under the house. The country smells seeping through the floorboards were too much for a city kid. I was never taken there again.

Nights were tough. Then anguish swept over me, just as in the cell, and I cried silently, twisting Aunt Hania's silk scarf in my fingers. As days slipped by, I lived in an odd state of suspense, talking and playing, yet watching and waiting, though for what precisely I was not sure. Perhaps with a child's intuition, I felt that I could not stay there forever, that some time Adam and Zofia were bound to come? Darker possibilities, like an orphanage, were unknown to me.

A fortnight passed and yet another policeman showed up. He took me back to the police station and upstairs to a second-floor office where Zofia and Adam seemed to be chatting amicably with a man in civilian clothes. Our battered suitcases stood against the wall. As soon as I came in the man rose from his chair, shook hands with my guardians and everybody smiled politely. We were escorted back to the border crossing with our suitcases, but the large one that Adam carried seemed strangely light now. All the while I kept puzzling over grown-ups who were capable of smiling at each other, even when they were badly treated and locked up in a cell, as we were. We crossed the bridge, passed the border guards, and were back on Polish soil. That night we slept in a small hotel by the railroad station and the next day we returned to Bytom. After two weeks in Czechoslovakia, my flight to join mother was over. Needless to say, Uncle Zbyszek and Aunt Hania were shocked, but hugely relieved, when we showed up at the door. It was clear that uncle's concerns over the escape were justified.

A few hours of rest and washing-up, a quick meal that my aunt prepared, and Adam and Zofia left for an unknown destination, but not, however, before telling uncle Zbyszek that we owed our release to the gold Adam carried in his shoddy suitcase. Gold ingots, he explained in a hushed tone, that he had buried before the war in his garden. *"I intend to stay abroad and the gold would have helped me start a new life in England. If the Czechs had turned us over to the Polish UB, they would have had to return everything they found on us, including the gold. They didn't want to part with it, you see."*

19

As I listened to Adam, I wondered what these gold bars that paid for our freedom looked like. Were they like the bars of Swiss chocolate in the care packages mother sent? And if they took Adam's gold bars, why did they send us back to the bridge on the River Olza? I never understood, even in later years, why Czech generosity did not extend so far as to let us continue on to Germany. Masaryk was still alive. They could have kept the gold and let us go on. Clearly, higher reasons prevailed.

Adam also told my uncle, on the side, as overheard by my snooping self, that my mother never asked that I should go with them alone. *"She insisted that the three of you should come,"* he confessed sheepishly, *"but we knew how desperately Zofia wants to get Ewa back."* So here I was now, a hero to my family. *"She never gave away her identity,"* Aunt Hania kept repeating tearfully to the four walls, since there was no one else to hear it, while I basked in this glow of admiration. It was good to be back at home, to be back with my doll, my teddy bear, my stuffed little bulldog, and books on dwarfs and fairies. But something was lacking. The excitement of that failed escape left me restless and life felt dull. My uncle firmly laid down the law that I was forbidden to talk of my adventure to anyone. Absolutely. So, what was I to do with this thrilling collection of words such as *tajniak, zielona granica,*[3] and *cela,*[4] all part of an exploit which had to be concealed from the world? Not that there was much of a world to whom I could have bragged about it, actually just old Mrs B., but even she would have done in a pinch.

Soon I heard Aunt Hania's footsteps on the staircase. I grabbed my doll and took off with a shout *"auntie's back,"* but she had already closed the door by the time I reached it, so I beat on it with my fist. The visitor stood so close behind me that it made me uncomfortable, while a curious Mrs B. peered from across the landing. *"I'm coming,"* Aunt Hania called out. She opened the door, staggered backwards as I breezed past her quickly calling out on the way: *"Auntie, there's a lady to see you,"* and I made straight for the bedroom. The front door slammed shut with unusual violence. I plopped down on the bed on my stomach and got on with my reading. There was no sound of voices in the flat, but I paid no attention to that. After a long while, Aunt Hania came in. *"Do you know who that lady is who came here this afternoon?"* She asked. I looked up from my book and saw that she had been crying, her eyes were red and her

---

[3] Slang for secret agent and illegal border crossing
[4] jail cell

cheeks were wet. But I was annoyed by the intrusion. *"Yes,"* I answered sullenly, *"she's an old friend of mummy."*

Aunt Hania shook her head. *"No,"* she said quietly, *"she is your mother."*

Chapter II
Leopolis, the City of Many Nations in the Kingdom of Galicia and Lodomeria

My parents lived in a very prestigious part of town, no.2 Plac Akademicki. They had their law office there as well. Both were lawyers, graduates of the Jan Kazimierz University of Lwów, or Universitas Leopoliensis as it was known by its Latin name. My Father, Maksymilian, Maks for intimates, held a doctorate in law; my Mother Zofia, called Zosia by friends and family, had a master in law degree. At the time when they were born this land was called the Kingdom of Galicia and Lodomeria, crown lands of the Habsburg monarchy, part of the Austro-Hungarian Empire.[5] When the First World War broke out, my father who had just then enrolled in law school, was called up for military service in the Austrian army.

In letters which she wrote to me many years later, my father's sister Ludwika or Lusia, my aunt and godmother, reminisced about that period: *"At that time,"* she wrote, *"Maks was first sent to Czechoslovakia and from there to the Italian front where he spent three years. It was a very dangerous front going through the Alps. Occasionally soldiers and officers were given home leave and Maks came home a few times and even managed to take some exams at the university.[6]"*

The Kingdom of Galicia and Lodomeria, known in earlier times as the province of Lesser Poland, became part of the Habsburg Empire when Poland

---

[5] The official name was Königreich Galizien und Lodomerien mit dem Großherzogtum Krakau und den Herzogtümern Auschwitz und Zator. Kingdom of Galicia and Lodomeria with the Grand Duchy of Krakau and the Duchies of Auschwitz and Zator. It became just Galicia after Lodomeria was separated.

[6] Although my aunt referred to it as Czechoslovakia, before WWI it would have been Bohemia or Moravia.

was torn apart, bit by bit throughout the eighteenth century, by its neighbours – Austria, Russia, and Prussia. The country had become weak and ungovernable through internal strife, corruption, and overweening ambitions of its elites, and when it became incapable of governing itself the three neighbours moved in for the kill. Each partitioning power had a reason of sorts for taking part in the dismemberment: Russia, because that was what Russia did: invade and grab to expand. Prussia, because the Prussian monarchy felt threatened by the Polish liberal constitutional movement influenced by the American Bill of Rights and the French Jacobinism. Although the absolutist King Frederick died in 1786, before the Polish Parliament adopted a liberal constitution on 3 May 1791, the great empires were sufficiently shaken by the French Revolution, in full swing at the time, deeming it more prudent to nip the nascent Polish liberal movement in the bud by invading and partitioning the country. And although the Austrians did not have a very plausible reason to join in the kill, they may have felt the time was right to erase an uncomfortable debt of gratitude, for having been saved from the Turks a mere hundred years earlier by none other than the Polish army under King John III Sobieski. Not only was Austria then saved from becoming part of the Ottoman fiefdom, but so was most of Europe.

My father was part of the fifth generation of Poles born under foreign domination. By then the Austrians had been entrenched in that part of Poland for well over one hundred years, with its capital city of Lwów or Leopolis, City of Lions in Latin, renamed Lemberg in Austrian times. Its origins went back to the thirteenth century as a fortress built by the Ruthenian Count Danilo for his son Lew (Leo). Hence the name. Through dynastic connections, it passed to the Polish Crown a hundred years later. For centuries it served as a bulwark of Christianity for the defence of Europe's eastern borders against Tatar invasions. Sitting on the caravan trails between the Black Sea and the Baltic, it became very prosperous over time attracting an ethnically diverse merchant class from all over Europe, while Polish rulers actively encouraged these newcomers to settle by implementing the Magdeburg Laws for the cities and by adopting religious freedom. By the time my father was born, the population of Lemberg comprised of Poles and several minorities: Ruthenians, Jews, Germans, Armenians, Czechs, Hungarians, even Roma also called Romani, with a smattering of Tatars, and Austrians of course, since this was part of their empire.

Until that time the various ethnic groups coexisted in a relative symbiosis, but things were on the way to changing. The Ruthenians, an ethnic minority with long-established roots in these lands, were assuming a new identity now calling themselves Ukrainians. Since the annexation by Austria, throughout most of the nineteenth century, there were major and minor uprisings by the Poles. To counter them and to stifle any burgeoning Polish liberation movements, long before WWI broke out, the Austrians began encouraging a growing Ukrainian nationalist movement, even arming them to some extent.

As soon as the war started winding down and an armistice was in view, the Austrian contingents began to pull out of the city. At that point the Ukrainians took advantage of the lull to launch an armed coup in Lwów on 1 November 1918, overrunning the principal installations throughout the town. It so happened that the city was hosting a gathering of university students from around the country and they were the first to go into action. Soon high school pupils, young factory workers, peasant boys from the countryside, and a large group of girls joined in. These youthful defenders, later known as the Eaglets of Lwów, were very young indeed. Fourteen-year-old Jurek Bitschan was killed at his post in the historic Łyczaków Cemetery on 21 November, the same day the Ukrainians abandoned the city. Not for nothing, the city's motto was *Leopolis Semper Fidelis Tibi Poloniae.* Even after the Ukrainians pulled out, they continued a blockade for seven more months, until June 1919 when regular Polish army units under General Józef Haller broke the siege.

Aunt Ludwika left a first-hand account of the conflict: *"When the world war ended in 1918 and Poland again became an independent country,"* she wrote, *"the conflict with the Ukrainians broke out and returning from the Italian front, your father enlisted straight away in the Polish army and as a lieutenant joined the 30th regiment of infantry known as the 'Children of Lwów'[7]. They were sent to the Ukrainian front which cut across the city. The Ukrainians were entrenched in the Citadel, close to where we were living. The battles were fierce and bloody. Each night at around ten o'clock the Ukrainians would start bombarding the centre of the town, just below the Citadel. Maks was on duty day and night. Once he was sent home for twelve hours, because he was worried about mother and me. He came home around nine o'clock at night, exhausted by lack of sleep, dirty, barely able to stand, and immediately crashed like a log onto his bed and fell asleep. He could not wash any way since the water system had been destroyed. An hour later the Ukrainians started their usual concert, guns were*

---

[7] The regiment known as The Children of Lwów – Lwowskich Dzieci – took its name from the fact that 14 and 15-year-old boys joined it.

pounding the city more ferociously than normally and I began to be afraid. First, I prayed, but when the furious cannonade continued, I started calling my brother: Maks, Maks, are those our guns or Ukrainian? Since he didn't stir, I called even louder. Finally, Maks barely opened his eyes and growled: 'Just shut up!' And fell back on the pillow."

Since my father was known for his courteous and urbane manners, the effect on aunt Lusia was staggering. *"At that moment,"* she wrote, *"I stopped being afraid."* It must be said that the next day he neither remembered that she had woken him up, nor believed that he could have spoken to her in that way.

After the Polish-Ukrainian conflict was settled, my father continued to serve in the army. In 1920 when, after the October revolution Russia advanced on Poland, he fought in the Polish-Bolshevik war and took part in the expedition against Kiev by then occupied by the Soviet Union. Finally, in 1922 he was demobilised in the rank of captain but remained in the reserves. Only then was he able to complete his studies, get the doctorate, and do the required two-year practice in a law firm before being admitted to the Bar.

The Hoffman family had deep middle-class roots and had been settled in Lwów for at least two hundred years. Family records go back to the eighteenth century. My great-great-grandfather Emil Waydowski owned a small factory of metal articles, gardening tools, rakes, spades, wheelbarrows, hammers, screwdrivers, and saws as well as articles for the home, like irons and bronze pestles with mortars used for grinding vanilla beans, cinnamon, pepper, and paprika, all popular spices in the lvovian-Austro-Hungarian regional cuisine. The Waydowski's daughter, Izabella, supposedly a great beauty, was born in 1830 and married Jan Hoffman, a small landowner who leased the land with a manor house, Malechów, from the city of Lwów.

The next generation of the Hoffman family had no interest in farming and mainly pursued liberal professions, but remained in and around Lwów. Jan and Izabella had one daughter and three sons. The daughter married an Austrian army officer, one son became a school teacher and eventually headmaster of the high school where he taught for fifty years. A second son, a lawyer, became a county councillor for the city of Lwów. A third son, Władysław, my grandfather born in 1866, was an employee of the treasury department in the k.k. office of city monuments.[8] He and his wife Paulina had two children, my father and his sister Ludwika.

---

[8] Kaiserliche-kőnigliche – imperial

Paulina came from a family long settled in Lwów and it was a large family indeed. Her grandparents Stanisław Nałęcz-Skałkowski and his wife Maria had three daughters and five sons, producing an endless array of aunts, uncles, and cousins. It was also the time of the third and final dismemberment of Poland by her neighbours, and that dismal reality reverberated across all the partitioned lands and across all the strata of society. One of the Skałkowski sons, Marceli, who grew up in the time of armed insurrections, executions, and Siberian exiles, composed a sort of prayer-song:

God, our Father, we your children
Beg you for a kinder fate.
Years go by, yet tragic bondage
Continues as our miserable state.
Lord, your very words had taught us,
'Every hair has been counted on your head',
Count our weeping widows, mothers,
Count our graves and our dead.[9]

Although the exact date of this prayer is not known, it was clearly inspired by the November Uprising of 1831, the period of Romanticism that gave Poland some of its greatest poets as well as Chopin's music.

One of Marceli's younger brothers at all costs wanted to become a physician, but for that he would have had to enrol at the university in Vienna. Since he had no money to hire horses to get there, he covered six hundred kilometres on foot to reach Vienna, where he eventually got his medical degree. This legendary feat survived in the family lore and was passed on to the younger generations as a shining example of will power and dedication. Aunt Lusia remembered how her mother made ample use of the story whenever she tried to coax my father out of bed in the morning: *"My Uncle Władysław,"* she would say, *"walked from Lwów to Vienna to get his education, while you, Maksio, are dragging your feet and your school is so close by."*

As in any family, ours did not lack eccentrics. Marceli's son married one of his cousins whom Lusia described as a most lovable oddball: *"They were both my mother's first cousins. Auntie Jadwisia was exceptionally ugly, highly educated, an atheist, and a very charitable, plain-speaking person. Together*

---

[9] Trans. from Polish by Eva Hoffman-Jedruch.

with her husband she travelled extensively across Europe and around the Mediterranean, hated beds, slept her entire life on a dining room couch, and bore eight children – four sons and four daughters." Clearly, the dining room sofa had been put to very good use.

On Grandmother Paulina's side, the family had mixed roots. While predominantly Polish, they did include a few Ruthenians[10] some of whom became totally *polonised* and converted to Roman Catholicism, while others remained true to the Greek Ruthenian rite – not an uncommon phenomenon in this complex society. Like many other families in this part of the world, my father's family embodied a veritable kaleidoscope of the ethnic, cultural, and religious diversity of people who from times immemorial inhabited these lands on the Marches of Poland. Passionately attached to their beloved city, they were an organic part of that unique warp which was the population of Lwów and its environs until 1939.

My grandfather Władysław Hoffman died in 1898 at the age of thirty-two leaving his young widow with a six-year-old daughter and a five-year-old son. After his death, Paulina decided not to remarry, but with the help of her spinster sister, devoted herself to her children's upbringing, which was not an easy task for a young woman with scant material resources. Judging by the frequent changes of address, their financial situation was fragile in spite of modest assistance from the family. Aunt Lusia wrote that after her father's death, *"our material situation changed. Mother received a widow's pension for herself and for us. Her brother, Uncle Włodzimierz, was our legal guardian and for many years, until the outbreak of WWI, each month he sent us 30 crowns for our school needs, books and uniforms. Every six months mother also received some interest on an insurance premium that my father had purchased before his marriage. We still had a parcel of land that daddy owned on the outskirts of Lwów, close to the world-famous Baczewski liquor factory. I don't remember who advised mother to sell this lot since surely she would not be building there. She sold it for eight thousand Austrian crowns. This helped a little with our domestic expenses, but a short time later the Austrian government decided to build a railway line right through that piece of land and paid the new owner one hundred thousand crowns. It's easy to see how sorry mother was to have sold it."*

---

[10] Ruthenians, inhabitants of Red Ruthenia, eventually morphed into present day Ukrainians, those of White Ruthenia into Byelorussians.

In spite of limited finances, in the early years following her husband's death, Paulina took her children for summer vacations to different beauty spots around Eastern Poland. Their favourite was Jaremcze, known as the Pearl of the Carpathians, but there were many other picturesque locations scattered along the River Prut. They trekked through woods replete with berries and mushrooms, picnicked on delightful glades, picked wild strawberries on clearings where the air was saturated with intoxicating scents of forest plants and flowers, of bluebells called Campanella, sweetly smelling wild orchids, and exuberant ferns and bushy grasses. In Jaremcze over a waterfall named after Poland's greatest poet Adam Mickiewicz,[11] Polish engineers built a viaduct considered in its time a marvel of technology. Aunt Lusia wrote that when one stood under it, trains passing overhead appeared like toys.[12] When heavy rains fell in the mountains the River Prut swelled, and its waters rose dangerously as they rushed along, swirling and overflowing the banks.

On a limited income, it was not possible to go away for lengthy vacations, so part of the summer was spent in the city. Lwów was famous for the beauty of its parks where vendors roamed the paths with baskets of baked wares slung across their backs, offering pretzels and sweet buns and rolls. At the entrance to the park, peasant women sat on low stools at small tables with all manner of fruit, cherries, raspberries, blackberries, blueberries, and strawberries, spread on large cabbage leaves. "*We loved the cherries most of all*" Aunt Lusia wrote, "*mother would buy us each a bunch. The fruit was sweet and juicy. There would be about twenty cherries in a bunch which cost one cent.*"

Flying kites was another popular summer pastime, allowed only on the outskirts of the town for fear of getting the kites entangled in telephone wires. At any hour on a sunny summer day, dozens of colourful strips of tissue fluttered above the treetops and green meadows.

As the family's money problems grew, even modest vacations had to be abandoned. There remained Janów, closer to Lwów, where granny's unmarried sister lived and worked as a teacher. It had a large deep pond, beautiful woods, and tenuous connections to Polish history through the Royal Mountain, so named after a visit from King John III Sobieski.[13] In the woods, Lusia and Maks picked

---

[11] Adam Mickiewicz. 1798-1855
[12] The bridge was blown up during WWI, rebuilt and destroyed again in WWII.
[13] John III Sobieski of Poland (1629 – 1696). Most famous for his victory over the Turks in the 1683 Battle of Vienna. Following his victories over the Ottoman Empire, he was called by the Turks the "Lion of Lechistan".

mushrooms and wild berries while granny bought golden honey in honeycombs from local bee-keepers.

For centuries, the month of May in Poland was a month dedicated to the Virgin Mary. The whole family attended church services held in her honour, although Maks invariably fell asleep sitting on the steps of the altar. In November, novenas were said to St. Stanislaus Kostka one of Poland's beloved patron saints, and Paulina took the children to the Jesuit church of Saints Peter and Paul. Aunt Lusia remembered how the church filled to capacity on these occasions. At the end of the service, the congregation sang the hymn to St. Stanislaus based on the tune of the Polish national anthem forbidden by the Austrian authorities. It was a patriotic manifestation intended as an antidote to the *Volkshymne,* the song performed in honour of the Austrian Emperor:

Gott erhalte, Gott beschütze	God support, God protect
Unsern Kaiser, unser Land!	Our Kaiser and our Land!
Mächtig durch des Glaubens Stütze	By the shield of faith protected
Führer uns mit weiser Hand!	Let him lead us with his hand!
Laßt uns seiner Väter Krone	We shall shield his sacred crown,
Schirmen wider jeden Feind	Turn away all enemy threat.
Innig bleibt mit Habsburgs Throne	For with Hapsburg throne united
Österreichs Geschick vereint	Is forever Austria's fate. [14]

At home, my grandmother played patriotic songs on the piano inspired by the November Uprising. Paulina Hoffman, the elder of two sisters, was musically talented, and since her parents were well-to-do, they spared no expense on her education. She attended a boarding school for young ladies in Tarnopol, spoke French fluently, and took piano lessons from Mieczysław Sołtys – the best teacher in Lwów, student of Karol Mikuli who in turn was Frederic Chopin's disciple and his right-hand man in Paris. Aunt Lusia told me how much her mother regretted not being able to teach music in schools, which would have been one of few professional occupations acceptable for a proper young lady. For a while after her husband's death, Paulina tried to shore up the family budget by giving piano lessons privately.

Ice skating was a favourite winter pastime of both Hoffman children, in addition to strolls around town and window shopping. Toy stores were a huge

---

[14] Translated from German by Eva Hoffman Jedruch

attraction, but mostly off limits due to the family's scant income. Aunt Lusia remembered that *"mother would not go along too often with that sort of an expense. Fortunately, there were other compensations: at various points around town Italian, Romanian, or Bulgarian vendors offered chestnuts called marrons, roasted in their hard brown skin on small iron stoves and sold two for one cent. Mother would buy us ten chestnuts each, hot and sweet, rolled into a tube made of newspaper. Another delicacy was the so-called Turkish honey, a hard and sticky cream-coloured concoction displayed in lumps on small tables; a vendor would cut off little pieces and serve them on bits of paper. This 'honey' glued our teeth together for several minutes until it dissolved in the mouth. Never again in my life would I taste anything so delicious as the roasted chestnuts, Turkish honey, and pretzels in the winter, and sweet, plump cherries from the peasant women in Park Stryjski in the summer."*

The modest resources of the Hoffman household did not allow my grandmother to employ a live-in servant, so the doorman's wife from their apartment building came to do the housework. Overall, it was a happy and serene home, the children got on well with each other and knew that money was tight, so their expectations of toys and games were modest. Aunt Lusia mused about the special dinner treats during the carnival that her mother prepared once they were older: a hot frankfurter with mustard and a slice of bread, three 'pączki's'[15] filled with the rose preserve, and tea with raspberry syrup. Granny was most particular about proper eating manners, but as Aunt Lusia remembered, *"If mother wasn't around, we'd dispose of the bread first, then had the frankfurters just with mustard, and the pączki with tea at the end."*

Paulina loved flowers and had the greenest of thumbs. She grew plants in clay pots and wooden window boxes and the pride of place went to two exotic members of her collection: a palm and a fig tree that produced a few sweet figs every year. When the family was away, the doorman's wife took care of them. But one very hot summer, upon their return from vacations, they found both plants withered. During their absence the woman fell ill, there was no one else to water granny's 'garden' and so the palm and the fig tree were lost. Granny was inconsolable since they were given as presents to my grandfather before their marriage, and had survived at home for twenty years. The death of the palm

---

[15] Pączek, Doughnut, Berliner Pfannkuchen in German. Dating back to 16th c when Berlin's population grew fast, bakers began deep-frying the pastries in pans over open fire to satisfy growing demand. Popular in Central Europe and Germany.

and the fig tree occurred just before the outbreak of the First World War, symbolically closing a unique era in Lwów's history.

Theatre was my grandmother's great passion and she took the children often to plays, operas, and operettas. At the time many outstanding actors, some of them world-renown, performed in Lwów. Aunt Lusia recalled that, *"In spite of her widowhood your granny loved life. She always claimed that she was contented with her lot, never bored, and usually serene. She liked to dress elegantly and as long as we lived at home, she was most particular about our uniforms and dresses."* Paulina's social life revolved around her large extended family, and she would take the children along on visits to their Grandmother Izabella, and her brothers, but rarely to Uncle Tadeusz and Aunt Jadwisia, the one who throughout her life slept on a sofa. Aunt Lusia recalled these visits with mixed emotions. *"We sat around a large table and were bored to tears because mother didn't like it when the children whispered among themselves,"* After one such visit, Lusia squealed on her brother by telling her mother that *"Maks says Auntie Jadwisia looks like a frog."* Granny took this very much to heart, because she and Aunt Jadwisia were fond of each other and enjoyed playing cards and patience. From then on, she mostly visited the Skałkowskis alone, which was no big loss for Lusia and Maks, since returning from visiting her cousins their mother always brought cakes and tortes for them; and with aunt Jadwisia's eight children, there were enough names-day parties throughout the year. Outside of their family, the Hoffman children led a social life of their own. Schoolmates, boys and girls, came to the house often, granny served them tea and cakes, and once they became teenagers, Lusia's girlfriends played piano duets for four hands while Maks's school mates accompanied on mandolins.

Books on travel and stories of the American Wild West fired my father's imagination. In 1906 Buffalo Bill with his cowboys came to town and lasso in hand, standing on their ponies, they performed acrobatics on the exhibition grounds in one of the parks. My thirteen-year-old father became fascinated with the show. Aunt Lusia remembered how *"he ran to the park each day after school to watch their antics. Finally, sad and pale, he informed our mother that he intended to join them because he loved their way of life, and that he wanted to leave school and go off with Buffalo Bill's cowboys. Mother was most upset because Maks started to slack off in his studies. Mercifully one day the cowboys left and your daddy could not run off with them."*

31

By then my father was in high school, while Lusia went to a private teachers' college. At that time secondary schools were identified by numbers and, starting with first class, students wore strictly prescribed uniforms: black trousers, navy jackets cut in military style, and tall peaked caps marked with the letter 'G' or 'R' and a Roman numeral; the letter indicated either a humanistic *gymnasium* with Latin and Greek, or *Realgymnasium,* with no Latin or Greek, but laying stress on mathematics and natural sciences. The number of stripes embroidered on the stiff collar of the jacket indicated the class, silver for I-IV, and gold for V-VIII

In spite of modest circumstances, granny took great pains to give the children a good education. Both took private piano lessons and French, an indispensable qualification for Polish *intelligentsia*, although my father would surely rather play with his buddies than practice scales. His grades were very good; he excelled in Latin and mathematics to a point that his teachers recommended him as a tutor in both subjects when he was barely fifteen. *"I remember,"* wrote Aunt Lusia, *"that one year for helping a teacher with her Latin he earned seventy crowns, and so could buy a beautiful English tennis racket and a set of tennis balls. He was then barely fifteen years old. He had learned to play tennis while vacationing with our cousins, who had a large orchard which was partly converted into tennis courts."*

Young people from families of modest means had no money of their own unless they earned a few cents by tutoring, if qualified, or if not serving as altar boys at Mass. Aunt Lusia recalled that *"students from II to IV class, once they learned the liturgy, would go to churches early in the morning to serve as altar boys and receive 10 halers per Mass. At most they could 'earn' 30-40 halers per day. A school friend, whose father was an organist, talked Maks into going to the nearby church to serve, but your daddy did not like to get up early, so he quickly gave up that source of income."* Tutoring was what he was good at.

Once my father passed his baccalaureate and enrolled in law school at the University of Lwów, his uncle recommended him for a job with an insurance company and then he started earning real money. He loved light music, liked to dance, and was a good dancer. This was a time when the Argentine tango took Europe by storm and a craze born in Paris swept across the continent. The whole world sang and hummed lyrics and refrains about *"the most beautiful women who under the blue skies of Argentina seduce with the tango's divine charm."*

Maks spent his first month's salary on music sheets of the Argentine tango for his sister to play on the piano.

The first shots of the Great War were fired on 28 July 1914. Lwów was part of the Austro-Hungarian Empire and my father was drafted for military service into the Austrian army. Under his command, he had men of all nationalities that made up the sprawling Habsburg domain. He was stationed in Bohemia during the first few months, then on the Italian front that passed through the Alps. In her recollections, Aunt Lusia described the dangerous offensives in the middle of harsh winters. *"When an offensive was approaching, your father tried to send a few of his older soldiers on leave to Lwów, especially those who had families and children. He did only what military code allowed, but I remember how often after the war, when he was already a practicing lawyer, some of these men thanked him whenever they met him."*

Captain Dr Maksymilian Hoffman

1914. Austrian officers at the front. Maksymilian Hoffman second from the right.

Chapter III

The Austrian Garrison Town of Tarnopol

My mother's family came from the town of Tarnopol, also in Galicia. On her
maternal side they were landowners, some with extensive holdings, and others
with modest estates. My great great-grandfather, Bazyli Sas-Leszczyński, the
progenitor of the clan, was married to baroness Aniela Andler whose two sisters
had also married landowners, all country gentry with country estates.

Bazyli and Aniela had four children, three daughters and one son. One of the
girls, Maria, my great-grandmother, married Mieczysław Tapkowski, director of
the local mortgage bank and owner of two small stone quarries not too far from
the city. In turn, the Tapkowski couple had six children, three sons and three
daughters. When their father died, the oldest sister, Antonina a beauty with
stunning auburn hair, was already married to a physician, but the two younger
girls were still single. In time their mother would need to provide dowries for
them.

After her husband's untimely death Maria managed the estates herself, but
the family's finances were fragile. The only promising source of revenue was the
two quarries of a rare light-coloured yellowish-grey stone much in demand by
architects for exterior wall cladding of large churches. These quarries would play
a crucial role in the family's fortune.

Towards the end of the 1800s local newspapers carried many articles on a
much-debated project of a new church in Tarnopol. For over a century the parish
enjoyed the hospitality of the Dominican church, but now the pastor, Fr. Cyril
Janer (Jahner) decided his parish deserved a church of its own. In 1897 he formed
a fund-raising ladies' committee, chaired by the wife of a local magnate and
owner of a great estate, who had offered to donate one million bricks for the
building.

35

By January 1900 the project committee was ready to receive tender offers, but the scheme ran into stiff opposition from the public as well as from the city council itself, because of unacceptably high cost estimates, so the plan was shelved. When Fr. Janer died suddenly he was succeeded as pastor by Monsignor Bolesław Twardowski, an aristocratic and highly intellectual man, who promptly revived the idea of a new parish church and successfully garnered both the public support and that of the city fathers. The original design of the building was abandoned and a new one was prepared by Teodor Talowski, an eminent architect from Lwów. It was to be an impressive structure. As the local press informed, the plan was swiftly approved and the entire project entrusted to a thirty-six years old engineer-architect, Stefan Neuhoff, who was charged with negotiating the supply contracts for the construction materials.

Stefan Neuhoff was descended from a German family that came to Poland from Westphalia in the 1700s. They settled around the city of Bydgoszcz, in that part of Poland which fell to Prussia after the first partition in 1772. They were Lutherans of the Evangelical Augsburg church. However, when Antoni Neuhoff, Stefan's father, married Karolina Weinert, a German Roman Catholic, he converted to his wife's faith and moved to the Austrian province of Galicia.

For centuries Poland had been attracting newcomers from all over Europe who settled and in time 'went native'. Polish romanticism was a magnet for susceptible souls. One such man was Franciszek Jan Smolka, son of Vincent Schmolke, an Austrian army officer and of Anna Nemethy who was Hungarian. The young man came to Lwów to study law at the Universitas Leopoliensis. After graduating he stayed in the city, opened a law practice, and changed the spelling of his surname to Smolka. Soon he too caught the romantic bug and became involved in Poland's struggle for freedom. He joined a secret political group but was arrested in 1843 for conspiratorial activities, kept in solitary confinement for two years, and with twelve co-conspirators sentenced to death by hanging. However, in the end he was pardoned by imperial decree, although deprived of his doctorate and forbidden to practice law. When the wave of social unrest swept across Europe in 1848, his title was restored and he continued to actively support the cause of Polish autonomy. In 1870 he was elected member to the Austrian House of Deputies, and in 1881 became President of Austria's Imperial Council, holding this position for twelve years.

Franciszek Smolka – 1881

There was a story making the rounds at the time related to the patriotic initiative launched by Smolka of building an earthen mound to commemorate the three hundredth anniversary of the union between Poland and Lithuania that resulted in the Commonwealth of Two Nations in 1569. Hundreds of people from all walks of life took part in bringing soil from all the Polish lands in carts, drums, and wheelbarrows, to build the mound. This effort lasted for several years[17]. On one occasion when he happened to be in town, Smolka, now president of the Austrian Lower Chamber, put his hand to the task pushing a wheelbarrow filled with earth. He was dressed like a common labourer with his bushy moustache and wide-brimmed worker's hat obscuring his face. Two Austrian dignitaries from Vienna stood watching from the side lines. One of them approached Smolka and asked ironically: "When you are not pushing this wheelbarrow, what do you do for a living, my good man?" To which Smolka replied: "In my free time I manage the affairs of the Austro-Hungarian Empire."

In a similar way to Smolka, Antoni Neuhoff also became fervently *polonised* and in 1863 took part in the armed insurrection which broke out in the part of

---

[16] Under Wikimedia Commons license
[17] The Union of Lublin Mound – Kopiec Unii Lubelskiej in Lwów (1869-1890).

Poland annexed by Russia[18] The uprising was brutally crushed, participants were hunted down and either executed or exiled to Siberia, but Antoni managed to avoid arrest and escaped to the safety of Austrian Galicia.

Antoni and Karolina had eight children, three daughters and five sons. Stefan, their second child, was born in 1864, a year after the Uprising. The family was not wealthy and when Antoni died leaving his widow with young children, the burden of bringing them up fell on the shoulders of the oldest son. In 1882 Stefan enrolled in Lwów Polytechnic, an eminent school of engineering, where he co-founded the student cooperative known as Fraternal Assistance (Bratnia Pomoc). After getting his degree as engineer-architect he settled in Tarnopol and took a job with the Austrian railroads, but he continued to provide for his siblings. He made sure his four younger brothers got university degrees; two became lawyers, one a physician, and the youngest one an engineer. He married off two of his three sisters, providing them with dowries that included the indispensable pianos.

By now the industrial revolution that rolled off the textile mills of Birmingham in the 1700's had spread across Europe and the United States, setting in motion an unprecedented flourishing of technology that stirred the imagination of young ambitious entrepreneurs worldwide. They built factories, drilled for oil, opened mines, and started companies. Invention followed invention. In the United States Henry Ford, son of a poor Irish farmer, was putting into practice his ideas of a motorised vehicle. Andrew Carnegie, a Scottish immigrant, was launching his enterprise of steel production, and barges loaded with coal tugged down the length of Ohio River, furnaces spewed out streams of molten metal, while the night sky over Pittsburgh glowed red from huge slag heaps surrounding the city.

My grandfather, Stefan Neuhoff, was of that generation. An intellectual, professionally brilliant, energetic, and ambitious. By mid-1890s he launched his own engineering-architectural firm, while remaining as head of the railroads' technical department with the acquiescence of the administration of k.k. österreichische Staatsbahnen.[19] From his office on the first floor of the Tarnopol train station, he managed the railroad construction operations, while in his house he set up his own workshop, employing draftsmen and technicians who worked on his private commissions. He was heavily engaged in various engineering jobs

---

[18] January 1863. Known as the January Uprising.
[19] Imperial Austrian railroads

when the new pastor, Monsignor Twardowski, approached him with the offer of taking on the large construction project of the new parish church.

According to plans prepared by the Architect Teodor Taler, the church was to be built in the neo-Gothic style, very popular at the time in Austria, with secessionist and modernistic elements. Certain accessories, such as the pulpit, the altars, and the framing of doors and windows, required a particularly light-coloured stone and as Uncle Zbyszek recalled, *"Someone advised my father to search for such a stone in the quarries owned by the widow Maria Tapkowska. My father went to see her about the purchase of the stone. On his first visit, they discussed some generalities and agreed to meet again to conclude the deal. During his second visit, while they were talking in the drawing-room, the door opened and Maria's nineteen-year-old daughter ran in. Confused, she quickly retreated, but her mother called her back and introduced the visitor.*

Budowniczy kościołów we Lwowie Stefan
Neuhoff z małżonką

1902. Tarnopol. Stefan Neuhoff and Maria (Tapkowska) Neuhoff

"My father was instantly bewitched and fell hopelessly in love. A few days later he paid a formal visit as was customary, at noon, dressed in a morning

39

coat, and requested permission to call on the family socially." Permission granted, it was not long before Stefan asked for the young lady's hand and his offer of marriage was accepted.

Maria Włodzimiera, intimately called Włodzia,[20] was a classic beauty, with an oval-shaped face, a Grecian nose, green eyes, and a serious disposition beyond her age. Although eighteen years Stefan's junior, their personalities were admirably matched.

They were married in January 1902 in the ancient Dominican church and took up residence in a small single-storey house which my grandfather had bought while still a bachelor. A year later a son, Zbigniew Jan, was born, and two years later on 5 March 1905 a daughter, Zofia Maria Bożena.

Reminiscing about his early childhood, Uncle Zbyszek wrote: *"I was born on 8 March 1903 in Tarnopol in an old single-storey house belonging to my father, located at the foot of an ancient iron bridge with a paved surface through the middle and footpaths on both sides. From this bridge in 1910, we watched Halley's Comet. After my parents were married, they made their home in that house owned by my father. Six rooms had fashionable Viennese-style furniture, a wedding present from my great-grandmother, replacing my father's bachelor furnishings. The entrance to the house was not from the street, but from the courtyard which transitioned into a vegetable garden. There was a well with a hand-pump in the yard since at the time Tarnopol still had no waterworks. The front door opened onto a small hallway, from there other doors led to the kitchen on the left, and family rooms on the right. The first was a small drawing-room adjoining a large salon with two sets of sofas, armchairs, and coffee tables. From there one entered the dining room, then my parents' bedroom and finally the nursery. My father's study was next to a large workroom with three drafting tables. The windows in this house were not large, so in the winter when they were covered with ice very little light filtered in. I remember from my childhood the fantastical patterns that the frost painted on the glass, and the thick icicles that hung from the eaves, transparent as crystals. Naphtha flare lamps were used for lighting, there was no electricity as yet, and the house was heated with large ceramic-tile wood-burning stoves set in the corner of each room. Some tiles were plain, other quite elaborate, embossed, or decorated with patterns of flowers or scenes of country life.*

---

[20] Pronounced Vuogia.

The last room in the house was reserved for Andzia, the seamstress, and for Mrs Julia, an elderly lady who came every few weeks to mend my and my sister's underwear. She also darned socks and stockings. Andzia was short, plump, quiet, modestly dressed, and worked fast on our Singer sewing machine. In those days we had quite a few servants: the cook, two housemaids, a boy who helped with chores around the house, and Basia Jawna (Yavna), our Ruthenian nanny. The domestics lived in another part of the house, closer to the kitchen. An old retired railway worker took care of our gardening.

Stefan with Zbyszek   Włodzia with Zosia

We had a huge acacia bush in the garden and in the summer when it bloomed, the scent from its flowers filled the house. It was my favourite plant. In the wintertime, when the garden was covered with a thick layer of snow and the temperature outdoors dropped well below zero, I would sneak out and place a slice of bread at the foot of the acacia, so that the poor bush would not starve. Next day I checked to see if the bread was still there, and of course, it was not, since the sparrows ate it. But my childish heart rejoiced at the thought that the bush would not go hungry through the winter.

Our nanny, Basia, was dedicated solely to caring for me and my sister, she took us for walks to the municipal park or to our private garden located at a fair distance from the house, surrounded by a tall wooden fence, with a hexagonal arbour in the centre, overgrown with cottage ivy. There was a wooden table in the middle of the arbour and wooden benches along its sides. The flowers in our garden were quite ordinary: pansies, carnations, mignonettes, lupines, and balsam, but there were no roses, and the paths, covered with pale grey gravel, harmonised with the brilliant colours of the blooms. This was our private paradise. We played there, Zosia and me, while our nanny napped in the arbour. Sometimes Mrs Julia took us there on warm sunny days bringing along her basket of stuff to mend. Mrs Julia was our special favourite because she told us beautiful stories. As soon as we overheard our mother sending for Mrs Julia, we were beside ourselves with joy. We could look forward to a day of stories of Sleeping Beauty, Cinderella, Hansel and Gretel, and dwarfs and fairies – some she borrowed from Hans Christian Andersen, others were of her own invention.

Whenever Mrs Julia was expected, first thing in the morning we would drag our little chairs from the nursery and place them close to her armchair. She was a widow, quite elderly. Her hair was white; a black bonnet with a black ostrich feather adorned with black bows covered her head; the bonnet was tied under her chin with a wide black ribbon. She wore an old-fashioned dress with wide puffy sleeves and a floor-length skirt and she carried a small black cloth sack where she placed the leftovers of food that she was served throughout the day. As soon as she arrived, she was offered a breakfast of coffee and buns and rolls with butter. After that, she would proceed to her armchair, put on her spectacles, and start sewing. Zosia and I would then pull our chairs even closer to her and beg for stories. Those were among the most beautiful memories of our childhood. In the evening, when it was already dark, Mrs Julia would leave, taking away a bulging black sack."

Once a week Władzio, the son of poor local peasants, came to do odd jobs around the house. He was a bright boy who lived in a boarding school and well-to-do neighbourhood families would invite him for meals. In the wintertime, when the ponds were frozen, Władzio took the Neuhoff children skating, and my uncle was always amazed at how fast and nimble he was[21].

---

[21] After WWII, my mother met Władzio in London. He was a major in the Polish Army.

In the old house by the bridge days flowed according to a well laid out pattern, as befitted the notion of family life. My grandfather's world centred around his wife and children, and after work he headed home to spend the rest of the day with them. He frequently brought large paper bags filled with fruit, candy, and other delicacies from Aszkenazy's store. Uncle Zbyszek recalls how one evening, *"as we were sitting around our square dining room table, Zosia across from our mother, I across from our father, he turned to mother with a little conspiratorial smile and said: 'Włodziu, could you please fix that lamp, dear'. Mother got up to reach the lamp and gasped: a diamond pendant on a platinum chain was dangling among the crystals of the chandelier."* Stefan adored his wife.

My grandparents ate breakfast alone, the children had beakers of milk brought into the nursery, but they sat down to dinner and supper with their parents on the strict understanding that *"fishes and children have no voice."* After supper their nanny took them to bed and after they were settled, my grandfather came to say prayers with each one in turn and tuck them in. A small coloured lamp in the doorway of the nursery stayed lit at all times so that he could come over during the night whenever one of the children woke up or cried. On the whole, it was a peaceful life. Uncle Zbyszek remembered that after supper his parents usually stayed in the dining room for a long while, *"mother doing embroidery, father reading the Viennese newspaper Neue Freie Presse, which he bought each day in Mrs Gottlieb's bookstore. He would often take out a pencil and sketch miniature gothic portals and windows in the margins. He worked on plans for the parish church in his study where he had three tables and only there he would smoke a cigar as he sat in his armchair, deep in thought. On other evenings my parents retired to the drawing-room and mother sat at the piano and played Chopin or melodies from operas."*

Tarnopol, a small Austrian garrison town of some thirty thousand inhabitants, was the capital of the region of Podolia. Uncle Zbyszek described this world kaleidoscopic in its make-up, where an amazing variety of cultures intermingled. Poles and Jews were a majority, Ruthenians a minority. Poles worked as civil servants in the administration, judiciary, postal services, and in free professions as physicians, engineers, to a lesser extent as lawyers, and only sporadically in trade which was perceived as a lower-class occupation. Since it was the seat of the regional government, upper-echelon bureaucrats formed part of the town's elite, and many a young lady viewed marriage to a *referendarz*, or higher government official, as a most desirable match.

Jews in Tarnopol were prominent in free professions, like physicians and lawyers, and dominated the trade from large elegant boutiques to small stalls from where they sold sand and lime for construction. Ruthenians were mostly government employees, teachers, and clergy. And to complete the picture there were the Austrians, military and government officials, solidly embedded in the Polish segment of society.

My grandfather had excellent relations with the local Jewish *kahal* and was much esteemed by its members. When he was elected to the town council, a large crowd gathered in the street in front of the house; people cheered, and Jews performed a celebratory dance. Uncle Zbyszek remembered that day as he and his sister accompanied their parents onto the balcony and my grandfather thanked the public assembled below. Among orthodox Jews, one of the most highly revered was old Goliger who wore a silk robe and a skull cap, and his beard reached down to his waist. He visited my grandfather always accompanied by his son-in-law Babad, who held a prominent position within the *kahal* and travelled all over Europe. A couple of times he brought my grandfather gifts from his trips, once it was a marble statuette from Florence, another time a secessionist sculpture of horses. Every year before the Jewish holidays he would come with an enormous platter of *gefilte* fish and *matse.* Old Goliger was greatly honoured by my grandparents and, on his visits, always treated with torte and wine.

At the other end of the social spectrum, among the impecunious members of the local Jewish community was Mr Weintraub, owner of a small grocery across from my grandparents' house at the foot of the iron bridge. It was a tiny dwelling, rickety with age, with hardly any goods on its shelves. A bell attached to the door by a thick spring announced the arrival of a customer. On 4 October, Emperor Franz Joseph's saint's day, Weintraub displayed the monarch's framed photograph in his shop window flanked by two candles stuck in beer bottles, which were lit in the evening.[22] My grandmother sent to Weintraub for penny purchases, but serious shopping was done in Mr Skowroński's grocery establishment.

---

[22] Traditionally in Central and Eastern Europe, in preference to birthdays, people celebrated the day of the saint in the Catholic calendar, also known as names-day or Namenstag in German.

This *tarnopolian* world was small, socially, professionally, and business-wise contained within an area of a dozen or so streets – some commercial, other residential of single-storey houses or villas. As Uncle Zbyszek remembered that *"it was fashionable at the time to have a little garden in front and to grow roses which were tied to wooden stakes and adorned with large coloured globes. One main street led from the railroad station to the centre of town, another one from the baroque monument of St Anne to the parish church, and the third one of Trzeci Maj* [23] *was purely commercial with two-storey buildings. Finally, the last significant street was Świętojańska, where the military hospital was located and there at number 3, my father built a two-storey house where we moved in 1908 from our original home by the bridge. Our family occupied one entire floor."*

My grandfather firmly believed in the virtues of real estate property. After he and granny were married, apart from the house on Świętojańska Street built for the family, he started on the construction of a second house which he intended to sell. Both buildings in the style of Austrian secession had plain unadorned façades, and balconies giving onto the street with ornate iron railings of leaves, branches and flowers. There were two entrance doors, one led to the main staircase, the other to a side stairway and smaller flats and servants' quarters. Sometime later my grandfather bought three additional buildings on the two main streets and eventually added one more, four in total, all with flats on the upper floors and shops on the street level. The shops and boutiques were among the most exclusive in town: Singer sewing machine dealership, an elegant jewellery store belonging to Mr Teichmann – my grandparents' chief provider of table silverware, and a shop with sewing materials and accessories. After the First World War, a large Italian ice cream parlour also moved in. One building was rented out to the county court and for the county attorney's offices. A shoe shop owned by Mrs Kaczka was a local institution. When shopping for shoes if one were asked: *"where are you going?"* The answer was simple: *"to Kaczka"* [24].

A popular place in Tarnopol was a buffet-delicatessen owned by Mr Ostrowski and patronised by gentlemen who after office hours, before heading home to supper, would drop in for *schnapps and herring*. My grandfather was wont to quote a little ditty about the restorative properties of vodka, *"vodka cools, vodka warms, vodka, never, never harms"* but, personally, he favoured

---

[23] Street named to commemorate 3 May 1793, date of the first Polish constitution, which precipitated Poland's partition by her absolutist neighbours in 1795.
[24] In Polish 'kaczka' means duck.

wines. Next to Mr Ostrowski's buffet-delicatessen was the Skowroński grocery that maintained its original name, although it had been owned for many years by Mr Borecki. Nothing changed that readily in Tarnopol. The next store belonging to Mr Lang sold porcelain and china. Beyond that, the last shop before the baroque arched gate leading to the back yard and buildings of the Jesuit monastery, was the optician Dornbaum who not only sold spectacles, opera glasses, records, and record players but also repaired watches. A large gramophone with an enormous phonograph cylinder, one metre in diameter, stood in the middle of the floor and propped up against it was a picture of a fox terrier, his head cocked sideways, listening to his master's voice. It was the trademark His Master's Voice record label. The picture was of a fox terrier called Nipper, painted by the English artist Francis Barraud. The painting was titled: *Dog looking into a phonograph and listening to his master's voice.* A sign under it read: *Die Stimme seines Herrn.* Above the entrance to the shop, at a right angle to the street, by way of advertisement hung a huge pair of blue eyes in *binocles,* electrically lit. Dornbaum imported records of Viennese opera singers from Austria.

Uncle Zbyszek described the second family home on Świętojańska Street, which was furnished *"with amenities that were very modern for those times: we had our own water and electricity. Generally, naphtha lamps were still being used to light homes; electric power came first with carbon filament bulbs and only much later with the German incandescent Osram bulbs produced by Siemens, my father introduced electric lighting in all his buildings. Cables were drawn along the outside walls, braided and tied together with coloured silk threads. He also installed running water in every one of his houses through a network of pipes supplied from a well in the cellar. At the turn of the century, in the early 1900s, there were still no central waterworks in Tarnopol. The pumps in our houses were handled by the doormen and water was pumped into a huge tank in the attic. All the flats had bathrooms with large tubs, a novelty, and were heated by tall, round coal or wood-burning stoves. Each tub was equipped with a shower, its pipe protruding directly from the stove. Water to bathrooms and kitchens flowed from the attic tank. Our first-floor apartment was spacious, six large rooms, and my father designed a wall cabinet for wines in the dining room as well as a special wine cellar in the basement for wines which he ordered from Austria, Hungary, and Germany.*

The entire life of the Tarnopolian beau monde was concentrated along Mickiewicz Street which served as a Corso. At noon and at six in the afternoon, people met in a large café called Boulevard. It was also fashionable to stroll along Świętojańska Street and my mother often stood on the balcony from where she greeted friends and acquaintances who leisurely sauntered along the pavement below. One such lady, the wife of General Patraszewski, wore hats richly adorned with artificial flowers that always attracted my attention. There were several wooden boxes filled with flowering plants on the balcony, lined along the railing, and a watering can next to them. One day as the lady was passing by, I picked up the heavy watering can as high as the balustrade and tipped it over, sending a goodly stream of water on the garden of artificial flowers below. My parents were mortified, of course, obliged to pay a visit to Mrs Patraszewska expressing their sincerest regrets, while at home I got a thundering admonition from my father. We were never slapped, neither I nor my sister Zosia, although we surely richly deserved it once in a while, being regular little devils at times.

In those days Mickiewicz Street was illuminated with arc lamps strung up along the middle, and at night their white light attracted a myriad of beetles that crashed onto the pavement and died with a crunching noise under the pedestrians' feet. The parish church stood at one end of the street, at the other a tall tower, with a clock lit electrically from inside. This illumination caused a sensation when it was first introduced. Next to the tower, in a little wooden shack with a tin roof, Fonio Schneider sold soda water mixed with fruit juices. Hefty siphons sat on the floor, two large glass tubes filled with juice stood on the counter, one was raspberry flavoured, the other lemon, and glasses were lined alongside. Serving his customers with a flourish, Fonio first splashed some juice into a glass, and then squirted the sparkling water from a siphon. There were also wafers with lemon or chocolate filling stacked in cardboard boxes along the wall. An iron fence behind Fonio's establishment separated the pavement from the military hospital. Mr Fonio was a local institution, in the same way as Mrs Kaczka, she of the shoe store, and when asked: 'where are you going?' It was enough to say: 'to Fonio's'.

Boulevard, a popular coffee house, was patronised by the local civilian elite. Uncle Misio, my mother's brother, was a frequent guest there, with his wife and his friend, Mr Seweryn – a Tarnopolian bon vivant, who sported bushy sideburns, emulating Emperor Franz Josef. Austrian officers assigned to the local garrison were not permitted to visit the café. However, in the evening, when the real Corso started, they strolled along the pavement, usually on the Boulevard side of the street, filling the air with friendly greetings, of 'Servus Fritzi', 'Servus Hansi'. Those were mostly young men, up to and including the rank of captain, in smartly fitting uniforms, often leading pure-bred dogs on a leash so trained as to walk in step with their masters. But the evening Corso was a daily social event mostly enjoyed by civilians. The street was lined with chestnut trees, in the summer the slim candle-shaped flowers delicately outlined against the deep green of the leaves in the daytime and the ink blue of the sky at night. The older generation of the Tarnopolian society did not stroll in the Corso, it was simply not done. On the other hand, it was quite acceptable after Sunday Mass to pop into the confectionary shop for a tray of mouth-watering pastries to be taken home."

There were two establishments on the town's main square that catered exclusively to men: Thieb Ghienel, the barber, who attended the *gentlemen of the bourgeoisie*, and the tailor Kotlar, who for many years made my grandfather's suits, even long after the family moved away from Tarnopol. The beautiful baroque Dominican church rose on one side of the square and at the right angle to it stood the Austro-Hungarian Bank, the municipal savings bank, and the teachers' seminary. Uncle Zbyszek recalled its headmaster, Mr Michałowski, *"a tall man with a long black beard, who always dressed like the insurgents of the 1863 Uprising, in a distinctive coat called czamara that symbolised their readiness to fight to the end. The barracks of the Austrian garrison were located across from the bank, on the opposite side of the square and when I was a pupil in the first class of grade school, every day I would watch the soldiers returning from their drill to the sound of a military band. Two white pillars crowned with winged globes flanked the entrance to the barracks."*

When the Neuhoff children reached the proper age, Zbyszek was enrolled in grade school which also included, as a separate institution, a seminary for primary school teachers. Reminiscing about his childhood, my uncle wrote: *"Our school was modestly equipped with primitive furnishings; there were some sixty pupils; we hung up our coats and caps on hooks nailed into the walls. The schoolrooms were large, bright; the walls whitewashed with lime, and the large windows gave out onto Sobieski Square. Benches made of coarse boards were lined up in four columns separated by aisles, the teacher's table stood in front of the blackboard over which hung a crucifix with the figure of Christ and a portrait of Emperor Franz Josef I in a general's uniform. Pupils did not wear uniforms; we each had a satchel, a writing tablet in a white wooden frame, an ABC primer, a writing stylus, and a wet sponge tied to the satchel with a string. After our initial writing with the stylus on tablets, we progressed to exercise books and pencils, eventually to pen and ink in small bottles which sat in special round holes in the desktop.*

The teacher held a rod in his hand and used it to point out letters and numbers on the blackboard, and not infrequently to smack our hands. I sat on the first bench with the son of Colonel Zerboni von Dispozetti, the highest-ranking officer in Tarnopol, chief of the local garrison; later on, I shared the bench with the son of Doctor Lenkiewicz, headmaster of the high school. When I turned seven my father gave me a Roskopf watch which I brought to class. During the lesson when the room was silent, the only audible sound was the cheerful ticking of my watch and suddenly I grew very ashamed, though why I don't know. The only teacher in our school of whom we were terrified was Father Urban who taught religion and gave bad grades. My Sister Zosia went to the convent school run by sisters of St Joseph who also managed an orphanage. I frequently saw girls from the orphanage led by a nun, walking in pairs through town dressed in their cheap grey dresses and large straw hats. These girls were being trained for work as maids and seamstresses."

Tarnopol had all the institutions one would expect of a small town and its inhabitants took an active part in urban life. The town hall resembled an overturned box, bottom up, with a square tower topped by a covered gallery on top. The city emblem was painted on the tower – a yellow star on the right, a yellow crescent on the left on a blue field. The tower served as a fire lookout and a volunteer fire watchman was permanently stationed in the gallery. The fire department was located next to the town hall and the equipment at its disposal was primitive: four drum-wagons -- popularly known as *"feuerpompen,"* simple iron water tanks mounted on carts with canvas hoses and bronze nozzles attached to them. Each bronze accessory was polished to a high shine. When the fire alarm was sounded, the wagons rolled out through the town hall gate at a gallop, pulled by a pair of white horses, and raced down the street. The driver, sitting on a raised box at the front, held the reins in one hand and in the other a trumpet which he blew constantly to warn pedestrians; the firemen stood on footboards mounted on either side of the wagon and held onto wooden railings. The chief of the volunteer fire brigade was Teodor Moroz, a master cobbler, who lived in the basement of my grandfather's house, where he also had his workshop. Moroz, as did all the other firemen when on duty, wore an outfit modelled on military uniforms, complete with a helmet adorned with bronze stripes.

Uncle Zbyszek remembered him fondly:

"Teodor Moroz not only repaired shoes, but he also made new ones and was considered the best cobbler in Tarnopol. His living quarters consisted of two rooms; one was the bedroom, the other was the kitchen combined with his workshop. A single small square table covered with tools sat on a high platform by the window, the master officiating on one side of it, his apprentice, Pietrek, across from him. Lasts were lined by size along the edge of the platform and a cobbler's sewing machine stood next to the kitchen stove. Moroz and his wife had a beloved fox terrier mutt, a smart little beast that pulled handkerchiefs out of customer's pockets. This workshop was my favourite hideout. I would sneak out of our flat and sit there for hours listening to the master's learned exposés on ways and methods of shoemaking and repair, or tales of his exploits in fire emergencies. Many years later, whenever I returned to Tarnopol from Lwów, I would spend long hours visiting with the couple. The cobbler's wife – short, thin, and not very pretty – was very fond of me, most likely because they had no children of their own. She gave me delicacies to snack on which she herself prepared. It is not certain that the Apprentice Pietrek ever mastered the cobbler's craft because every day he had to sweep the floor, chop firewood, and go to the market before he sat down on the bench at the work table."

A few bitter memories that reflect a sad reality of the impoverished Galician countryside creep into Uncle Zbyszek's normally sunny childhood recollections. *"Across from the town hall, there was a local travel agency of the Blue Star Line shipping company. A two-chimney ocean liner displayed on a poster in the window invited passers-by to dream of faraway places. Inside the locale was furnished with the agent's desk and some chairs. One day as I was passing the agency with my mother, I saw a group of boys and girls, fifteen or sixteen years old, sitting on the curb, each with a small trunk painted green. Those were peasant children, the girls dressed in their Sunday best, colourful skirts and poor cheap blouses, and strings of coloured glass beads around their necks, their greatest treasure. The boys wore canvas trousers and jackets. Only years later, as an adult, I understood the meaning of what I then saw. Galician villages, with their desperately poor peasantry, were frequently visited by agents recruiting young people ostensibly for work in South America, but the girls more often than not ended in brothels, the boys doing unpaid labour in the fields. Their parents, ignorant of reality, were only too happy to give their offspring a chance for a better life in a distant land, while also relieved that there would be fewer mouths to feed off the miserable acre of land and the sale of milk and cheese from the one and only cow they owned. In my mind's eye, the image of these youngsters and its tragic significance recur frequently."*

In the Austro-Hungarian Empire, the onset of railroad transportation played a big role. Trains pulled by teams of horses appeared as early as 1810, and the line Vienna-Cracow, the *Kaiser Ferdinands Nordbahn*, financed by the Rothschild bank, was built in 1837. Over time certain segments of the Austrian railway system were sold off to private investors, but after the financial crash of 1873 many went bankrupt and were bought back by the state, becoming the *kaiserliche-königliche Staatsbahnen* Imperial Royal Austrian State Railways, which contributed mightily to the economic development of the Habsburg Empire. Railways were the carriers of the future and the reason why my grandfather took the job as his first employment to become head of the Construction Section. A string of railroad bridges across Galicia was built under his management.

Towards the end of the nineteenth century and early twentieth in every major city whether London, Paris, New York, Vienna or Lwów, train stations became a vital element of urban planning and objects of lavish architectural design with marble wall claddings, ornamental clocks, elegant waiting areas, and fine restaurants. Modest Tarnopol wanted to make its own mark with an impressive station and Uncle Zbyszek described it in some detail: *"The station was located in a large building with an enormous round window of thick pale green glass and the platform was kept impeccably clean by a few old retired railway workers who walked around all day with brooms of thin twigs. I was fascinated by the traffic office, where some twelve or fourteen telegraph machines tapped constantly, spewing out narrow paper ribbons covered with dots and dashes. Along one wall a large black leather sofa with a wooden frame painted yellow, a standard fixture of Austrian office furniture, allowed the telegraph operator to rest while on night duty.*

Above all, I was impressed by the traffic controller in a red cap and uniform who approached the first car behind the locomotive, spoke to the engine-driver or 'zugführer', blew a trumpet signalling the train's imminent departure and waved a small red flag to alert the conductors waiting by the carriages that the train was about to leave. His name was Mr. Grabowski. He was married to Helena, daughter of a fitter from the engine workshops popularly called 'heitzen', which were not far from the main train station building. I knew the fitter's family well: the parents, two daughters Helena and Zosia, and a son Janek. They had a small black mutt and I remember the crazy games Janek, then a high school student, used to play with the dog. Janek went on to study law at the University of Lwów, got his doctorate, became a judge, and was assassinated by Ukrainian nationalists just before WWII. His sister Zosia then lost her mind. The mother's name was Minka; she spoke a broken Polish, often interjecting German words.

Tarnopol had a large transfer station where old steam engines shunted cargo cars from one siding to another. Open cars called wagons were loaded with sacks of wheat and customs officials checked the contents by sticking sharp hooked needles into the sacks to verify that they were indeed filled with grain. The station had two types of signal systems: large bells strung up on a tall turret with iron hammers that made them clang when the apparatus was activated, and several signalling systems placed in between the tracks enclosed in thick opaque glass cases, lit from inside. Offices of the station manager and of the technical staff were located on the upper floor of the main building. In the winter, during heavy snowfall, locomotives were fitted with triangular iron ploughs to cut through thick layers of snow.

The line Lwów-Tarnopol was one of the marginal lines running regular passenger service, but no express trains. Vintage carriages had individual doors directly from the platform to each compartment forming separate units without connecting passages. The trains stopped on all minor stations between Tarnopol and Lwów. Along the way, for several kilometres, the line ran along a steep scarp. Small tunnels had been cut out to provide a crossing, large enough for a horse-drawn cart to go through, as well as for pedestrians. The gaps in the embankment were covered with iron bridges for the train.

My father's office on the upper floor of the main station building was furnished with typical Austrian government office furniture: a heavy sofa and armchairs with yellow frames and black leather upholstery, a large desk with stacks of folders and ledgers, a long extremely precise chronometer hung on the wall next to a gigantic map of railway networks."

There were several churches in Tarnopol, each catering to a different public. The town's elite, dignified members of local society, went to the Jesuit church at eleven, or to the beautiful late-baroque Dominican church which my grandfather had rebuilt *pro bono*. He also had restored the Jesuit church and was thanked with an elegant silver cigar box, inscribed: *To Stefan Neuhoff, may God reward you. Jesuit Fathers. Tarnopol. 1908.* The parish church served the "broad masses." It was not unusual for my grandmother's brother, Michał – Misio to the family – to call on my grandparents after Mass with his wife Irene, a highly educated and intelligent lady, my uncle's and my mother's beloved auntie Runia. Occasionally another brother also came, one married to an "inappropriate" woman according to granny. An opulent *second* breakfast would be served, lasting for hours, often stretching into mid-afternoon.

The clergy in Tarnopol took an active part in the town's social life. In those early 1900's the head of the Jesuit congregation was Reverend Haduch, a friend of our family. He travelled to Lwów frequently and as Uncle Zbyszek reminisced *"he often brought us various things. I recall in particular our first gramophone with the large tube and the little dog listening to His Master's Voice."* The Ruthenians, predominantly Greek Orthodox, had a beautiful church in Tarnopol where Reverend Gromnycky officiated, a man universally respected and liked. And then there was Monsignor Bolesław Twardowski, the pastor of the Catholic parish church, and a personal friend of our family. In a curious twist of fate, his first cousin Kazimierz Twardowski, professor of the Lwów University and one of the most brilliant philosophers of his day, was an avowed atheist.[25]

For the younger generation, the *Corso* was very much a part of their social life, but local patricians limited themselves to visits and receptions "at home" and these were governed by strict rules of etiquette. Lithographed invitations were sent out by mail, three weeks prior to the date of the reception; each male guest invited to the house for the first time had the obligation to pay a short visit three days before the event and then to call three days following it. My grandparents would typically invite between forty and sixty guests. The invitations read, *Mr and Mrs Stefan Neuhoff, have the pleasure of inviting Mr and Mrs...*

To prepare the sumptuous meal they would engage a chef, and the local florist was entrusted with the floral decorations. Receptions had a very formal character. The seating order of guests was of utmost importance, and missteps in

---

[25] Kazimierz Jerzy ze Skrzypna-Twardowski (1866-1938) Polish philosopher and logician. Studied philosophy in Vienna. Established the Lwów-Warsaw School of Logic, starting the tradition of scientific philosophy in Poland.

the arrangement could cause serious offence. My grandparents' guest list was a miniature cross-section of the local society. My great-grandmother, Maria Tapkowska, usually presided at the head of the table, next to her sat Monsignor Twardowski, others followed according to seniority in age and position. Karol Sochaniewicz, the owner of the toy shop, was a frequent guest as was the Lawyer Rosenfeld, who was married to the daughter of Doctor Liebling. Uncle Zbyszek remembered Mrs Rosenfeld who was deemed to be one of the most beautiful women in Tarnopol. Since attorney Rosenfeld had travelled twice to Vienna to defend legal cases in the Supreme Court, his fame as *"the best criminal lawyer"* was unchallenged. *"He was short and plump, with few hairs elaborately combed to cover the baldness and he had an artificial eye. He dressed elegantly, always carried an ebony cane with a silver head. Another frequent guest at the dinners was Mr Hess, general manager of the Tarnopol branch of the Viennese bank, who many years later committed suicide by jumping from the train on the Lwów-Tarnopol line."*

After supper, the gentlemen stepped out for a cigar, while the ladies remained at the table. Then the older men retired to another room where card tables had been already set up and crystal wine glasses placed next to each player. It was preference or whist with cards from a new, freshly unsealed pack. Candles in heavy silver candelabra stood on the tables, electric light being unacceptable as Uncle Zbyszek noted *the atmosphere would not be right.* The players, elderly distinguished-looking men dressed in black, treated the cards not as gambling but as a social game. Losing one's temper would make one a pariah and such incidents were unthinkable. Silence reigned in the room, rarely broken by an odd word, as the players concentrated on the game. My grandfather did not take part in card games in his own house, he merely walked around refilling the glasses and offering cigars.

In the meantime, in the drawing-room, under the watchful eyes of aunts and mothers who sat on sofas, young gentlemen entertained young ladies with games such as blindman's buff, while the matrons chatted and silently concocted marriage plans. According to the fashion of the time, women's dresses had puffed sleeves and long skirts that swept the floor and were tightly gathered in the waist with stiff corsets. The older the lady, the more plunging her neckline, while the young ones were buttoned up to the chin. Hairdressers created fancy hairdos with artificial bits to widen or raise the structure and tortoiseshell combs were fashionable as decorative accessories. Life flowed according to well-defined canons, leaving no doubt as to what was proper and what was not.

There was a casino in the municipal park and an arbour where all summer long a military band played on Sundays. Each year two balls were held in the casino and granny ordered her ball gowns for the occasion either in Lwów or in Vienna where she travelled with my grandfather. For the Neuhoff children, the day of the ball was one of pure enjoyment. The house oozed excitement, the subtle scents of perfume and eau de cologne mingled with the inevitable odour of fumes from the portable alcohol heater used for metal curling irons. Uncle Zbyszek recalled how on one occasion he walked into his parents' bedroom just as the maid was curling his mother's hair. *"My mother was sitting in front of a mirror and in the dim light I saw the reflection of her delicate face and neck, while the air in the room was permeated with the typical smell of heated metal and vapours of alcohol emanating from the little stove."* Grandfather wore his tailcoat, granny her newest evening gown, God forbid that she should be seen in a previous year's model; the florist delivered flowers ordered for the occasion. One year, grandfather had sprigs of mimosa ordered from Nice as a corsage for granny's dress.

For years the host of the ball was Jasio Warzeszkiewicz, politely addressed as captain, though when and where he had served remained a mystery. He was the master of ceremony during the New Year's Eve ball. At the stroke of twelve the door to the ballroom would swing wide open and Captain Jasio, dressed as a chef in a toque, entered preceded by an enormous punch bowl rolled in on a cart. The punch was then lit and with a huge ladle in hand, he officiated pouring the punch into glasses that waiters handed around to welcome the New Year. Pan Jasio performed another important function: at Easter for the Resurrection Mass at the door of the church he commanded an honorary guard of soldiers. He was light-hearted and good-natured, he had a pleasant voice and happily obliged with fashionable drawing-room hits such as Stanislao Gastadon's "The Forbidden Song" or Mendelssohn's "On the Wings of Song". Pan Jasio was a welcome addition to all social gatherings.

All this time construction of the new parish church proceeded briskly. Work on foundations had begun in 1903 and the cornerstone was laid a year later. Already it was possible to start planning the stained-glass windows as well as a life-size copy of the painting that was to be placed above the altar. Eventually, my grandmother posed for the painting of the Madonna, flanked by both children as two cherubs. Three portrait pictures were taken in Lwów and the stained-glass window was executed by glassworks in Kraków.

On 4 April 1905, the local newspaper carried an article on the general assembly of St. Joseph's Society of 25 March 1905, where Monsignor Twardowski reporting on the status of the parish church construction said that the author of the plan, Architect Mr Talowski, was delighted with the progress and calibre of the work and given that his project was in the capable hands of the engineer, Mr Stefan Neuhoff, he saw no further need of supervision on his part. He then expressed his gratitude to the manager of the project and stressed the disinterested nature of his contribution.[26]

Although my grandfather did receive an honorarium of 9000 crowns, it was a tiny sum for the enormous, five-year effort, a fact underscored many years later by Archbishop Twardowski, who said that grandfather's compensation was minimal compared to the huge amount of work involved. In total, the cost of the project came to 360,000 crowns[27] and the construction, finished in 1908, up to that point consumed 1,500,000 bricks and 2000 m^3 of cladding stone, partly financed by the member of parliament, Rudolf Gall, partly supplied at 'a significant discount' from the Zaścianka and Dyczków quarries, my great-grandmother Maria Tapkowska's property.

The dome of the church was crowned with a three and a half metre high cross. A copper engraving of the image of the Virgin of Częstochowa designed by my grandfather was placed in the patibulum, and a commemorative document was inserted in the golden globe at the foot of the cross. On Sunday 11 October 1908, the archbishop of Lwów, Józef Bilczewski, consecrated the church and this was followed by a processional transfer of the miraculous picture of Our Lady of Perpetual Help from the Dominican church to the provisional main altar of the new temple.

The local press also reported that in the afternoon at a reception held in the main hall of the casino, Archbishop Bilczewski announced that for his efforts in promoting the construction of the church, Fr Twardowski has been granted by the pope the title of Papal Prelate, and Mr Stefan Neuhoff has been awarded the Knight Commander's Cross of the Order of St. Gregory the Great. The ceremony

---

[26] Kościoły i Klasztory Rzymskokatolickie Dawnego Województwa Ruskiego. Vol. 16. p.230. Międzynarodowe Centrum Kultury w Krakowie. Kraków. 2008.
[27] In 1900, 1 US dollar = 2.1375 Austrian crowns (krone)

was accompanied by a display of posters with the image of the new church, organised by the building committee.

1908. Tarnopol. Parish Church of Our Lady of Perpetual Help [28]

On that occasion, Archbishop Bilczewski came to Tarnopol with an entourage of thirty or forty canons and after the official celebrations, another grand reception was offered in the evening by my grandparents. My five-year-old Uncle Zbyszek remembered it well. *"In our house, the table had been extended across two rooms, and laid with porcelain and silverware from end to end, when for no particular reason, I took a bucket, stuffed it with newspapers, lit them with a match, and slipped the smouldering pail under the table, just as Archbishop Bilczewski and his entourage were due. The house filled with smoke. My father was racing home to greet the archbishop on the doorstep, while the*

---

servants were frantically waving wet sheets to clear the air, and fortunately succeeded to do so before the distinguished company arrived.

But my devilries were not over yet. In Tarnopol, at that time there was a young Jewish man, off his rocker so to speak, who walked around in colourful women's dresses. They called him "crazy Josio". When the archbishop arrived in his canonical garb, my father brought me and my sister to him to introduce us. I observed the kindly smiling hierarch for a short while, then I turned to my sister and said: 'look, Koziaczku,[29] this is crazy Josio'. I don't remember how the archbishop reacted, or how my parents covered up the embarrassment after which the banquet proceeded without a hitch.

Stefan Neuhoff with the Order of Gregory the Great

However, I was still on a wild roll and while the dinner was underway, I swiped a wine glass from the table, filled it with wine, olive oil, and vinegar, and took it to Mr Grodzicki, the chef, saying 'Daddy sends this for you'. Mr Grodzicki

---

[29] Uncle Zyszek called my mother "Koziaczek" an affectionate diminutive for somebody courageous, who also loved frolicking.

liked his liquor and he was also preoccupied with the food that was being served, so he downed the drink in a single gulp. Luckily for me, my father was in such a good mood that day on account of the order of Gregory the Great that I got off with only a minor scolding." Uncle Zbyszek would have had no idea what his concoction could do to Mr Grodzicki's digestive system, but to the chef's credit the dinner was a success to the end and my grandfather compensated him handsomely for the damage done.

The Order given to my grandfather included a papal blessing for the entire family of Stefan Neuhoff, down to the fourth generation. It was a handwritten document of large format on grey paper in a beautiful handmade frame of light-coloured wood with a gold border. It was stipulated that upon my grandfather's death, the document should be returned to the Vatican.

At the age of four Zbyszek had contracted scarlet fever, a common illness in those days, frequently fatal. The source of the contamination, his doctors suspected, to be a funeral cortege that passed by the house of a child that had succumbed to the illness. The notion that the wind 'carried' the bacteria was not quite as outlandish as it may sound since now it is known that these particular bacteria are transmitted through inhalation. In those days when antibiotics did not exist, survival was a toss-up. The prescribed draconian treatment consisted in keeping the patient in bed for nine months, applying daily baths of warm water, then wrapping him in cold wet sheets for several hours. Eventually, as a side effect of scarlet fever, Zbyszek developed an eye condition that required treatment and since Tarnopol did not have an eye specialist, his parents decided to take him to Lwów to see Doctor Emanuel Machek, considered to be one of the best ophthalmologists at the time.

My uncle's first train ride with his mother was memorable. *"Preparations for the trip started several days before our departure,"* he wrote. *"Two large leather suitcases were brought down from the attic and packed with new clothes, soaps, toothbrushes, clothes brushes, and so much other unnecessary stuff. The kitchen turned into a beehive of activity. Chickens were roasted and wrapped in greaseproof paper and packed into cardboard boxes, together with small buns. Food was necessary since the journey would last many hours. On the beautiful summer day of departure, I wore a new outfit with a sailor collar, my mother an elegant dress and a large straw hat with ribbons and artificial flowers; father took us to the train station in a hansom cab. The platform was empty when we arrived because few people travelled from Tarnopol to Lwów. Suddenly I heard a bell indicating the approaching train and majestically a long line of archaic carriages rolled into the station, preceded by an equally archaic locomotive. A puff of smoke rose from its tall chimney wreathed by a crown. The porter lifted our suitcases, father gave mother and me a kiss and helped us into the carriage. The stationmaster stood next to the locomotive, a trumpet in one hand, a red flag in the other, watching the platform, then waved the flag and blew the trumpet. Slowly, laboriously, with the clang of metal bumpers and squeaking of wheels, the train began to move. A little while later mother reached for the food and we started on our mid-morning breakfast. I spent the remainder of the trip standing at the window, mesmerised by the novelty of the passing landscape, the telegraph poles, the meadows and pastures where peasant children were minding the cows, and country cottages with wells in the yards, and cartwheels on thatched roofs for storks to build their nests in."*

In those days the trip from Tarnopol to Lwów by passenger train lasted about four hours. In winter floors in the coupé cars were very cold, so train attendants would bring in thick metal sheets heated with hot water and lay them on the floor. *"Finally, we rolled into the glass-domed railway station in Lwów. I was overwhelmed by the chaos, the crowd of people hurrying in different directions; I had never seen anything like it. On the street, I noticed a policeman in a navy-blue uniform wearing a small bronze shield shaped like a moon quadrant with a number engraved on it. Years later I would see this very image in a painting by Tondos. We took a cab from the station to the hotel on the prestigious Karol Ludwik Street and there for the first time in my life I saw a horse-drawn streetcar. The porter at the door wore a knee-length black jacket with a yellow trim, and a round cap adorned with a gold band. Our Francuski Hotel used naphtha lamps for lighting. After registering at the reception desk, we were taken to our room. We rested, freshened up and unpacked, and proceeded to my aunt's house, a short distance away. Another surprise awaited me there. As daylight faded and the room grew dark, Aunt Helena took a match from the box, lit it, and walked up to a hanging lamp, touched a small net shaped like a plum with the match and presto! With a tiny explosion of gas, the lamp was lit. In our hotel room, all we had was a candle that mother put out for safety when we went to bed. Next day on our way to breakfast at the famous Sotchek café, we passed a tall column with a figure of a man next to it, and what I perceived to be a large moth hovering above his head."*

Lwów-Lemberg. 1915. Odo Dobrowolski. Lithograph[30]

What Uncle Zbyszek described was a city on the eve of modernisation. Streetcars were still horse-drawn and a small rivulet ran down the middle of the fashionable Akademicka Street, but all that was soon to change. The bed of the stream was excavated, deepened, and encased in concrete; the water channelled into concrete pipes and paved over. A tree-lined island down the middle of Akademicka ran its entire length, with a lawn and benches, and wide pavements on either side in the mode of Parisian boulevards. Soon horse-drawn streetcars were replaced with electric tramways. But what would remain unchanged was the column that Uncle Zbyszek saw, a tribute to Poland's most revered poet, Adam Mickiewicz. Uncle's *moth* suspended over the poet's head was none other than the allegory of a winged muse crowning the bard with a laurel wreath.

"The following day, we headed with mother and Aunt Helena to a hat salon located in the most prestigious hotel in town, The George Hotel. The shop was on the first floor, a large rectangular room with mirrors lining one wall, each mirror with its individual small shelf and a chair facing it. I was told to sit in the corner, while mother and my aunt gave themselves up to the delights of trying on hats. Actually, it was only my mother since Aunt Helena came merely as a fashion advisor. As soon as mother sat down, a young woman appeared and my

[30] Odo Dobrowolski (1883-1917) Wikipedia. available under the Creative Commons Attribution-Share-Alike- License

aunt offered a lengthy, rather detailed explanation of the desired hat. Soon the girl returned with a stack of round boxes and mother began trying on hats, one by one. It seemed endless. Aunt Helena standing on the side assessed each hat with a critical eye, cocking her head to the side, pursing her lips and offering comments, while the tireless shop attendant, with a fixed smile, held a hand mirror for mother to see herself from the back. Finally, a hat was picked out and my aunt gave instructions to have it packed and delivered to our hotel. By then I was desperately bored and quite cranky, so by way of consolation I was promised that the next stop will be a toy shop. And indeed, that was where we went, to the only toy shop in Lwów, which seemed a paradise to me. There were wooden rocking horses, dolls with porcelain heads and wigs of real hair, toy soldiers, all manner of weapons and cardboard towers and castles, and even small printers with rubber types for children that already could read and write. After lengthy deliberations with my mother, I settled on a miniature locomotive activated by a spring mechanism. It rolled on circular metal tracks. Not until late that afternoon we finally reached the consulting rooms of the university professor, Doctor Machek. So ended my first visit to Lwów"

During those early years of mother's and uncle's childhood, certain family traditions were fixed points on the calendar. One of them was their parents' trip to Vienna. *"Every year before Christmas, my parents went to Vienna for a week or so, travelling through Lwów, always staying in the same hotels: in Lwów it was the Francuski Hotel, in Vienna the Klomser on Herrengasse, in the first "bezirk," across from the literary coffee house, the Café Central patronised by celebrities, from Hugo von Hofmannsthal to Sigmund Freud and Leon Trotsky. In Vienna, my parents enjoyed the theatre, but the real purpose was shopping for toys for Christmas, while my mother also bought her dresses, and more importantly, her hats. My sister and I were left in the care of our nanny and of the cook."*

Some years later, when my grandfather became an advisor to the ministry of railroads in Vienna and the family moved there, the Klomser hotel was a scene of a dramatic espionage affair that had far-reaching repercussions across the entire Austro-Hungarian Empire. Alfred Redl, born in Lwów, the son of a modest railway clerk, graduated from the cadet academy. He was intelligent, had a gift for languages and he made a brilliant military career, reaching the rank of colonel normally reserved in the Austrian army for members of the privileged classes, the gentry and nobility. In 1900 Redl became head of the counter-espionage in Vienna. He was a homosexual and when the Russian tsarist secret service in Warsaw, under Colonel Batyushin, discovered his leanings, they procured for him young lovers and then blackmailed him into committing treason. From 1902 to 1913 Redl was Russia's master spy in the Austrian counter-espionage, well paid for the services rendered. His lifestyle was extravagant, out of proportion to the government salary. He acquired several properties in Vienna and a palatial residence on the outskirts. His Russian paymasters had a low opinion of him, disdainfully calling him in their diplomatic correspondence a "cynical debauchee," more cunning and false than intelligent.

Redl betrayed Austria's top-secret strategies, including plans for war with Serbia. In 1912 he was appointed chief of staff of General Baron von Giesl, head of the army corps in Prague. Major Maximilian Ronge took over as his successor to the post of chief of counter-espionage. In March 1913 by sheer chance, two compromising letters containing a large sum of money were discovered in the *poste restante*. A trap was set for the unnamed recipient with an identical letter left in the same *poste restante* box. When the individual showed up to claim it, the detectives who were lying in wait tried to grab him, but he evaded them by jumping into a taxi. Though they gave chase, they lost him. As luck would have it, within minutes the same taxi returned to the stand at the post office. The policemen ordered the cabbie to drive them to wherever he took his previous fare, which turned out to be the Klomser Hotel, where the shocked detectives recognised their erstwhile boss. How many Austrian intelligence agents lost their lives through Redl's treason is hard to tell, but they were many because he supplied information liberally to his tsarist paymasters.

Scandals were resolved discreetly in the Austrian army, even more so when they involved high ranking officers. That same rainy afternoon in May, two colonels arrived at the hotel and privately met with Redl, who was writing farewell letters in his room. They left and two hours later a shot rang out. Although the government tried to hush up the affair, it was impossible, there were too many witnesses. Hundreds of secret documents were handed over to Serbia, Austria's greatest enemy, still more were uncovered in Redl's Prague residence. His sister changed her name from Redl to Rados and moved to Lwów. Later it was found that she was running a house of ill repute and had in her possession albums with pictures of young "candidates". A sensational trial followed, presided over by Judge Majer, during which the chief of police,

Konarski, gave evidence. The attending public was treated to a titillating moment when during his testimony suddenly Miss Rados stood up and asked whether perchance mister Konarski had not been one of her customers. History did not record the policeman's answer.

When the Neuhoff children were still very young, their parents took them on vacations to a spa near the Carpathian Mountains, to take the "waters". Grandfather rented a villa in a beautiful spot in the midst of larch forests. But granny tired easily of places, so next came Zakopane, at the foot of the Tatra Mountains. There Zbyszek and Zosia embarked on a lifelong love affair with the mountains. *"Zakopane,"* wrote my uncle in his recollections, *"is unquestionably the most enchanting spot in Poland. The delightful road to Kuźnice lined with guelder-rose trees, their clusters of red berries that inspired many a romantic folk song adding a splash of colour to the severe greyness of the rocks. The Giewont massif with the overwhelming beauty of its three peaks appeared enormously powerful and heroic as their stark coldness gave birth to the legend of the sleeping knight who only wakes up when Poland is in danger. There was a sanatorium in Zakopane for tuberculosis patients. They would come hoping for a cure in the pure mountain air, but tragically the outcome usually was the same: emphysema and death."*

At the time Zakopane was a small village of unpaved roads offering as the only mode of transportation highlanders' carts drawn by ponies. Since granny strongly believed in the curative powers of mineral waters, her adoring husband would also send her periodically to Karlsbad *to improve her health*. According to family tradition, Włodzia was deemed as the most delicate and fragile of six siblings. She outlived them all.

Neuhoff children: Zosia and Zbyszek

After some years, grandfather changed course and opted for the family's vacations further afield, for two or three months on the Adriatic coast. One year it was Abbazia on the eastern coast of Istria, at the foot of Monte Maggiore, in the midst of laurel woods. It was considered the most elegant spa on the Adriatic and attracted the great and not necessarily the good, but certainly the wealthiest clientele from all over Europe. My grandparents found it too flashy for their taste, so the following year they removed to the nearby more modest Lovrana, which also offered vacation villas. Grandfather rented half a villa called Carmen, owned by Dr Kiel, a Viennese physician, who lived in the other half of the house with his wife and two daughters. *"Our apartment,"* Uncle Zbyszek remembered, *"comprised of two large rooms and a glass veranda. It was a miniscule paradise;*

the garden railings densely covered with white passion flowers; our veranda windows looked out on two small islands, Grande and Piccolo. The hot wind, Sirocco, blew across the sea from the Sahara Desert, driving tall waves with crests of white foam. We ate supper with the Kiel family. Every day, at the end of the meal, a servant brought a selection of cheeses with small slices of pumpernickel bread on a tray. In those years I was already given to telling jokes, and one evening after something I said, my mother nearly choked on that dark bread. Thereafter I was forbidden to tell jokes at dinner." Uncle Zbyszek did not say whether granny was choking because the joke was funny, or because she deemed it otherwise.

Lovrana. Familienbad

In Lovrana, the beach was divided into three parts: *Damenbad* for ladies, *Herrenbad* for men, and *Familienbad* for families. A near-accident happened there once which granny still remembered with a shudder years later. She was sitting on the beach in a wide-brimmed hat, under an even wider parasol. She was appropriately dressed in a long skirt down to her ankles and a blouse with puffy sleeves, engaged in lively conversation with ladies from the hotel; meanwhile five-year-old Zosia and eight-year-old Zbyszek played in the sand under the eye of their governess, Käti Lueger, a young lady from Graz. Zbyszek

66

splashed around in shallow water on the edge, but Zosia got bored with sandcastles and climbed onto a jetty that stretched far out into the sea. Another governess joined Käti and, in the meantime, Zosia was running up and down and wandering further away until she reached the end of the pier. As she bent over the edge to look below, she lost her footing and fell into the deep water. No one on the beach saw this, but a Hungarian lady who was swimming nearby noticed Zosia's yellow bathing cap easily visible in the sun, bobbing over the waves. She reached her with a few powerful strokes and pulled her out of the water. Granny's anger at the governess and her panic at what might have been would be hard to describe. *"We are leaving,"* she announced and that same day sent a telegram to my grandfather: *"Zosia nearly drowned. Stop. Come at once. Stop. We are going home. Stop. Włodzia."* His answer came promptly the very next day: *"Stay the rest of the vacation. Stop. Immediately arrange swimming lessons for Zosia. Stop. Stefan."*

Vacations in Lovrana. Granny with Zosia and Zbyszek

Vacations in Lovrana were followed by other in Venice where the family took a charming villa on the Lido with boat rides across the lagoon to visit the

Murano glassworks, and to Burano, where the most exquisite lace in the world was made in picturesque colourful houses. Thus, at an early age, the Neuhoff children were getting a wide exposure to the world. My grandfather would travel with the family, settle them in, and after a week or so return home. On the way there and back, they always stayed for a few days in Vienna at the Klomser Hotel.

Chapter IV
From Austrian Lemberg to Polish Lwów
(1910–1918)

In 1910 Stefan Neuhoff resigned his position as technical director for the imperial railways and moved his construction firm to Lwów. He rented a second-floor flat in a building on Kleinowska Street at number 3 in the vicinity of the park known as the post-Jesuit Garden on account of having once been part of the Jesuit monastery. Kleinowska was a very prestigious street and many of those who lived there belonged to the who-is-who of lvovian society: professor of literature Bronisław Gubrynowicz, brother of the publisher Ludwik Gubrynowicz; Count Scazighino; Austrian General Lamezan; Professor Count Leon Piniński, a man of phenomenal culture and erudition, an authority on Roman law, and former Governor of the Province of Galicia. One entire corner of the street was taken up by the gardens belonging to the palace and the library founded in the mid-nineteenth century by Count Wiktor Baworowski – a bibliophile, patron of arts, translator of Byron and other romantic writers, and a poet in his own right. He turned his library over to the public in 1900. On the opposite corner stood another palatial residence of Count Brunicki, situated on a slope covered by a dazzling mass of tulips and hyacinths in the spring. In my grandparents' apartment building the flat on the first floor was occupied by old Countess Suchodolska, while my grandfather took over the ground floor premises for his firm as indicated by a marble plaque at the entrance: *Civil Eng. Stefan Neuhoff. Engineering office.* Here he would work on the plans for his first major engineering job in Lwów, the expansion of the passenger railway station and the construction of a new cargo terminal.

At this time Lwów began to modernise. Although as yet the streets were lit with antiquated gas lanterns and at dusk a lamplighter, employed by the gas company, walked from lamppost to lamppost lighting each lamp in turn with a wick on a long pole, and the streetcar on Karol Ludwik Street was still horse-drawn, but already new tram lines were being introduced and the city illumination was being electrified.

This most multi-ethnic of Polish cities, Lwów, otherwise Leopolis, or Lemberg to the Austrians, like Rome, is situated on seven hills. The violet hue of its sunsets was perfectly captured by the local painter Odo (Otto) Dobrowolski, whose winter landscapes reflected the curious lilac shades of the snow. Three hillocks and the star of the Vatican were added to the city's coat of arms in 1586 by Pope Sixtus V in recognition of the defence of Catholic faith against Tatar invasions.

By comparison with Tarnopol, Lemberg was a great deal more worldly and cosmopolitan. It was the seat of power and of provincial authority, where all three branches of government were located: the governor of Galicia resided here as did its legislative body, the unicameral Seym,[31] and the judiciary with courts of first and second instance. Like Kraków, Lwów had an autonomous municipal government with a president and a council. Galicia railways were under the control of the ministry in Vienna, but the management boards were located in Lwów and in Kraków. The Austrian police were headquartered on Smolka Place and its director, Doctor Josef Reinländer, lived with his family on Sykstuska Street and was favourably disposed towards Poles, often most helpful in matters of delicate patriotic nature. Austrian infantry and cavalry garrisons were stationed in Lwów, as well as a company of guardsmen that occupied a small building with barred windows in the centre of town and performed a ceremonial changing of the guard every day at noon.

Syskstuska Street, which at one end intersected the street where my grandparents lived, was interesting because it consisted of two very different parts: one half purely residential, the other in the opposite direction, purely commercial. Uncle Zbyszek knew it particularly well since as a teenager he had a crush on Doctor Reinländer's daughter and strolled down that street at every opportunity.

"There were mostly apartment houses along the residential half of the street, except for three small shops: the grocery of Itzek Kandel, a store selling various

---

[31] Known as Sejm Krajowy, Parliament of the Land, it was the Diet of the Kingdom of Galicia and Lodomeria – Landtag von Galizien und Lodomerien, formed in 1861 as a result of the struggles for regional autonomy

grades of naphtha run by miss Matilda Matuszkiewicz, and a bar belonging to Aaron Reiter. In Miss Matuszkiewicz's shop, two large metal containers stood labelled 'ordinary naphtha' and 'drawing room naphtha'. The owner of the establishment, a small round person with a pleasant smile and hair neatly gathered in the back, expertly slipped a large funnel under the container's spout to fill the customer's bottle. In 1911 a young Jewish couple rented the small empty store without a display window, next to Matilda's, and opened a grocery shop under the name of Itzek Kandel. When the World War broke out, Kandel was drafted into the Austrian army and almost immediately killed in action. His wife managed the store alone and when a larger locale became available, she moved there, grew her business, and continued running it by herself. The third shop, Aaron Reiter's bar, was small and quiet, more of a club where local doormen popped in for a 'one stiff shot' and a chat. Its owner, by then middle-aged, maintained his establishment in proper order as befitted the neighbourhood.

One of the houses at that end of the street displayed a large plaque of white marble at the entrance, with a Persian emblem: a reclining lion holding an antique sabre in its front paws; the inscription below it read: 'Dr Reinhold, personal physician to the Shah of Persia and court physician of the Grand Duke of Baden, attends to illnesses of throat, ears, and nose'. On sunny summer days, every Thursday, an old man, slightly bent, shuffled past the plaque of the Persian shah's physician carrying a large black box on his back, and a street organ with a frayed green parrot on it. In his left hand, he held a folding stand which he used as a support. He walked with a tired step and entered those doorways that did not carry a sign: 'Entrance to beggars and street vendors forbidden'. Once in the inner courtyard, he would put down his stand, set up the organ, and soon the scratchy tones of the waltz from The Merry Widow wafted across the open space. The green parrot sat on the organ, next to the black box, pulling out little scraps of paper inscribed with words of wisdom and vague promises of future happiness. At that point, kitchen windows on all the floors would be flung open and small change wrapped in bits of paper rained down into the courtyard. Maids and cooks ran down the service stairs to have their fortune told by the parrot. After his rounds, the organ-grinder collected his stuff and headed for Aaron Reiter's bar, where he would drop down on the bench, pour some food for the parrot on a small tin plate, and shore up his strength with a stiff shot of vodka. Nobody knew whence he came or where he went.

Begging took on a different form in the other half of Sykstuska, its commercial segment. Here it was very busy, with heavy pedestrian traffic along the pavements and streetcars that rolled this way down the middle of the road, up to the corner of the residential part, where they turned. The organ-grinder would not have been able to walk here with his load. Most shops were Jewish and they had their own method of alms-giving, while the beggars had theirs of alms-taking. On warm summer days when the doors were open onto the street, small tables were set up on the threshold and coins, usually Austrian cents, would be placed around the edge. Beggars knew that they were allowed to take only one coin. They took it and shuffled on. In the winter, when the doors were closed, the coins were lined up on the counter closest to the entrance. An emaciated hand, covered in wrinkled yellow skin, would push the door a crack, slip in, quickly grab a coin, and disappear. Bookstores on Batory Street which were owned by Jews practiced the same method of giving alms. In non-Jewish stores, the shopkeepers simply gave alms directly to beggars waiting at the entrance."

Other colourful figures in Lwów that my uncle remembered well were Jewish 'handeles', *"Jews who bought used things from private homes. Old men, with no other means of support, in wretched clothes and shoes many times repaired, walked from house to house and from inner courtyards announced their presence, calling out: 'handele, handele'. When summoned by an apartment dweller, they climbed the service staircase and the bargaining would begin. They bought everything but mostly used clothing and shoes, which they inspected carefully because they then resold the stuff to shops dealing in second-hand goods in the part of town behind the Lwów theatre. Whatever they bought they stuffed into sacks and continued on their way. It was a tough way to make a living. With loaded sacks on their back, these old men shuffled along in blistering summer heat, climbing several flights of stairs, often without success. They worked during morning hours and were never seen in the afternoons. Occasionally doormen in apartment buildings barred their way, and those who were allowed probably had secured some 'payment' deal."*

After the family moved to Lwów, Zbyszek went to second grade at the only private school for boys, founded in 1909. It included the lyceum and the high school and was reputed to be the best boys' school in town. Pupils wore grey caps with a crimson band and a badge depicting a hand holding a torch against the backdrop of the Polish eagle. The school's motto was a line from Adam Asnyk's poem: *Empty regrets are useless.*[32]

Six-year-old Zosia was sent to the convent school of the Sacred Heart, where she acquired all the social graces indispensable to a young lady of good breeding, including the art of getting in and out of carriages. One afternoon her father came to fetch her and as he waited, he watched his daughter, gently holding the edge of her skirt with the tips of her fingers, run up and down a set of wooden steps placed in the centre of the school courtyard. He made a mental note of it for the future since he felt that the ability to read, write, and count, surpassed in usefulness the aptitude of stepping gracefully in and out of a carriage.

After the move, the Neuhoffs' cultural life grew richer, since Lwów was directly influenced by Vienna. The city's theatre, which at this time was flourishing, offered wonderful entertainment. Its traditions went as far back as the seventeenth century. Poland's preeminent drama writer, Count Aleksander Fredro, dubbed the *Polish Molière*, debuted in Lwów in 1815 with his comedy, *A Quick Intrigue,* and from the on, most premières of his plays were performed there as well. At that time Polish actors did not enjoy the same rights as German actors until 1837 when Count Stanisław Skarbek did battle for them in Vienna, securing equal privileges. He then founded a new theatre known as the Skarbek Theatre. A young budding actress, Aniela Aszperger, became its star performer. She was born in Warsaw, but moved to Lwów in 1840 with her husband, a stage director, and inaugurated the new Skarbek theatre in the lead role of one of Fredro's plays. Aniela Aszperger remained in Lwów for the rest of her life, but she made a gift of her talent to the world in the person of her great-grandson. Her younger daughter Leontyna Aniela, brought up in a Paris boarding school, married Adam Gielgud, a Polish journalist, and moved with him to England. Their son, Francis, married Katherine Terry of the famous acting family and it was their son, John, who became one of England's greatest actors.

In spite of the privileges officially granted to Polish actors, at first, they were still obliged to share the theatre facilities with the German ensemble on unequal terms. Their spectacles were relegated to less attractive days of the week and not until 1872, when the province of Galicia won its autonomy, would the Polish ensemble get full control of the theatre premises. In 1900 the new Great Theatre was erected in the style of the Paris Opéra Garnier, and Tadeusz Pawlikowski

---

[32] Adam Asnyk, (1838-1897) Polish poet and dramatist, one of the most prominent men of culture in partitioned Poland.

took the lead as its first general manager. He was an amazing thirty-nine-year-old stage manager who studied in Vienna, Leipzig, Weimar, and Meiningen and was encouraged by Franz Liszt to take up stage direction. He was a superb innovator. In his first season, he put on 71 plays, of which 28 were premières, performed during the first three months. The following six seasons, until 1906, saw 302 plays – half by Polish, half by foreign authors. His repertoire included the latest and the greatest, plays by Henrik Ibsen, Gerhart Hauptmann, Arthur Schnitzler, and Maurice Maeterlinck.

The opera repertoire was equally rich and offered performances by outstanding foreign singers, mainly Italian, although the lead dramatic soprano, Janina Korolewicz-Wajdowa, was Polish and a student of an extraordinary pedagogue, Walery Wysocki. Another singer who came out of the same school was the great bass-baritone, Adam Didur. His debut did not take place in Lwów, but at La Scala in Milan in 1903, followed in 1908 by the Metropolitan Opera in New York where he continued to perform for the next quarter of a century. Didur was much in demand by the most prestigious opera houses around the world. He sang in Cairo, Buenos Aires, and Rio de Janeiro. But his vacations were spent in Lwów and there he sang in the Great Theatre for the home public. My mother remembered him as Mefisto in Gounod's Faust. His satanic laughter in act II was an inimitable art, which Didur made uniquely his own.

By the time my grandparents moved to Lwów, the theatre was run by the outstanding Stage Director Ludwik Heller and the opera by Edward Okoński. The most beloved diva then was Amalia Kasprowicz, a singer 'for all seasons', who sang opera as well as operetta. But the real queen of the operetta was Helena Miłowska-Niewiarowicz. Both the theatre and the opera played a big part in the Neuhoff family's life and Uncle Zbyszek remembered it fondly, *"During those years after we moved to Lwów, we went often to the theatre because my father had a box for all the operas and operettas; my parents did not care so much for plays. After the performances, we would go to the Imperial restaurant which was patronised by opera singers. Korolewicz-Wajdowa often came there with her husband. She had an admirer, ophthalmologist Alfred Burzyński who was also my doctor. He was madly in love with her and sent her huge baskets of flowers after each performance. He was a bachelor, lived with his widowed mother, and one day disappeared from Lwów. Word got out that he went to Egypt, but committed suicide on the way. Supposedly it was a case of an 'American' duel as it was then practiced; a black ball and a white ball were placed in a top hat, and whoever pulled out the black one was in honour bound to shoot himself."*

Saturday matinées in the theatre were reserved for the young audiences, with many eminent actors taking part. These performances covered a broad repertoire of Polish comedy writers, such as Fredro and Bałucki, as well as dramas by Ibsen and Strindberg. There was also a Jewish theatre with plays performed in Yiddish. Its general manager, Jakub Gimpel, brought in troupes from Russia, with Esther Rokhl-Kaminska in Dybbuk. In this cultural hothouse, encouraged by their father, Zosia and Zbyszek acquired a taste for music and theatre and a lifelong love of literature.

1912. Lwów. The Neuhoff Family

By now Zbyszek was displaying a promising musical talent, so he was enrolled at the Galician Conservatory of the Music Society for piano lessons. Back in 1858, its director was Karol Mikuli, Chopin's pupil. The director's mantle passed on from him to one of his students, Mieczysław Sołtys – a conductor, composer, pedagogue, and author, whose works included a famous oratorio. The Music Society did not have a permanent orchestra, it was assembled ad hoc. There was a Ukrainian conservatory as well, managed by Wasyl Barwiński, a good composer, who also taught at the Galician Conservatory and was Uncle Zbyszek's first teacher of harmony.

When cinema came to Lwów it instantly became a huge success. The first silent movie shown was Quo Vadis, based on the novel by Henryk Sienkiewicz. It was so popular that tickets had to be bought days in advance. To celebrate the event, the painter Henryk Siemiradzki produced a realistic picture of a naked Ligia tied to the back of a bull in the Roman circus. But the city fathers deemed it to be far too risqué, so the painter was obliged to cover up the heroine's nakedness with little blossoms and a flowery wreath.

One manifestation of Vienna's influence on Lwów was the ubiquitous coffee-houses. Those who loved to sit at little tables for hours over one demitasse, conversing, debating, or reading the newspapers available to the habitués on wooden frames, were jokingly called 'kaffee-pflantzen', implying that these café plants had put in roots there.

Karol Ludwik Street was a very prestigious thoroughfare and boasted Sotchek's café, the most elegant in town. Uncle Zbyszek described it in detail: *"Sotchek's café consisted of two medium-sized rooms, one with a Viennese-style counter with trays of pastries and slices of tortes lined up, the other an elongated rectangle fitted out with small round tables and white metal chairs. The furnishing was archaic. Tea was served in glasses in metal holders on metal plates, pastries on small metal trays. The walls were blank except for one at the end of the room which was covered by a large painting of a young woman in a fantastic costume; a white shawl was slipping off her head as she walked down a country lane, straight towards the onlooker. In one hand she held a cane and in the other a jug of water, her eyes were closed, she was blind. The path was cutting across a field of golden wheat dotted with red poppies that brushed against her skirt. Why this painting was hanging in the café and what it symbolised remained a mystery to me."*

A daily *Corso* on Karol Ludwik Street passed in front of Sotchek's café and guests sitting at tables by the window could watch the strollers and acknowledge friends with a gentle nod. Sotchek had close ties to the Great Theatre and managed its two buffets, one in the foyer for the theatre public, the other backstage for actors and staff. Every day around eleven actors from the operetta came to the café, and this continued long after the *Corso* moved to Akademicka

Street where other coffee-houses took the prime. One of Sotchek's loyal habitués was Helena Miłowska, the operetta's leading diva of whom it was said that the Viennese waltz coursed through her veins. A dark blonde with an oval-shaped face and delicate features, she possessed a beautifully trained voice, an inborn musicality, discreet humour, and a personal charm that captivated her audiences. Uncle Zbyszek nostalgically remembered her walking onto the stage *"in a triple metre step; she was justly called the queen of the waltz. She was brilliant in Lehar's Merry Widow and the Gypsy Baron. I was nine years old when I saw her for the first time in Strauss's Night in Venice, and I still remember with emotion her silken voice and silvery laughter. Later on, I heard her as Siegel in Gounod's Faust with its waltz aria. Her stage name was Miłowska, in private life it was Niewiarowicz; her husband was an employee of the Mortgage Bank. I also knew her son Roman. Initially, he followed his mother onto the stage, but soon gave it up and turned to writing comedies, staging several of them quite successfully."*

The inhabitants of Lwów were a peculiar lot, known for their unique brand of humour and lack of reverence for celebrities. They loved their local heroes, but not slavishly. In 1901 the city fathers decided to erect a statue of Count Agenor Gołuchowski, a prominent politician, on one of the public squares. Thrice viceroy of Galicia and imperial regent, he promoted statutes on the abolition of serfdom; in his last administration he successfully rid the government bureaucracy of the German language, replacing it with Polish. Much of his work aimed at protecting Polish landowners and gentry.

1901. Lwów. Monument of Count Agenor Gołuchowski. [33]

The site chosen for the monument in a beautiful park, was prestigious; it was close to the regional parliament, the Galician Seym. Unfortunately, it also happened to be in the vicinity of a public toilet, popularly called "the municipal crap house". The unveiling was planned with much pomp and ceremony in the presence of invited guests, prominent citizens, and high dignitaries. After the speeches were delivered the cloth covering the sculpture was dropped and Gołuchowski emerged from under it in a tin chamber pot on his head, with a large roll of toilet paper in hand, and a rhyme scribbled on a piece of cardboard in *lvovian* slang, that loosely translated as:

Toilet paper in one hand,
He stands by the crap-house,
But what good is it to him,
Without a hole in his arse?

Amusing ditties and limericks on various topics and in varying shades of literacy and good taste abounded not only among the local low-life and street

---

[33] Source: Wikipedia. Creative Commons License. Photo from 1901. The monument has been destroyed around 1950.

slicks but among respectable bourgeoisie and aristocracy as well, although among the latter in a more refined vein. An occasion that gave rise to such a creative effort came after one of the Austrian archduchesses became pregnant out of wedlock. To remedy the situation, the Viennese court searched high and low, but mostly low, for an appropriate husband and found one in Lwów, in the person of a certain count Łoś, son of minor nobility with an unimpressive title. A hurriedly arranged wedding, with all due pomp, was followed by a sumptuous banquet and a ball at the Hofburg. Among the invited guests were two Polish aristocrats from Lwów, Count Dzieduszycki and Mrs Rey. As they passed each other on the dance floor Dzieduszycki murmured:

Did a surprised Łoś care?
That someone had already been there?

To which Mrs Rey replied without missing a beat:

Had that someone not been there,
He'd have no reason to care.

Apart from ribald rhymes and courtly poeticising, Lwów celebrated many emotional events. My Aunt Ludwika remembered a visit to the city by Ignacy Jan Paderewski.[34] As he walked from his hotel to the theatre for a concert, the eminent pianist was surrounded by an adoring crowd. Aunt Lusia described him as *"a tall, lanky man, with a mane of hair like burnished gold and a face marked by deep spirituality."* Another major happening was a visit by Henryk Sienkiewicz, one of Poland's leading writers, whose historical novels aimed at sustaining the public morale during the partition period.[35] Aunt Lusia also witnessed this occasion: *"it was already late in the evening, and with our mother, we came out into the street. One felt the electric current of excitement running through the crowd. Then his procession came into view. The horses had been unhooked from the carriage and it was being pulled by university students. There was no end to ovations by the crowd."*

---

[34] 860-1941. An eminent pianist, and composer and the first Prime Minister after Poland regained independence in 1918, Paderewski represented Poland at the Versailles Peace Conference in 1919, with considerable support from President Woodrow Wilson.
[35] Henryk Sienkiewicz 1846-1916. Nobel prize for literature 1905.

Similarly, in 1910 the funeral of Poland's pre-eminent poet Maria Konopnicka,[36] turned into a virtual patriotic manifestation. She was not a native of Lwów but lived there towards the end of her life and that was where she died. The city went into deep mourning and gave her a royal send-off. Street lanterns were draped in black crepe, bells rang in all the churches as the funeral procession proceeded towards the Łyczakowski Cemetery. From the main gate, students carried her coffin on their shoulders. Thousands lined the streets paying tribute to the dead poet.

Moving to Lwów, my grandparents changed their vacation venues to Austria, Italy, Switzerland, and Bavaria. Their social life in Lwów was more subdued than in Tarnopol, limited to receptions for their extended family and a handful of friends. Some of granny's relatives had moved to Lwów as well, hers was a very clannish family and she was close with her sisters, the younger redhead Helena and the older chestnut-hair Antonina. By then also her two brothers lived in Lwów.

On my grandfather's side, his siblings were scattered all over the Austro-Hungarian Empire. One brother, a lawyer, settled in Lwów, and was department head at the Treasury. A second brother, who never married, was a judge but committed suicide at an early age for unexplained reasons. A third brother was a doctor. He graduated from the medical school at the Jagiellonian University, joined the Austrian army, and was a colonel in the cavalry regiment. He never married and lived permanently in Budapest.

The youngest brother, a hydraulic engineer, worked on the regulation of waterworks of two rivers around Cracow in the vicinity of the Frank chicory factory. Of grandfather's three sisters, the oldest Janina was married to an Austrian and lived in Vienna, where her husband was the postmaster general of the Vienna post office. The second sister, Paulina, had married an engineer, Franciszek Kuhn, the inventor of the recycling system for steam engines. The third sister, Sabina remained single.

---

[36] Maria Konopnicka 1842-1910. One of Poland's most influential poets.

Grandfather's brother Colonel Dr. Wladyslaw Neuhoff

The family ties varied, they were very intimate with some members, with others limited to weddings, christenings, and visits at Christmastime. Granny was closest to her younger sister Helena, but with such a large extended family, the Neuhoff children enjoyed an abundance of aunts, uncles, and cousins. Granny's amanuensis, the irreplaceable Basia Jawna, moved to Lwów with the family and was ruling the household with a firm hand, a holy terror to all the maids. Basia was not very tall, nor very stout, and at all times wore a kerchief on her head knotted at the back. She was Ruthenian of peasant stock and came from the village of Hłuboczek where she had a brother, Wasil, and a sister. Since she was semiliterate, it fell to my teenage mother to write Basia's letters to her family. Regardless of content, every letter started with the same sacrosanct formula: *"A little fly is buzzing around my little ear, I'm writing this letter to you from the bottom of my heart."*

Basia was devoted to granny, but her deepest love was reserved for my mother, Zosia, her beloved *dońcia*.[37] She was a Greek Catholic but attended Mass at the nearby Roman Catholic church of St. Nicholas. When Andrzej Szeptycki, the grandson of the playwright Aleksander Fredro, became archbishop metropolitan of the Greek Catholic church in Lwów, there were strong pressures on the Ruthenian population to attend the services at Saint George's Greek Catholic cathedral. Granny told Basia that's where she should go, which she did until her first Easter confession when the priest sharply reprimanded her for her faulty Ruthenian. An indignant Basia left the church in a huff and informed my grandmother that she will never set foot there again. She returned to St. Nicholas where her brand of Ruthenian-Polish *Esperanto* was courteously accepted.

Uncle Zbyszek recalled that in his parents' home *"all Church rules were meticulously observed. We went to Mass unfailingly, at first to the Jesuit church, then later on we switched to the church of Saint Mary Magdalene. Fridays were meatless days of abstinence, Christmas and Easter were solemnly celebrated. For the traditional Polish Wigilia on Christmas Eve, we sat down to dinner with all the domestics. It was an intimate family affair. On Easter Sunday, my parents entertained the family and December 26th, my father's names-day, the feast of St Stephen his patron saint, was celebrated with a large reception. But on Easter Monday it was Aunt Helena's turn to give a dinner party, a custom that continued after her first husband died and she had remarried. Throughout the year there were many occasions for family gatherings, some were even weekly affairs: granny's brother Uncle Misio and Aunt Runia often came for brunch after the twelve o'clock Mass at the Jesuits, as they used to do in Tarnopol, and that leisurely meal dragged on for hours."*

The 'twelve o'clock' at the Jesuits' as it was popularly known, was mostly attended by local landowners and aristocracy. It was a quiet Mass with organ music. A red carpet was laid all the way from the main door to the altar and chairs for the most distinguished members of the congregation were set up close to the main altar. Typically, the collection plate filled with generous donations of silver coins.

---

[37] Darling in Ruthenian

For Easter granny ordered potted hyacinths and cineraria from the florist and grandfather arranged them himself, one of his few 'domestic' chores. On Holy Saturday, a priest from the nearby church of St Mary Magdalene came to bless the table and as he left, grandfather would slip a hefty banknote into the pocket of his cassock. Strict fast was observed until after the Resurrection Mass when it was time for hams and sausages, rich *babas* and tortes baked throughout that entire week leading up to Easter.

Among the immediate family, my grandfather was the wealthiest. Indifferent to the prestige of country estates and rural land ownership, he considered urban real estate, apartment buildings with office space and shops, as the most worthwhile investment. Relatives came to him with their money problems and time and time again he would bail out the younger ones who wallowed in gambling debts and obligations.

Although Stefan Neuhoff had retired from his position with the railways after moving to Lwów, in 1913 he was offered the post of a counsellor to the Ministry of Railways in Vienna. It was a tempting proposition and hard to turn down a prestigious assignment, so he accepted. For the duration, Basia Jawna was to stay with her relatives in the village of Hłuboczek, while in Vienna the family would reside with grandfather's sister, Janina Terlecka, in Währingbezirk where the Türkenschanz Park marked the site of the old Turkish entrenchments. For the next two years vacations would be spent in Viareggio in Tuscany, with stops in many cities on the way, for Zbyszek's and Zosia's cultural enrichment.

The First World War broke out on 28 July 1914 surprising them in Viareggio. They returned to Vienna post-haste, my grandfather resigned from his position as advisor to the ministry and moved the family to Innsbruck. Uncle Zbyszek spoke with nostalgia of the years he spent in that charming town. *"Our apartment was located on the south side, on the ground floor, with windows giving onto the Wilten monastery. The view was of the Alps, of three peaks, Patsch, Serles, and Seiler and the electric mountain railroad Stubeibahn ran the length as far as the Stubei valley"* Zbyszek was enrolled in the second year of the gymnasium and the music studies that he started at the Viennese conservatory under Seweryn Eisenberger, the best professor at the time, were resumed in Innsbruck with another well-known pianist, Leo Sirota. Music would remain my uncle's lifelong passion, but for my grandfather mathematics held the pride of place, a subject Zbyszek heartily detested. To his disgust each day he was forced to give it many hours under his father's watchful eye. These evenings over the hated algebra became entwined with the memory of the mountain train, with its windows lit, as at eight o'clock precisely it wound its way along the Alps, announcing the end of the mathematical torture. Zosia displayed no such hard feelings towards arithmetic and happily attended a primary school run by nuns. My grandfather continued his professional life, and during that time won a competition for a project of two churches in the vicinity of Innsbruck, one in Mutters, the other one in Natters. In the midst of the conflagration raging across Europe, Innsbruck became an oasis of quiet and normal life, although that panacea would not last.

During the family's stay in Austria, two events of great significance seemingly presaged the shattering of the existing world order. Pope Pius X died in 1914 and Emperor Franz Josef in 1916. By the end of that year, the Neuhoff family said farewell to Innsbruck and returned to Vienna. At the beginning of 1917, my grandfather went back to Lwów for two months where he found his properties in Tarnopol in good order, but the Lwów apartment had been ransacked and looted. He rented a large second-floor apartment on Sykstuska Street and set up his office on the first floor of the same building. The house belonged to Count Agenor Gołuchowski and a few years later my grandfather bought it from him. The Cieński family, one of the wealthiest landowners in Galicia, lived across the street in a beautiful residence and Uncle Zbyszek remembered their two daughters – very devout, prim, young ladies always soberly dressed, with their hair pulled tightly to the back, as they pottered in the garden. The older sister, Magdalena, married a university professor; the younger Anna, an agricultural engineer, and both would eventually share my mother's fate at the outbreak of WWII.

Chapter V

Lwów After WWI. Portrait of a City

That same year, 1917, my grandparents returned to Lwów with my mother, leaving Uncle Zbyszek behind in Vienna with Aunt Janina to continue his studies at the conservatory, at least until he finished high school. But the political situation forced them to change those plans. Whether out of fear that the war which was to be over by Christmas according to popular wishful thinking, but had already dragged on for three years, or a sudden shift in the balance of powers between the fast crumbling empires, would separate the family for a long time, or perhaps over concerns for Zbyszek's weak health, for whatever the reason my grandfather brought him back to Lwów at the start of the new school year and enrolled him in the elite and snobbish Adam Mickiewicz gymnasium founded by Doctor Karol Petelenz.

My mother was sent to the private school of the Sisters of the Holy Family of Nazareth founded in 1908 as a middle school, which became a full-fledged eight-year humanistic high school by 1915. Zosia was now old enough to go by herself on the tram that wound its way across town and left her at the door. This tram continued up the Tall Castle Hill, a favourite spot for students playing hooky. From its top, a panoramic view of the old town spread below with the graceful red Korniakt tower built in 1580 deemed one of the most beautiful Renaissance towers in all of Central Europe, the green dome of the Dominican church, and the roofs of houses submerged in the sea of treetops, because Lwów was an eminently green city with countless parks and squares. While at mother's new school there was no practice of graceful alighting from carriages, it boasted a team of outstanding teachers and educators. Religion was taught by Fr. Eugeniusz Baziak, the future archbishop of Lwów, a brilliant intellectual and outstandingly good-looking man, a fact that added much charm to classes of catechism in an all-girls' school.

The war ended in November 1918 and after one hundred and twenty-three years of partition, Poland recovered her independence and became a single country. However, renewed fighting broke out immediately because on 1 November armed Ukrainian groups overran all the major public installations in Lwów. Furious battles raged all over town, with snipers from both sides shooting from the rooftops. It lasted until 21 November when the Ukrainians abandoned their positions and pulled out but continued to lay siege to the city.

My grandfather joined the Municipal Citizen Guard entrusted with maintaining order and safety at night. The guardsmen were issued rifles and were given police authority. Regular army units now went into action and on 21 April they were reinforced by regiments under General Haller. The struggle went on until June, while the construction of the Eaglets' Cemetery was started in one section of the Łyczakowski Cemetery to bury the young defenders who fought and died in the early days of the conflict.[38] In the meantime, on 14 March 1919, the Polish-Russian war broke out, not with the tsarist regime which was now gone, but with the newly minted Soviet Russia bent on bringing its brand of international communism to the entire world proletariat. According to Lenin, Warsaw was not just the hub of the bourgeois Polish government and its capitalist republic, but the centre of the entire imperialist world system. For the duration of the war, Stefan Neuhoff moved his family to Kraków. In his reminiscences, Uncle Zbyszek wrote that they spent the war in the village close to Kraków. *"It was a beautiful place, in the middle of pine forests, close to Kalwaria Zebrzydowska, famous for its Via Crucis, a string of tiny chapels spread over a few kilometres."* Zbyszek went into town almost daily, wandering through the ancient city, exploring old nooks and streets, visiting antiquarian booksellers, and starting his lifelong romance with Kraków.

---

[38] Known as Cmentarz Orląt. The youngest of the Eaglets buried there was thirteen-year-old Antoś Petrykiewicz, posthumously decorated with the Cross of Virtuti Military, Poland's highest order for valour. Another one was 14-year-old Jurek Bitschan On 11 November 1921 Marshal Piłsudski decorated the city of Lwów with the Order of Virtuti Militari.

1920. Lwów. Uncle Zbyszk

An armistice was concluded on 12 October 1921 and a peace treaty signed on 18 October in Riga. Lwów resumed its daily normal life and nineteen-year-old Zbyszek was now given a room with a separate entrance. He dreamt to become a concert pianist and when the famous Dutch pianist, Egon Petri came to town, Zbyszek got from him a positive and encouraging evaluation.

But my uncle's plans ran into stiff opposition from my grandfather who saw an artistic career as a slippery road. *"First, get yourself a solid profession,"* he advised soberly. Zbyszek's health was not robust after illnesses suffered in childhood and Stefan was aware that a career of a pianist, with long hours of practice and exhausting concert tours, could easily undermine his son's physical condition. Giving in to pressure, Zbyszek settled for law school at the Jan Kazimierz University of Lwów.

At the same time, Zosia's demanding baccalaureate finals were approaching. On 18 June 1923, she completed the cycle of examinations with flying colours, and *"based on the outstanding results, [was] declared competent to pursue academic studies,"* as stated in the diploma.

Finally! A chorus of aunts and cousins exclaimed enthusiastically in unison. After achieving such brilliant results in her *matura,*[39] it was time for Zosia to get serious about marriage. But the horror of horrors, Zosia displayed no such inclination. On the contrary, she was contemplating following her brother into law school. Family fireworks exploded, aunts reached for smelling salts, and raised an anguished cry: Impossible! Zosia, lingering among old musty books, would assuredly end as an old maid. My grandmother just clasped her hands in desperation, but she felt helpless to save her daughter from the impending disaster since Zosia's own father was wholeheartedly encouraging the headstrong girl in this reckless pursuit. *"Old Neuhoff has gone mad, going along with such crazy whims,"* the aunts declared darkly, giving Zosia up for lost. In spite of these gloomy prognoses, in 1924 my mother enrolled in law school and contrary to her aunts' predictions the Neuhoff household filled with suitors.

Mother's appearance in the first year of law created a stir, as Uncle Zbyszek remembered, *"as soon as Zosia entered the university, most young unmarried members of the lvovian Bar and of the faculty fell in love with her en masse and flocked to our house."* Even though she was determined to pursue her studies, an abundance of candidates provided much food for fascinating debates. Years later Uncle Zbyszek mused about these *"late night chats between my sister and our parents, sometimes lasting 'til wee hours of the morning. Although none of the rejected suitors committed suicide out of hopeless love like young Werther, the next world war took care of most of them."* But at that time nobody thought of future cataclysmic events. The world was awakening to life after the bloodletting which killed sixteen million and maimed twenty-one million more, and WWI was hailed as the war to end all wars. What followed were madly exuberant *roaring twenties*, bursting upon Europe from America with Dixieland jazz born in New Orleans, the craze of the Charleston, and the Argentine tango.

The Victorian era, which for so long set the standards of social mores among the wealthy bourgeoisie of Central Europe as much as it did in Great Britain, now definitely came to an end. New ways displaced old ones, dancing parties gained in popularity, women's fashions became more daring, lace collars, puffed sleeves, floor-length skirts, and tight corsets went out the window, hems rose to mid-calf, long strings of beads became all the rage, short hair replaced long

---

[39] Polish for baccalaureate

tresses and elaborate coils. These were baby steps towards women's emancipation which Zosia wholeheartedly embraced. In Poland, women were granted the right to vote and to stand for election in 1918.

Mother never lacked for suitors…

… but always duly chaperoned

Still, balls continued to be the proper social venue for well-bred young ladies of good families, and my mother surely did not lack for dance partners. The social club known as Municipal Casino and Literary Circle still organised elegant balls during the carnival season which Zosia attended, duly escorted by granny and uncle Zbyszek, since by now my grandfather had left the responsibility to his son. As in bygone days, mothers, aunts, and chaperones sat on sofas along the walls, and certain social niceties had to be observed, such as a young man introducing himself to mamma before asking the daughter for a waltz.

After WWI Vienna's influence on Lwów waned giving way to trends set by Warsaw. The city changed physically. The old electric wiring stretched between poles was replaced with underground cables, and automatic street gas lighting was installed. Akademicka, the poshest thoroughfare in town, was remade into a wide avenue with a lawn, trees, and benches running through the middle. Modern multi-storey structures, such as the Sprecher Building, replaced old two-storey houses. But apartment buildings were as yet quite antiquated, bathrooms were heated with wood or coal, there were no bidets, water closets were separate units from the actual bathrooms. Kitchen stoves burned coal, although, modern double-burner gas stoves were increasingly coming into vogue, which were set up on metal shelves fixed to the walls.

In 1922 the newly restored Polish Parliament or Seym was debating a bill on pensions for railway workers, and my grandfather frequently travelled to Warsaw, lobbying for the approval of a Central Union of Railway Pensioners for the Lwów region. His aim was to secure better pensions for railway workers and ways and means that would give them added sources of income. A union was created and the institution of 'Red Caps' or luggage carriers was introduced at the main railway station in Lwów. Retired railwaymen carried passengers' luggage from trains to cabs for a fee, supplementing their meagre pensions.

Lwów's cultural and social life revolved around the Municipal Casino and Literary Circle. The Casino had nothing to do with gambling, and the name derived from military officers' mess that was once located there. Uncle Zbyszek visited it often but noted that over the years the earlier level of sophistication of events that were organised was dwindling. And while gentlemen still dined in the upper floor restaurant, balls were held during the carnival season, and lectures, and concerts all year round, among the city elite interest in topics such as philosophy, art, or politics was waning. There was an exception though, Zbyszek wrote, *"among my many young Jewish acquaintances our discussions and debates were truly satisfying, although their life views were often tinged red."* In the park across from the Casino stood a bust of Kornel Ujejski, the last great Polish romantic poet. He had his back to the building, and malicious tongues asked: why was he turning his back on the Literary Circle?

Apart from the Casino and Literary Circle, there was also the Horse Casino, an exclusive club for the aristocracy and local landowners, where, as my uncle ironically remarked, *"normal mortals were not readily admitted."*

In 1923 grandfather's friend, Monsignor Twardowski, erstwhile pastor of the parish church in Tarnopol, became archbishop of Lwów. Another old friend, the apothecary Marian Krzyżanowski, joined my grandparents' intimate circle when he moved to Lwów and bought a pharmacy in the Mikolasch gallery. In the nineteenth century covered galleries like the Passage Jouffroy in Paris, were in vogue throughout Europe and Lwów built several of them, mostly named after the original owners: there was the Andriolli Passage, the Hausmann Passage, the Fellers' Passage, and the Mikolasch Passage built in the 1890's that became a fashionable place for strolling, meeting in the café, and shopping in elegant pricey boutiques. In time it also acquired a cinema. Daylight poured in through the glass dome of the roof, illuminating the stained-glass windows; in the evening the gallery was lit with artificial light, and in the winter, it was heated. A fountain graced by a marble nymph stood at the entrance to the passage and the largest pharmacy in town, *Under the Golden Star* which Marian Krzyżanowski bought, occupied the first building of the gallery at number one.

This pharmacy had been established by Piotr Mikolasch in 1828 and remained in his family for one hundred years. In 1846 a young pharmacist apprentice, Jan Józef Ignacy Łukasiewicz[40], son of an impoverished aristocratic family and an ardent patriot, was involved in subversive political activities, and he was arrested and jailed in Lwów by the Austrian authorities. Though he was set free for lack of evidence, he remained suspect and was not permitted to leave town. It was then that he became employed in the pharmacy. Its owner, Piotr Mikolasch, soon realised the young man's enormous scientific potential and after some time, through his persistent efforts, Łukasiewicz was allowed to enrol at the Jagiellonian University in Kraków for four years, supported financially by Mikolasch. He went on to study in Vienna and after receiving his doctorate, returned to Lwów and to the pharmacy, where he ran experiments with naphtha lamps and distillation of oil from natural oil seeps in the region of the Carpathian Mountains. Łukasiewicz can be truly called the father of the petroleum industry and the pharmacy 'Under the Golden Star', its undeniable cradle.

---

[40] Jan Józef Ignacy Łukasiewicz 1822-1882.

Uncle Zbyszek might have detested mathematics, but he loved chemistry and was a frequent visitor at the pharmacy. His parents' friend, Marian Krzyżanowski, was an apothecary of the old school that prepared its own drugs, potions and pills, miraculous creams against freckles, reviving smelling salts, and all-healing waters. The pharmacy had large personnel, and the apothecary's son Fredzio, after he got his degree in pharmaceutical sciences, also worked with his father. White porcelain jars with hand-painted flowers and Latin names of the stuff they contained lined the shelves along the walls, next to green and amber glass bottles, also labelled in Latin. A scale in a glass case took the pride of place on the counter; garnet crystals scattered on one plate served as tare, and microgram balance weights for precision weighing sat in a wooden box alongside. Marian Krzyżanowski's office was next to the shop and there was a scale-chair that served to weigh people. In the laboratory on the upper floor, a couple of technicians mashed, grounded and measured ingredients for various concoctions in small metal and porcelain mortars.

My uncle's interest in chemistry stemmed from a hobby about which he was passionate – photography. From an early age, he had been making artistic photographs. His father allowed him to buy the chemicals needed for developing and to arrange a dark-room, where he prepared, retouched, and framed his pictures. Wet strips of film attached with clothespins hung on lines, a red light-bulb suspended over the basins with liquids spread a mysterious glow. That was Zbyszek's kingdom and other family members were barred from it since, God forbid, a streak of light could overexpose a film. He bought books, prepared solutions, pestered everybody to sit for him, and more often than not got his sister to pose in fancy hats.

Posing for her brother in fancy hats

His second hobby was clocks and watches which he collected since childhood, large and small. He made friends with other amateurs and one of them old Maćków, the doorman from a large house in the Market Square, was a collector of antique clocks in his own right. As Uncle Zbyszek wrote, *"[Maćków] was a particularly knowledgeable watchmaker. Sometimes he would come to our house to help me and after a glass of Baczewski nourishing nectar,[41] he expounded at length and taught me."* Another mate in this close-knit circle was an old watchmaker, Rosengarten, with whom Zbyszek spent many happy hours on a park bench, amid the chirping of birds and away from the noise of

---

[41] Baczewski was the best-known establishment in Lwów, selling wines and fine spirits. The vodka factory, dating back to late 18th century, was based in <u>Lwów</u> and until 1939 was one of two most popular Polish export goods.

traffic, discussing the secrets of timepiece movements. There were also Jude Schwert, a dealer in clocks, and Gerstin, the general importer of Swiss watches in Lwów. As a teenager, Zbyszek began to visit antiquarian shops, buying old wrecks, then spending hours poring over the table strewn with screws, springs, pendulums, and with almost Benedictine patience using tiny tweezers, he assembled the minute mechanisms.

After getting his law degree, my uncle opted to go to the Jagiellonian University in Cracow for his doctorate. In the meantime, my mother was getting close to completing her master's in law degree at the Jan Kazimierz University. It was a four-year curriculum, each academic year made up of three semesters ending in final examinations. Zosia was in the habit of studying aloud and the rhythmic chanting of Latin texts from behind the closed door of her room drove granny's housekeeper Basia to despair because she imagined that with all that 'wisdom' her darling would study herself to death. So Basia snuck into her room every few hours with a tray in hand.

But for Zosia, all was not hard work and no play. She still found time for social life and during the 1928 carnival season at a ball, she met Doctor Maksymilian Hoffman, good looking barrister, excellent dancer, good tennis player, who had a weakness for elegant ties. He was charming and she liked him a lot, above all for his easy unaffected manner and for his enthusiastic approval of her career plans. He for his part fell madly in love instantly. After a few months' courtship, he proposed in the middle of the dance floor at another ball. But Zosia still had one full year of law school ahead. Receiving no answer, he took it for a 'no', and the contact was broken off.

Lwów 1929. Zosia, Magistra Legum

On 9 July 1929, diplomas were handed out in the *aula magna* of Jan Kazimierz University. It was Zosia's hour of triumph, but also her father's because Stefan Neuhoff was immensely proud of this beloved daughter, who took after him in character and personality.

Mother's results were very good in every subject but outstanding in civil and procedural law, and they merited special mention with distinction. She became the third woman in Poland to graduate from law school. The young *Magistra legum* was showered with accolades and good wishes, yet she knew that this was not the final step. Two tough years of law practice awaited before she would be able to take her examination for the Bar.

For starters, she decided it was time to relax and enjoy a bit of social life. She was besieged by suitors, among them a brilliant anthropologist, professor of ethnology at the Jagiellonian University who was determined to win her hand. Zosia dithered. She was flattered by his attentions and much taken by his extraordinary intellect, but in love with him? Not really. In her mind, there was a serious obstacle to the union. Professor Jan Bystroń was a strict Calvinist, his unsmiling greeting of 'Peace be to this house', each time he crossed the threshold was a bit of a damper. She could not see herself living a strict ascetic life. She was a Roman Catholic, there could be no question of converting. Zosia was full of joy; she loved life and a good laugh. In her vivid imagination myriad adventures from thousand and one nights awaited, shimmering and beckoning. And a promising law career to boot. Evermore often her thoughts turned to Maks Hoffman, the easy-going barrister who danced well, wore beautiful ties, admired her independence, and had fallen so romantically in love with her, that he proposed in the middle of a waltz. Sadly, since her unspoken refusal, he had not renewed his attentions and their paths had not crossed again.

With tennis partners. Maks on the left in the rear

By this time my grandfather did little by way of professional work, devoting himself to the administration of his properties and to his great passion, history of ancient Greece. He was a prodigious reader; he bought and ordered a great deal of books. He also enjoyed his collection of paintings, mostly by contemporary Polish artists, with a few old masters thrown in, of which the most valuable one was by the Italian Baroque painter, Carlo Maratta, a portrait of a canon in a lavender scarf that hung in the *salon* above the sofa.

In the spring of 1930, the dire economic situation worldwide proved calamitous for Poland. My grandfather sold one of his properties to a nunnery the day before the stock market crashed and the next day the sum of money he received was worth a box of matches. For the third time in his life, Stefan Neuhoff started to rebuild his family's fortunes. At that time early symptoms of heart disease began to appear and my grandparents decided to move away from the centre to a quieter part of town. They bought a villa with a garden and an orchard slightly on the outskirts.

In the meantime, Zbyszek continued to prepare for his doctoral finals in Kraków, the dreaded *rigorosum*. Finally, the day arrived. His examiner was Professor Franciszek Ksawery Fierich of the Jagiellonian University, a renowned specialist in civil procedural law who was also president of the Polish Codification Commission of the Seym set up in Warsaw in 1919 to unify and reconcile all aspects of civil and criminal law for the country. On the eve of Armistice Day, Poland had no government, no parliament, and no constitution. The reborn Polish State came into existence practically overnight from three regions into which it had been partitioned since 1795. Józef Piłsudski, a military commander who launched the struggle for Poland's independence at the outbreak of WWI, became a temporary head of state. He was entrusted with forming a temporary government and immediately ordered elections to the Seym which took place in January 1919. The newly elected parliament then issued a call to all lawyers' associations from across the land to submit proposals for a new constitution. The most serious projects came from Jan Kazimierz University and the Polish Law Society of Lwów since Poles living in the Austrian Galicia had the most extensive legal experience thanks to the region's relative autonomy. The postulates presented had been worked on by an elite group of barristers, the crème de la crème of *lvovian* legal profession. Among them were Maurycy Allerhand, member of the State Tribunal and professor of Jan Kazimierz University, Roman Longchamps de Berier, eminent specialist in civil law, Kamil Stefko, member of the Polish Academy of Learning, and Julian Nowotny, an authority on criminal law.[42]

Doctoral candidates presenting themselves for the *rigorosum* had to adhere to a strict dress code. *"Can you imagine,"* Uncle Zbyszek told me, *"what it was like for a candidate to be dressed in a tailcoat and a tight collar while sweating*

---

[42] Maurycy Allerhand died in 1942 in Belzec concentration camp. Roman Longchamps de Bérier (1883–1941) the last rector of the Jan Kazimierz University of Lwów, murdered together with his three sons by the SS in 1941 in what became known as the Massacre of Lwów professors.

like a pig from sheer nerves? I was waiting in the library to be called. When I finally walked in, old Professor Fierich sat wrapped in a heavy overcoat. He was recovering from a bout of pneumonia. 'I was sitting on a bench in the park with the sun in the front and shade in the back, and I caught a cold', he complained."

My grandfather came to Kraków for the presentation of diplomas. The ceremony took place in the Aula Magna of the Academy. Zbyszek was ushered in by four attendants in black gowns carrying halberds, the *rector magnificus* Professor Henryk Hoyer, biologist, dressed in a red toga, presided on the podium, surrounded by deans in black togas. Two rolls lay before him on a table, a smaller one and a large one with seals. Uncle's promoter, the eminent historian Professor Władysław Konopczyński,[43] presented his *Vitae*, whereupon the rector read out the text of the diploma in Latin, addressing Zbyszek as *Illustrissimi Vir*, in the name of the *Serenissimae Republicae Polonorum*, he, *Henricus Hoyer Universitates Jagellonicae Rector Magnificus*, together with two deans, awarded *Virum Clarissimum Zbigneum Ioannem Neuhoff* the title of *Doctoris Iuris*. Academy of Kraków did nothing by halves.[44]

In the meantime, back in Lwów, Zosia weighed her chances of finding a law practice for a two-year apprenticeship prior to the Bar examination. She knew it wouldn't be easy, during the current economic crisis law firms didn't hire young applicants. On a beautiful July day, she sat on a streetcar deep in thought mulling over her dilemma, when the sound of the tram's bell jerked her out of her reverie. Jumping up from the seat she made a dash for the door, stepped onto the pavement, and bumped straight into a man waiting at the bus stop. It was Maks Hoffman. Both were flustered by the unexpected encounter, but he was quicker to recover; gallantly kissing her hand and as if afraid that the magic moment might elude him, he shot the question: *"Miss Sophie, don't you owe me an answer?"* This time it was a firm 'yes'.

They strolled arm in arm along the green island lined with trees that ran down the middle of Akademicka Street. Finally, they decided that Zosia would go ahead to tell her parents about their engagement and Maks would follow shortly

---

[43] Wladyslaw Konopczyński, (1880-1952) eminent historian, member of the Polish delegation to the Paris Peace Conference in 1919. During World War II, Konopczyński survived German imprisonment at Sachsenhausen concentration camp. After the war he was deprived of his academic post by the communist regime. He was awarded the French Légion d' honneur by the French government.

[44] Founded in 1364 by King Casimir III the Great, the Jagiellonian University is the oldest university in Poland, the second oldest university in Central Europe.

to ask for her hand. He walked her to the house and then made a beeline for the nearest flower stall on the street corner. The flowers arranged in baskets glowed in the sun with myriad colours, like one oversized bouquet. The florist, chewing on a long piece of straw grass, and his young helper sat on low stools next to the stand. Maks took out his card and scribbled the Neuhoffs' address. *"That's where the flowers are to be delivered"* he said, handing it to the man. *"Which ones?"* the vendor asked laconically. *"All of them,"* said Maks pulling out his wallet. The vendor took the money with a sphinx-like expression, only slightly raising one eyebrow. As Maks walked away, he heard the man saying to his assistant: *"Józik, hop-off with those flowers."* Then quietly, but still audibly, *"Can't you see the guy is as madly in love, as a March cat?"* clearly referring to the popular lore of March being the cats' mating season, even though it was August. My father could not help smiling at this accurate allusion.

Maks was twelve years Sophie's senior. After WWI ended in 1918, he volunteered for the Polish army and joined the officer corps of the 30th infantry regiment in the rank of captain. He took part in the defence of Lwów, then was transferred to the 39th infantry regiment and fought in the Polish-Russian war of 1920 and continued to serve for the next three years until 1922 when he was finally discharged, but remained in the reserves. Wars and conflicts took out eight years of his life. Throughout these years, whenever he was on leave from the front, he studied. He completed his master of law degree and went on to get his doctorate in 1925. His diploma carried the signatures of several eminent academics of the time: Włodzimierz Sieradzki,[45] *rector magnificus*, Oswald Balzer, an authority on the history of law and representative government systems, and Maks's promoter. It stated that VIRUM CLARISSIMUM, MAXIMILIANUM ADOLPHUM HOFFMAN, NATIONE POLONUM LEOPOLI ORIUNDUM,[46] had passed all the examinations and has been awarded the title of Juris Doctor with all the privileges, etc. that it entailed.

---

[45] Włodzimierz Sieradzki, professor of forensic pathology, murdered in July 1941 in a group of 41 *lvovian* professors executed by the German SS. Five more professors were executed later on in the same month, among them the eminent mathematician, Kazimierz Bartel, former prime minister of Poland.

[46] Native of Poland, citizen of Lwów.

Maks's doctoral diploma

Four fiscal stamps affixed to the diploma were intended, as inscribed, *for the purchase of gold and silver*. After the devastation brought on by the recent wars, Poland was straining to replenish her depleted national coffers.

In order to be entered on the list of practicing attorneys, two years of law practice were required before he could take his Bar examination. Soon Maks took a position with a law firm and by November 1927 presented himself at the Appellate Court for the finals. Those were tough three days of written examinations and one day of oral. He passed them successfully and in January 1928 was duly inscribed in the register of the Chamber of Lawyers and admitted to the Bar.

For Maks, 1928 turned out to be a momentous year. Not only was he now a full-fledged attorney working for the well-recognised law firm of Doctor Argasiński, but during the carnival season, he met Zosia Neuhoff – a third-year law student with whom he instantly fell in love. He confessed to his sister that she was the "one and only". He proposed, but his offer of marriage remained unacknowledged. In desperation, Maks swore to remain a bachelor to the end of his days.

Two years had passed since then and even though Lwów was not a large city, they never saw each other, until the day when by the sheer twist of fate, Zosia literally ran into him at the bus stop. My grandparents approved of her choice, although they had been surprised no doubt by this unexpected turn of events when their daughter went into town and returned home engaged. Preceded by a colossal basket of flowers, Maks asked for her hand. By now he had acquired doctor Argasinski's law practice and could offer his bride-to-be a reasonable livelihood. Still, the economic situation in the country was dire and the practice itself was not doing that well, so my grandfather offered to buy the engagement rings and presented the couple with two emeralds in heavy settings of white gold. Maks, in turn, explained with a soldier's directness that he simply had no time for long engagements. He and Zosia agreed on a wedding date in October. And what about her law practice he asked outright. Did she take her career seriously, or merely for amusement? Because right at that moment he needed a junior lawyer. Mother assured him that she was serious about her profession. So, it was settled that after the wedding, she would do her two-year apprenticeship in his office.

My grandfather's help was not limited to the engagement rings. He rented a flat for them at no.12 Kadecka Street. Up to that moment, Maks had been living with his widowed mother, while his sister Lusia had long been married to Karol Düring, director of the institute for blind children. The couple's only child, a little girl Jasia, died at the age of seven. My father was thirty-seven years old by then and granny Paulina was delighted that Maks finally decided to marry. *"Your grandmother didn't like old bachelors,"* Aunt Lusia told me, *"she was so happy that your mummy agreed to be his wife. A relative of your Uncle Karol met her shortly after the engagement and news spread like wildfire that Maks has a lovely fiancée."*

My grandfather's friend, Bolesław Twardowski, Archbishop of Lwów, offered to perform the wedding in the cathedral, but too many rejected suitors in Lwów created an awkward social dilemma, who to invite, who rather not. In the end, my mother opted for a quiet ceremony in the Gothic church of St Mary in Kraków. On 4 October 1930, the wedding party of fourteen family members and closest friends travelled by train to the royal city. My parents were married by the bishop at the main altar under the magnificent Gothic masterpiece, the triptych of Wit Stwosz (Veit Stoss). The bride wore a cream-coloured suit instead of a long wedding gown. Grandfather's friend, the apothecary Marian Krzyżanowski was the witness for the bride, and my father's best friend Doctor Stefan Margold was the witness for the groom. As a young man, Doctor Margold had lost an eye in an accident, and since then he wore a monocle, which lent him a very distinguished air. The reception was held in the Grand Hotel, a former residence of the Princes Czartoryski. The wedding party returned to Lwów that same day.

Kraków. St. Mary's Church, Veit Stoss Altar

Now that mother was married several of her suitors rushed to tie the knot and the following year abounded in a large number of weddings. Uncle Zbyszek was still unmarried, but he had already met the great love of his life at a masked ball during the carnival in the Literary Casino. Her name was Anna Dąbrowska, a twenty-five-year-old dark-haired beauty. At the time when uncle met her, Anna was working in the accounting office of the travel organisation, ORBIS. She lived in Lwów with a maiden aunt, Miss Maria (Misia) Demel, an activist in the National Democratic Party, a right-of-centre political grouping. For her social work, Miss Misia had been awarded the *Polonia Restituta*, Order of the Rebirth of Poland, one of Poland's highest decorations. After my parents were married

Uncle Zbyszek and Anna got engaged and made plans for their own wedding. But first, uncle had to secure a job position. Since he intended to be a judge, he completed his legal apprenticeship in the tribunals, and successfully passed his examinations. Now he could present himself, duly attired in a tailcoat, for an interview with the presiding judge of the Appellate Court. For starters he was offered a post in the prosecutor's office of a small neighbouring town, a post he happily accepted. Unhappily stormy politics at the time got in the way in the guise of Miss Misia's membership in the National Democratic Party. Although my uncle had no political affiliation of any sort, toxic fumes from the fierce wrangling going on between major political parties poisoned the lives of ordinary folk. Because of his fiancée's aunt, Uncle Zbyszek was turned down for the judgeship. Angry and disgusted he immediately returned to Lwów, resigned from the prosecutor's office, and opted for law practice.

As soon as the word got around that Zbyszek Neuhoff was professionally available, he was offered a position in the northern city of Gdańsk at the Danziger Werft shipyard that opened in 1921. It replaced the old Kaiserliche Werft Danziger shipyard. The consortium was financed by Polish, German, Danziger, and Dutch capitals. Its president was Dr Noe from the Gdańsk University, the commercial director was a Dutchman, De Vogl, and at the beginning of 1931 Zbyszek became head of the legal department, a position nominated by the Polish government.[47]

His wedding was set for 2 January 1932. *"I was living in the Continental Hotel in Gdańsk,"* my uncle recalled, *"and I was to return to Lwów by train on New Year's Eve during the night. That evening the owner of the hotel threw a lavish party to celebrate the opening of a new wing and I was invited to the reception. I got drunk, I didn't even know how I got to my room and when I woke up it was nine o'clock. My train was leaving at midnight and suddenly I realised that I had not contacted the church to announce the banns. I dashed off in a horse drawn sleigh to the nearest village where a priest agreed to read the banns in the morning. I caught the train for Warsaw at midnight and made the connection to Lwów."* Everything happened at dizzying speed for those times, and he arrived

---

[47] During WWII after occupying Poland, Germans built submarines – U-boot – for the *Kriegsmarine* – German Navy – in this shipyard and it was badly damaged by Allied bombs. In 1945 the shipyard was taken over by the Polish government and rebuilt as the Gdańsk Shipyard where the Polish trade union movement Solidarity was born in 1980's, which led to the fall of communism in Central and Eastern Europe in 1989 putting an end to the Iron Curtain.

on time. He and Anna were married in the beautiful Baroque church of St Bernard and my father served as a witness. After two days the newlyweds left for Gdańsk.

About that time my grandparents moved away from the centre into the villa and furnished their apartment on the first floor. The ground floor stood empty and the top floor was taken by grandfather's brother, Władysław who returned from Budapest. Basia Jawna had her room in the basement with a window giving out onto the garden. The property was separated from the street by a wire fence, a reddish colour from the minium, also known as red lead, in the paint. My grandfather planned the garden himself. He ordered yellow and blue iris bulbs from Holland and had them planted along the path all the way from the gate to the entrance door. Bushes of white and purple lilacs grew along the fence, shielding the garden from the street, and in the spring, tulips bloomed along the walls of the house. There was no formal rose garden, just one uninvited wild rose that planted itself in the middle of the lawn. The orchard behind the house had several fruit trees: a cherry, a pear, and an apple tree – the golden reinette; there were bushes of raspberries, gooseberries, and currents on the side. At the back in the vegetable garden, my grandfather installed a greenhouse for asparagus. *"I watched your grandpa walk slowly the length of the path, stopping by each blooming iris,"* granny told me. *"The garden gave him enormous joy."* Because of grandfather's creeping heart condition, Zbyszek decided to return to Lwów. By the end of 1934, he resigned from the position at the Danziger Werft.

Although Zbyszek had already passed his examinations for the judgeship earlier on, he still needed to get his two-year practice for the Bar examination. That done he presented himself at the Law Society. All this took place during the catastrophic depression of the 1930's and waiting lists of candidates for the Bar were basically closed. Zbyszek asked for a personal meeting with the President of the Chamber, Abraham Landes, an eminent lawyer. At some point during the meeting, Mr Landes casually asked my uncle whether he had any family connection to the civil engineer, Stefan Neuhoff. *"Yes,"* Zbyszek replied, *"that's my father."* He was startled when the dignified Abraham Landes jumped up from his chair, threw his hands up in the air, and exclaimed: *"There is nothing I would not do for the son of Stefan Neuhoff."* He then recounted an incident that took place in Tarnopol long before WWI, when my grandfather worked for the Imperial-Royal Austrian Railways. Landes's father was a lumber trader in Tarnopol. At some point, he had received a substantial order for sleepers for the railroad tracks. However, as soon as he delivered the consignment, the entire shipment was rejected because supposedly the wood was defective. For Landes that spelled financial ruin. And he demanded an expert opinion to evaluate the quality. My grandfather was called in to assess it and firmly decided in Landes's favour because there was nothing wrong with the lumber; it was good, strictly according to specifications. In reality, another trader had bribed the inspector. *"In our family, we will never forget the name of Stefan Neuhoff,"* Landes's son affirmed emotionally, as he ended his story and Uncle Zbyszek was promptly inscribed on the list of Lwów's practicing attorneys. Soon he secured a position with a law firm.

My grandparents continued to maintain lively contacts with their *Tarnopolian* friends who had also moved to Lwów. Archbishop Twardowski frequently invited the whole family to Obroszyn, the summer residence of the archbishops of Lwów, some 14 kilometres from the city. On one occasion Uncle Zbyszek remembered that 200-year-old Tokay wine was served after dinner in thin crystal glasses. "Savour it a drop at a time," the archbishop suggested. *"He then invited us for a boat ride on the lake and rowed one of the boats himself."*

After their return from Gdańsk, Zbyszek and Anna took a flat on Mikołaj Street at number 3, and my parents moved to a flat on Plac Akademicki 2, which was around the corner and the two apartments had connecting balconies. Zbyszek now hung his lawyer's plaque on the door, while my parents set up their office in their new apartment which was large enough to accommodate it. They arranged a waiting room in the entrance hall with a filing cabinet, a desk, and a typewriter for Miss Genia, the secretary. From there on one side door led to the dining room, on the other to a large drawing room with huge windows that gave onto the square. A set of Viennese furniture occupied the centre, armchairs and a sofa with brocade upholstery. There was plenty of space for my father to place his desk in one corner where he could receive his clients. A rich mahogany dining room set with six leather side chairs, two end chairs, and a glass cabinet for mother's collection of antique porcelain, was a present from my grandparents. Also, a magnificent sideboard was a gift from great-aunt Malwina Eckhardt. My father loved light music, so Uncle Zbyszek installed him a radio in the dining room.

These apartments in the heart of the city were well located for lawyers since Batory Street with the county, appellate, and criminal courts was a stone's throw away. While the court was a place of work, the real attraction of Batory Street lay in several bookstores across from the courts along the opposite pavement. The world of old engravings, lithographs, and drawings was a world apart from the daily humdrum existence of the twentieth century. Since his early student days, Uncle Zbyszek collected engravings and his musings about Batory Street carried a deep sadness for a paradise lost.

"Batory was not a long street. Across from the courts ran a row of booksellers, intersected only by the small dead-end Boulard Street; and up to the First World War, these small shops belonged to the Bodek family. By the 1920s they started disappearing and by 1930, only five of them remained. All were single room locales owned by Jews. The first one belonged to Rubin Bodek who dealt mainly in used school texts. The next one called Leopolia belonged to Doctor Maximilian Bodek who took it over from his father, the head of the Bodek clan. He enlarged and modernised the place, and he also dealt in school books. Maximilian Bodek was a tall lanky man with a pale face, large dark eyes, and quick nervous gestures. He moved very fast and could serve several customers crowding into his store at the same time, but always remained pleasant and smiling. His good humour was widely known among his clientele. One day I was walking behind two young schoolboys arguing loudly about the price of books that they intended to sell. Suddenly one of them called out: "Go to Bodek, at least you'll get some laughs." When I repeated this to the bookseller, he burst out laughing and kept saying: 'You see, you see, Bodek is Bodek.' But weightier reasons than selling used books drew high school students here: Bodek's book shop carried cribs.[48] These booklets with Greek and Latin texts translated into Polish rendered a huge service to untold generations of overworked pupils. The use of cribs was forbidden, but one could get them at Bodek's. And schoolboys were not the only ones to make ample use of them; it would happen that a leaf from a crib booklet would slip out of the master's book and flutter onto the floor. Nobody knew who were the authors of these texts, perhaps students of philology at Jan Kazimierz University, or perhaps some members of the faculty.

The third bookstore in the row belonged to Józef Bodek. It was small and dark with shelves along the walls made of thick planks and rough posts. In the old days before the war they were packed with many books, but as time went by they grew more and more depleted until they stood almost bare. At the time I

---

[48] Crib (British) or pony (American) is a translation of a language text, for the (usually) surreptitious use by students.

*knew him Józef Bodek was middle-aged, very pleasant and chatty; every morning
he opened his store, but nobody knew what he traded.*

*My own interest lay in the two remaining booksellers on Batory Street. There
were no school texts sold there; the shelves were stacked with texts on
philosophy, monographs on art and aesthetics, volumes on history and
sociology. Next to a complete edition of Ibsen, one could find Wund and Eisler.
One of these shops, on the corner of Batory and Boulard, had two large display
windows. I got to know its owner, Wilhelm Klaper, while I was still a student at
Jan Kazimierz University and over time our acquaintance grew into a friendship.
Klaper was a tall man, meticulously dressed, his gestures were slow, somewhat
deliberate, and he was always eager to assist and to counsel. He was an expert
on publishing, very much up-to-date on what works were coming out and by
whom. He knew the names of all publishing houses, maintained commercial
contacts with the largest ones, mostly German, and only rarely needed to consult
the huge catalogue that lay on the counter. He could find books that were rare
and out of print, and produced them as if by magic, as when he got me the almost
unavailable second volume of 'Geschichte der Philosophie' by Heinze-
Ueberweg. We talked about publishing matters and of books since Klaper was a
great reader. Every evening, just before closing, his wife came to the shop and
they walked home together arm in arm.*

*The last bookshop on that stretch of Batory Street had high ceilings; books
were stacked all the way up to the top on shelves along the walls and in piles on
the floor. There was no counter, but an iron stove stood in the middle of the room,
a pipe drew the smoke up to the ceiling and into the wall. Next to the stove
Zygmunt Igel, the owner of the shop, a large broad-shouldered man with a beard
trimmed neatly into a ducktail presided in an antique armchair. In spite of his
age, he walked ramrod straight. Behind thick concave lenses, his pupils looked
small like tiny coffee beans. He was almost blind and in order to read he had to
hold the book barely a few centimetres away from his eyes. He was a man of very
few words except when it came to old books, ancient manuscripts, and copper
engravings, then he could discourse on them for hours. Igel was a great
specialist in that field and was often summoned as an expert witness in court
cases. In the early 1920's when I began collecting old engravings and drawings,
he became my mentor. He taught me how to recognise an early or a late copy of
a copper engraving, or the continuity of a line in a drawing, or special
watermarks, and pointed out hundred and one details meaningful to any*

collector. He was a marvellous teacher and in his love of old books and drawings, he handled them with such delicate care as most precious objects."

It would be wrong to assume that the Bodeks were the only booksellers in town. In fact, Lwów had several and Uncle Zbyszek knew them all. On the corner of Akademicka Street, not far from my parents' first law office, there was a large bookstore of Bernard Połoniecki. It had two big display windows, one on each side of the corner, and further down the street there were more stores also belonging to Połoniecki that sold pianos and leased sheet music. There was another music store near the conservatory. The bookstore and publishing house of Altenberg had their headquarters at the George Hotel, the most elegant hotel in Lwów. Altenberg was a high-class establishment offering paintings, graphics, and drawings at exorbitant prices. Another bookstore and publishing institute of Gubrynowicz occupied a large building on Kilinski Street and it fell into the same category as Altenberg but specialised in topics on Polish culture; one of their authors was Kazimierz Kolbuszewski, professor of Polish history and literature and a great authority on the theatre.

My mother also suffered from a collector's bug, but her passion was antique porcelain. She loved to rummage through the antiquarian shops and easily distinguished the genuine from the junk, although in some cases good customer relations forced her to make concessions, bowing to the inevitable and accepting a worthless piece of porcelain as an undesirable gift of gratitude. As when a wealthy grocery store owner, a valuable client of the law practice, thanked her for a positive outcome of a court case by offering a kitschy pseudo-Rococo figurine *"that has been forever in granny's family,"* she assured my mother. Gifts like this one created a real headache, what to do with the little monstrosity that could not be readily disposed of since the client might show up at any time unexpectedly and wish to see her gift prominently displayed.

Mother's good taste in antiques was greatly appreciated by the family. Aunt Lusia wrote that *"your mummy was very knowledgeable when it came to antiques. Sometimes your Granny Paulina would say how sorry she was that she and her siblings got rid of their parents' antique walnut furniture for next to nothing. When I would ask if the furniture was nice, she would say that it was and 'even Zosia would have liked it'. Later on, whenever there was a question about antiques, your mother was always consulted."* On the other hand, when mother first saw a beautiful small Biedermeier table at her mother-in-law's house with slits along the edges, she was appalled to be told that young Maks used it to test the sharpness of his penknife.

Starting in the early 1920's, there was a growing interest in antiques among the *lvovian* intelligentsia, especially among doctors and lawyers. Some members of high society took up trading in antiques right from their homes, and these items became decorative fixtures of an expensive highlife. Certain carpenters worked exclusively on restorations of old furniture, two of the best known in town were the workshops of Karabin and of Michał Sarabach, who were both highly regarded specialists and very pricey.

However, antiques could be found not only in elite antiquarian establishments but also in modest shops owned by Jews, clustered behind the Great Theatre. Scattered among shops with cheap cotton fabrics and second-hand home goods, there were several shops where it was possible to find authentic hidden treasures provided one could bring oneself to rummage through piles of junk, sometimes not the most pleasant thing to do.

Uncle Zbyszek also loved antiques. His friend Doctor Dominik Olech introduced him to the mysterious world of second-hand stores in the Jewish quarter. Uncle Zbyszek remembered strolling with Doctor Olech: *"On a sunny summer afternoon, we crossed the large market square and entered a maze of narrow streets, nameless mostly since their nameplates had long since dropped off the walls. An old Jewish woman sat on a low stool on a corner selling pretzels and rolls spread on a piece of newspaper before her. My friend bought a couple of bagels and munched on them as we walked along; to my protestations that as a physician he should know better than eat that stuff crawling with bacteria, he answered drily: 'medicine doesn't know' and went on eating.*

Dominik told me that most shops dealing in used wares were owned by the Ritel family. He knew three of them, one belonging to Ritel father, another one to Ritel son, and the third to Uncle Ritel. The senior Ritel's store was spacious and bright with a clean display window and large candelabra suspended from the ceiling. It was an orderly place and the goods were neatly arranged. The walls were hung with cheap prints in rich gold frames, the choice adornment of bourgeois drawing rooms, and the pride of place, dwarfing all others in Ritel's shop, went to Siemiradzki's painting 'Lidia and Ursus', the two principal characters in Henryk Sienkiewicz's novel 'Quo Vadis'.

Kitchen naphtha lamps and copper pots hung interspersed among the paintings. Odd sets of cups, saucers, water goblets and wine glasses, decorative bottles and stacks of mismatched plates sat on small tables together with assorted cutlery – knives, forks, and spoons. Garden implements and plumbers' and masons' tools were lined up against the walls, separated into groups by large glass bottles of various colours. Under the Siemiradzki painting, padlocks and bundles of keys were strung together. Papa Ritel did not deal in used clothing. When I first met him, he was over fifty years old, he spoke slowly and with authority as befitting the head of the Ritel clan. His gestures were measured and dignified, he gave the impression of a serious well-respected merchant and that was the reputation he enjoyed. He was listed in the Civil Court books of experts on paintings and antiques and when Dominik introduced me, I was readily accepted as a client.

A few months later I became acquainted with the son's shop located in a two-storey house with a peeling façade, in a small and dark room where the window blinds were always closed. Opposite the door stood a huge black leather sofa with a yellows strip around the back, a typical piece of furniture from an Austrian government office. It was piled high with used clothing and underwear. Next to the wall on a three-legged dresser, the missing fourth leg replaced by a tin can, and covered with a rag stood all manner of tableware, glassware, and cutlery. On the opposite side, pairs of shoes and boots were lined up on shelves and below them hung trousers, jackets, and coats. A couple of chairs for customers completed the décor and a single electric bulb hanging from the ceiling and covered with a thick layer of dirt was the only source of light in this entire place.

Ritel junior was my age, blond and blue-eyed, he looked more like a sportsman that a salesman of second-hand goods. We struck up a cordial acquaintance as soon as he heard that I was his father's client. In time we became good friends and I could rummage in his shop to my heart's content. During that first visit, I discovered a glass Murano plate decorated with gold inlay, another time an early nineteenth-century candleholder, next came the three-legged dresser propped up on a can. It turned out to be pure Biedermeier walnut and I was overjoyed when the fourth leg turned up in a drawer. When I asked him why the Austrian sofa stood so far away from the wall, he said that there were old picture frames stacked behind it. I started pulling them out one by one, dusty and dirty, mostly worthless until I hit on two identical ones, which were handmade with a perfect finish and beautifully carved. It was hard to tell what was hidden under the glass since it was covered by a thick sticky layer of goo. After I cleaned them up at home, to my delight I discovered those were two *watercolours by an excellent Viennese painter, famous Leopold Löffler. When I told Ritel about it, he laughed and said: 'you were lucky.'*

The most interesting of the three stores belonged to Uncle Ritel. Narrow and dark in spite of the single light bulb hanging from the ceiling, its floor was densely covered with second-hand trousers, jackets, shirts, and underwear; a thin path cut through all this led to the back of the shop. A large hip-bath in the corner was filled to capacity with ladies' and men's shoes from the early 1900's and scattered along the walls were kitchen pots and pans and tin chamber pots. Above them, strung on wires hung wreaths of padlocks and keys. A huge gypsum bust of Poland's greatest poet, Adam Mickiewicz, presided on a pedestal in another corner, his neck festooned with hernia support belts, popular in medicine at the turn of the century. Looking at the poet's bust, I remembered a comment in an official's note reporting on an eviction. He wrote that 'from the debtor's shop with used things we confiscated three Mickiewiczes of whom one turned out to be a Słowacki.' [49]

A year after her wedding, mother thought she may be pregnant. It would have spelled a disruption to her law practice and a delay in the examination to the Bar for which she was preparing, putting on hold her dream of becoming a full-fledged barrister. She did not share her frustration with Maks, but distressed by this conundrum telephoned her father. He arrived with a large tray of exquisite pastries from Zalewski. He found Zosia in tears. For a long time, he tried to convince her how wonderful it would be to have a little Zosia or a little Maks while she sitting in bed simpered, emptying the entire tray of cream cakes. A visit to her gynaecologist, Dr Stanisława Duczymińska, showed that it was a false alarm, she was not pregnant after all. Moreover, it appeared that a certain anomaly in her reproductive system would prevent her from ever having children.

Were my parents distressed by the discovery? Not at all. They were sublimely happy and took this news in a stride, and were not unduly upset by the prospect of a childless marriage. Their personalities were so well matched. Father was calm and self-controlled; mother more excitable, political problems besetting the country at the time tended to set off emotional diatribes. Usually, he waited for the storm to blow over before saying: *"Dearest, spare your nerves,*

---

[49] Adam Mickiewicz (1798-1855) and Juliusz Słowacki (1808-1849): both considered Poland's greatest Romantic poets.

you can't change the world." His words worked like balm and mother would start to laugh.

Maks, Zosia, and Granny

Living as they did next door my parents and my uncle and aunt often went out on town together in the evening. Cinema was a favourite entertainment. Father loved light music and comic films; he had had his fill of real-life tragedies during eight years of war so he avoided heavy drama on the screen. A large selection of movie theatres had sprung up around town and one was located directly across from my parents' apartment building. The greatest hit at the time was the *Blue Angel* with Marlene Dietrich. After watching a film, the four of them would saunter over to a coffee house or to their favourite Italian winery where they could relax at one of the tiny white tables over wine and ice cream, and enjoy carefree moments of *dolce-far-niente*. Uncle Zbyszek smoked cigarettes; my father in addition to cigarettes also smoked a short pipe.

Faithful to its Viennese tradition, Lwów offered its coffee drinking public a large selection of cafés and *confiséries*, and the best confectionery shop in all of Poland was of the renowned *confiseur* Ludwik Zalewski; it was located in a neo-Baroque building on Akademicka Street from whence boxes of cakes and tortes were flown daily to Warsaw. Another excellent pastry shop of Hieronim Welz was closer to where my parents lived. Each coffee house catered to a different public. Roma café on the corner of Akademicki Square and Fredro was favoured by wealthy Jews. In the past, it also served as a home away from home for Lwów's mathematicians until they transferred to the Scottish Café (Kawiarnia Szkocka) with their leader, the self-taught mathematical genius, Stefan Banach.[50] At the Scottish, they entertained themselves with complex equations scribbled on marble table-tops, but since these calculations were erased each night as the tables were cleaned and records of previous day's discussions were lost, eventually they decided to copy the formulae into an exercise book which was handed at the end of the evening to the waiter for safekeeping.[51] The Scottish Café was also my uncle's preferred haunt.

Not everyone patronised cafés and *confiséries*. In his bachelor days, Uncle Zbyszek's favourite watering hole was a pub called the Atlas. The pub faced the main Market Square where, as Uncle Zbyszek wrote, *"Life started at dawn and ended just before sunrise. Mornings on the Market Square belonged to fishwives who sat on low stools offering their fresh wares: potatoes, beets, onions piled on rough sack-cloth, baskets of eggs, slabs of butter and country cheese. These ladies were known for their strong and colourful language, best described by a derogatory saying that 'she barks like a lvovian fishwife'. They had their own private sense of humour. An anecdote that made the rounds of the town back in Austrian times, told of a young man who bought a bowl of hot tripe. As he began to eat it, he suddenly called out, 'Hey, lady, there is a piece of a rag in these tripe'. To which the woman responded without missing a beat, 'So what did you expect for two cents? A piece of velvet?'*

On warm summer nights, in the feeble light of city lamps, the lvovian Market transformed itself. Gone were the din and the scratched walls of surrounding

---

[50] Stefan Banach (1892-1945) Polish mathematician, founder of the Lwów School of Mathematics, generally considered to have been one of the 20th century's most important and influential mathematicians.

[51] Lwow mathematicians, Stanisław Ulam,. worked on the Manhattan Project. After WWII the Scottish Café note book was recovered, English translation annotated by Ulam was published by Los Alamos National Laboratory in 1957.

houses. The gentle contours of buildings and the shadow of the massive city hall with its dancing tower became enfolded in a transparent spider's web of poetry, especially as one was leaving Atlas's pub just before dawn. Modelled on Parisian bistros, Atlas's pub was a temple of Art generously steeped in liquor. It was a large hall, poorly lit, with off-white walls, a stone floor, and a wide window protected by barnacles of dirt; its furnishings were simple: small iron tables and iron chairs. The air reeked of cigarette smoke and beer. Waiters in white jackets served with alacrity, expertly uncorking the bottles. Sitting at a table in Atlas's pub one came to realise that vapours of alcohol were an integral element of Art. During the daytime when the market was filled with people, occasionally someone might pop in for 'a swift shot'; in the afternoons it stood mostly empty and only filled up in the evening after ten o'clock when the last theatre performances ended. Drama and comedy actors had their own reserved table at Atlas's and the theatre's Hairdresser Rzeszutko, and the Stage Manager Stahl always tagged along with the rest.

The linchpins of this artistic circle were Henryk Zbierzchowski[52] and his wife Zadora. He was the most lvovian of all lvovian literati, who launched his career as a prose writer with a handful of novels positively reviewed in Brückner's history of Polish literature[53]. But Zbierzchowski preferred to substitute Atlas's pub for Parnassus. His short poems appeared in the morning paper under a pen name NEMO. He was a handsome man, his longish hair and an elegant profile, reminiscent of Romantic poets, won him general adulation. In our town, he was Mr Poet. Conversations around the table where he and his wife held court were never loud, except for an occasional outburst of laughter. Once I was sitting with a group of friends close to the artists when one of them uttered a rude word. Zbierzchowski stood up, walked over to us, bowed and said: 'Gentlemen, I apologise for the unacceptable word at our table'. I knew who had uttered it, but a battery of bottles on their table seemed a perfectly acceptable excuse. Zbierzchowski had his own version of Hamlet's 'to be or not to be':

To drink or not to drink, that elemental quest
With which humanity struggles in vain.
The answer we reach is obvious and plain,
To drink is pleasant, not to drink is best.

---

[52] Henryk Zbierzchowski (1881-1942).
[53] Aleksander Brückner (1856-1939). *Polnische Literaturgeschichte.*

But best for who, since we all have to die
Healthy or not, does not change the game.
Pushing up daisies for all is the same
So drink, brother, drink, and enjoy your life.[54]

One evening returning home late I was crossing the park when I met the poet and, as we continued on our way, we chatted about Lwów. I remarked that it was difficult to write about our town since it was both sophisticated and provincial. After a while, Zbierzchowski said: 'If you want to write about Lwów, write with your heart, not with the pen.'"

Two of the city's longest streetcar lines, number 1 and 4, passed by the equestrian statue of King John III Sobieski. It was the busiest stop in town, right next to the Wiedeńska coffee house (Viennese coffee house), a central location for *doing business*, as Uncle Zbyszek defined it: *"In the centre of the café stood an enormous counter arranged in Viennese style, scattered around the room were small round iron tables and iron chairs. The air was saturated with the aroma of coffee, beer, and tobacco, the clientele was mostly men and the talk was business. Here the 'black' stock exchange operated, houses and lots were bought and sold, flats rented, and large deals concluded. Businessmen came here looking for workers, and workers came looking for jobs. It was a place where 'agents,' mostly elderly Jews, acted as middlemen in large real estate deals. The bus stop took its name from the Wiedeńska (Viennese) coffee house and around King John's statue on a small green strip the city fathers placed several wooden benches. This became a miniature replica of the coffee house itself, a meeting place for old poor Jewish agents dealing in small properties. I knew two of them, one called Kalniczny and the other Łapajówker.*

---

[54] Translated from Polish by Eva Hoffman Jedruch.

Monument of King John III Sobieski[55]

One day at this stop where I often took the tram, a strange woman showed up, about fortyish, tall, slim, and dressed in a silk evening gown from the 1800's and a large straw hat richly adorned with bows and artificial flowers. In her hand, she held a tall hooked staff like a bishop's crosier decorated with bunches of coloured ribbons. She wore large dark glasses and people called her Blind Mincia. She then came to the bus stop every day and stood there all day until the evening. She was totally blind and moved slowly and when street urchins tugged at her sleeve, she swung her stick attempting to whack them, but by then they were beyond her reach. Then Mincia would let out a string of epithets quite out of character with her exquisite costume. At first, she was selling newspapers hoping that the customer would leave the change in her palm. That lasted a few months, but apparently did not provide sufficient income, so she changed her method of begging and started to play on a small harmonica. But even this did not work out, so she stopped playing and just stood there like a statue waiting for someone to slip a coin into the leather pouch hanging at her belt. Years went by, yet she came to her tram stop each day but rain and sun wreaked havoc with

---

[55] Photo from author's personal collection. Monument is now located in Gdańsk. Moved from Lwów after WWII, when that part of Poland was taken by the USSR.

her antique dress, her evening gown became tattered and covered in rusty spots, the ribbons and artificial flowers from her hat were gone, and only a straw skeleton remained on her head until one day she showed up dressed in a grey cotton shift and her head was covered only by strait mousy blonde hair. After many years Mincia disappeared, perhaps she was taken to a hospital, or perhaps straight to the Janowski Cemetery, the cemetery for the indigent."

The war that ended in 1918 brought huge changes to the world, imposed new trends in literature, music, painting, and the theatre. Pre-war stars stepped off the stage making way for new actors and new repertories. Still, the old ones remained in the nostalgic memories of their erstwhile fans and for my uncle, the unforgettable character was Helena Miłowska, the diva of the operetta and the queen of the Viennese waltz. *"Years after she stopped performing, one summer evening I was strolling down Kraszewski Street. The air was saturated with the scent of flowering linden trees, when unexpectedly I saw a woman wrapped in a shawl, sitting at a ground floor window, and listening to the chirping of birds from the nearby park. It was Helena Miłowska Niewiarowicz."*

Not all performances were limited to well-known actors or singers. Just like Paris, Lwów had its very own unmistakeable genre of street music and popular hits with a smattering of Ukrainian *dumkas*, folk songs. Sensational affairs and scandals became ready material for new street ballads. In 1912 a wealthy young man Stanisław Lewicki in a fit of jealousy shot and killed his lover, a popular actress and a married woman, Janina Ogińska. The family engaged a law professor to defend him, but the defence turned so academic that, as the papers reported, the defendant was being led straight onto the gallows. This lawyer was replaced by another barrister. This widely commented affair immediately gave birth to a ballad about the dark crime. In the event the murderer was not hung, he later committed suicide in prison, but the ballad, *You see, Lewicki, what love can do* survived and joined the repertory of many other low-life street songs.

Because of the ethnic diversity of the population, street music was quite varied. Uncle Zbyszek remembered another street *artist*, a small beggar who one day planted himself not far from Blind Mincia at the same bus stop. *"He was reasonably dressed and he stood there with his head hung low, staring at the pavement, then slowly looking up he began to sing a sad Ukrainian dumka[56] in a sort of Polish-Ukrainian Esperanto: Be well, my darling, Be well, my heart.*

---

[56] Folk song. *Buwaj ty zdorowa, moja ty myłeńko, buway ty zdorowa, moje ty serdeńko.*

Then his head would drop low again and for a while, he just stood still before starting all over again. But one day the public waiting at the stop was stunned by the familiar melody, but treated to words sung in Polish that were anything but the same. For the sake of decency, I cannot quote it in its entirety, but it went something like this:

Lady you have an inkwell,
And I have a long pen,
What say you we open an office.

I don't know what followed, because my streetcar arrived. After that performance, he resumed his original ditty for a few days, but then began to alternate them. The public was highly amused and the little beggar with a face of evangelical simplicity, knew exactly how to get coins tumbling into his cap."

A hugely popular gourmet delicatessen place in Lwów, a so-called 'breakfast room,' belonged to Zofia Teliczkowa, a lady of vast proportions. It was located on Akademicka at number 6, conveniently for my parents to stop on their way home from the courthouse, father for schnapps before dinner and mother for a herring canapé. Mother loved herring in any guise, smoked, pickled, or rolled into rollmops with onion and pickled dill cucumber. All these varieties were on offer at Mrs Teliczkowa's. One year a tightrope walker, popularly called a fly-man, came to Lwów to perform on a cable stretched across Akademicka Street, between Mrs Teliczkowa's shop and the Sprecher office building across from her. Tightrope walkers, fearless and swift as cats, were perceived by the populace as a class of super-heroes. Tragically the acrobat fell and was killed. Lvovian street did not fail to commemorate the tragic incident with a rhymed epitaph:

A fly-man came to Lwów to perform on a wire.
He climbed on Teliczkowa and promptly expired.

As a child, apart from swimming and ice skating, my mother practised no other sports, but from her earliest age, she loved Zakopane, the small mountain village at the foot of the Tatra Mountains where the family used to vacation. My father played tennis but he too loved the mountains, so mother was happy to spend their vacations on the mountain trails.

She told me about that first time: *"When I went with your daddy for our first hike in the Tatras, I bought myself an elegant outfit for mountain climbing that made me feel quite superior. A veteran climber looked at me with pity and noted: "It's easy to see, madam, by your dress, that you are a novice.' He was right. After a week, I didn't look quite so impeccable."*

On the trail in Tatra Mountains

My grandfather no longer accepted engineering commissions, but he gave in to archbishop Twardowski's pleas and in 1931 agreed to take on the construction of the new church of Our Lady of Ostrabrama in the district of Łyczaków. Not that there was a dearth of churches in Lwów, each Christian denomination had its own cathedral and its own rich history. In the Roman Catholic cathedral of the Assumption of Mary, King Jan Kazimierz Vasa made his vows in 1656 during the Swedish invasion of Poland. [57] The small fourteenth-century Armenian cathedral of the Holy Trinity surrounded by houses, founded by a merchant from Caffa, had marvellous frescoes by Jan Henryk Rosen representing the burial of Odilo, the great eleventh-century abbot of Cluny. At the time, the archbishop of the Armenian Church in Lwów was Józef Teodorowicz and its bishop Władysław Bandurski, an extraordinary speaker and author of a biography of Poland's Queen Jadwiga[58] whose canonisation he championed. Bishop Bandurski had served as a chaplain in Marshal Piłsudski's Legions during WWI. A few paces from the Latin cathedral stood a pearl of late-renaissance architecture, the chapel of the Boim family founded in the early 1600's by Jerzy (György) Boim, an officer from Transylvania, merchant, city counsellor, and secretary to King Stefan Bathory. The tallest of all sanctuaries was the beautiful rococo Greek-Catholic cathedral of St George sitting on a hill whose metropolitan archbishop of Lwów, Andrzej Szeptycki, was the grandson of Poland's greatest comedy writer, Aleksander Count Fredro.

The place chosen by Archbishop Twardowski for the new Roman Catholic Church under the calling of the Virgin of Ostra Brama was not accidental. It was to be a votive church, funded by the citizenry of Lwów in thanksgiving for the city's survival during the wars of 1918 and 1920. The first artillery shells from Budienny's Soviet cavalry fell on that spot. The church was to be given to the Salesian Fathers of Don Bosco as part of a school for underprivileged youth.

Calculations for the project were made under the direction of Tadeusz Obmiński professor of Lwów Polytechnic. The cornerstone was consecrated on 7 October 1931. The following year, after the foundations had already been laid, my grandfather discovered a serious error in the calculations of the structure's design. According to my grandmother, he spent three days and three nights in his study not eating, drinking only black coffee, smoking his Trabucco cigars, and recalculating the project. He then sent his calculations to the Polytechnic with his observations. Tragically, Professor Obmiński suffered a heart attack and died. He was replaced by a younger man, Wawrzyniec Dayczak, but the responsibilities for the project were not clearly defined, and Mr Dayczak

---

[57] Known as The Deluge, part of Northern Wars of 1655-1661.
[58] Queen Hedwig. Jadwiga in Polish: 1373/4-1399) queen of Poland from 1384. She belonged to the Capetian House of Anjou, and was the daughter of king Louis I of Hungary and Elizabeth of Bosnia.

attempted to take over total control. Conflicts arose that put a great strain on my grandfather, aggravating his heart condition. He knew exactly where the errors lay and what needed to be done to salvage the construction. According to the original calculations, the church was to have two towers, but an incorrect soil coefficient had been applied and the foundations would not have supported such a weight. The design had to be changed and while Mr Dayczak was also aware of it, he blocked my grandfather's initiatives. Construction of the church was proceeding briskly and by May 1934, work on the façade and the walls was finished. Several decorative elements were ready and the electrical system installed. But then, it became clear that Dayczak had made changes to the original design on his own without consulting the project committee. The construction site was sealed off, work was suspended, and city hall ordered a new revision of the plans in order to reach a consensus. Dayczak was instructed to prepare the necessary adjustments which were to be presented for approval to my grandfather. Finally, the church of Our Lady of Ostra Brama was consecrated on 7 October 1934. Relics of the bishop-martyr Stanisław Szczepanowski and St Jozefat Kuncewicz were placed under the altar. That same day the Society of St Francis Sales took possession of the church for perpetuity.[59]

The Lwów Polytechnic, school of engineering, in their journal *Technical News* dedicated one entire issue to my grandfather's projects, railway bridges and railway serpentines in particular. These were his specialties. As a student at the Polytechnic in the final oral examinations, he was given a problem to resolve, but his solution was rejected by the panel of examiners, which was tantamount to failure. My grandfather requested a public hearing to present his results and, in an auditorium filled to capacity, developed his solution step-by-step. Not only did he pass with distinction but his method became part of the technical literature.

My mother's examinations to the Bar were set for 1936. She was studying with her usual passion, just as she did in her student days. Suddenly, overnight, her face became covered with small, flat flesh-coloured spots. Her doctor diagnosed *verruca plana juvenalis*. *"I looked dreadful,"* mother recalled, *"not even your granny wanted to be seen with me in public. Only your daddy was not ashamed to be out in the street with me."* The condition persisted for weeks and though mother consulted several physicians, none were able to help. She grew

---

[59] After the war when Lwów became part of the USSR and the Ukraine, the Soviets turned the church into a warehouse. In 1992 the church was reopened and given to the Greek Orthodox order of Salesians.

very depressed and also stressed out by the approaching examination, so her doctor prescribed a bromide powder as a tranquiliser. *"The next morning my spots began to fade from one hour to the next as if somebody had applied a blotting paper to an ink stain."* She passed her oral and written examinations with distinction in January and became a full-fledged barrister, admitted to the Bar in the city of Lwów on 24 September 1936. From now on, she could defend her cases in court under her own name.

My parents ran their law practice jointly, many of their clients were large firms and corporations, and father was legal counsel for the oil company Premier where his friend Dr Stefan Margold worked. But not all clients were large, some were small and among those was a monastery whose important benefactor was a rich lady butcher. One day a quarrel broke out between her and a neighbour whose parting shot was: *"You, grey rag!"* Enraged by the insult, the butcher took her neighbour to court and the monks brought the case to my parents. It created a dilemma for my father who was too senior to prosecute a mud-slinging verbal attack, but now he had a newly minted barrister as a junior partner. He asked mother to take it on.

The case might have sounded like a joke, but a client was a client, and mother had to figure out a strategy. She decided to play up the word 'grey', *"Your honour, my client feels deeply hurt by the insult hurled at her by the accused. She considers that her honour had been called into question. It was not the word 'rag' per se that was objectionable, for what is a rag? A piece of cloth made of cotton, or wool, linen, or silk. But grey? Now that is another matter. The core of the insult lies in the colour. Because what does grey imply? Pale as a shadow, devoid of expression, something without character. My client claims that through the word 'grey' she has been deprived of her personality."* The presiding judge, the clerks, and the court officials, were biting their lips, but the offended lady received her satisfaction, a few zlotys' compensation and a formal apology for the injury to her pride. *"You are the best lawyer in Lwów,"* she gushed as she thanked her youthful attorney.

Sadly, a long shadow of sorrow hung over Zosia's joy from her new career status. Her father's heart condition, aggravated by the exertions over the construction of the church, worsened alarmingly. He contracted pneumonia and a blood clot formed perforating his lung. Stefan Neuhoff died on 26 November 1936, at the age of seventy-two. For two days his coffin stood on a catafalque in the church of St Bernard. On the day of his funeral, the city authorities ordered all the lamps along the street, leading from the church to Łyczakowski Cemetery, to be lit and wrapped in black crêpe. A long column of monks and nuns from various monastic orders stretched for several hundred meters, preceding the hearse pulled by six black horses, towards the cemetery. Archbishop Twardowski, in white, headed the funeral procession on foot. Granny, my mother, and Uncle Zbyszek walked behind the hearse, followed by my father and Aunt Hania. Halfway up the long Piekarska Street, the procession stopped. The Archbishop got into his car and another churchman took over. When the hearse reached the cemetery, Twardowski was waiting at the gate and accompanied the coffin to the gravesite. For the Neuhoff family, grandfather's death closed an epoch. One year later my Grandmother Paulina Hoffman died. *"It was the only time in my life that I saw your father cry,"* mother told me.

Grandmother Neuhoff was a wealthy widow, but she worried that neither of her children had any offspring and it didn't look likely that they ever would. Zosia had been married for eight years, and Zbyszek for six. So it was a welcome surprise in February 1938 when my mother was found to be in her second month of pregnancy. Her regular physician, Dr Duczymińska was away and another gynaecologist saw her. Zosia was well built, the very picture of health. *"Madam, you should have half a dozen children,"* he joked. But after examining her, his expression turned serious. He mentioned that childbirth might be difficult.

For the first seven months mother felt well, regularly attended court sessions and her pregnancy hardly showed. Then it became quite visible. *"I suddenly blew up like a balloon,"* she told me. A private room had been reserved in the exclusive Salus Clinic, Dr Duczymińska was in attendance, together with a midwife. Even though problems appeared at the start with the first labour pains, mother refused to allow the use of forceps for fear of deforming the baby's cranium. The horror lasted from Wednesday until Sunday. My grandmother prayed for the baby to be born on Sunday, because *Sunday* babies were supposed to be lucky. I finally obliged and made my appearance a few minutes before midnight, but after the traumatic birth, my mother started to haemorrhage uncontrollably. Doctors seemed unable to stop the bleeding, the situation turned critical. My father, totally shaken, kept watch at the door of her room. Realising she may not survive, my mother asked that I be baptised right away in the clinic's chapel. A priest was hurriedly summoned from the nearby church of St Nicholas, Uncle Zbyszek and Aunt Lusia stood as godparents, and I was christened Ewa

Krystyna. Twelve hours later the physicians were able to stop mother's haemorrhaging.

My parents' house now had to be adapted to the new reality and thanks to mother's excellent organisational skills, she could combine a limited legal work load with motherhood. Miss Genia, the secretary, was now in charge of Smyk's afternoon walks while mother intensely perused baby literature, strictly adhering to instructions imparted by experts

Miss Genia with Smyk

A paediatrician, Dr Brichta, made regular house calls to check me. Mother took me to the botanical gardens and Uncle Zbyszek went along whenever he could. As of January 1938, he had been working for the city government and also teaching civil law at the Academy of International Commerce, the only academic institution in Poland preparing candidates for diplomatic service.

Father worked from the house and my uncle remembered how *"Maks would often drop whatever he was doing and run over to the bedroom where your cot stood, just to look at you."* Because of the way I cried, *ay, ay, ay* father called me Ayka, and the nickname stuck. After mother's traumatic childbirth, he decreed that *"there will be no more children."* I was well on the way to being an only child in the nearest family and a little heiress to boot. Life promised to be nicely predictable.

The only surviving baby picture with my mother

A young nanny was engaged to take care of me during the day, and my parents were already making long term plans for my future. Father was determined to walk me to school every day and carry my books, while mother insisted that I would not go to a private high school, but to the excellent public school of Queen Jadwiga which she deemed to be more democratic.

It was Christmas 1938, the first and the only one that we would celebrate together. Among mother's papers, I found a short reminiscence: *"That evening was sad, the weather was freezing, and the empty streets were snow-covered. Once in a while, the silence was disrupted by bells on sleighs taking people* home; calls of night watchmen offered a reassuring sense of security. The year was 1938 in the city of Lwów, a town replete with historical buildings that testified to Poland's past splendour, a border town that prospered on flourishing trade whose inhabitants, full of verve and good humour were known for their welcoming hospitality and readiness to help any newcomer. The one and only Polish town ever decorated with the order of Virtuti Militari for bravery.

I was walking arm in arm with my husband down a narrow street mostly inhabited by the poor Jewish population trading in anything that could be sold. There one could buy marinated herrings straight out of a barrel, fresh eggs, onions and radishes, down filling for pillows and quilts, silk sheets. Furniture, new and used, lamps, candlesticks, electric irons and also old ones heated with coke. In one shop window packed with second-and stuff in the pale light of a street lamp, I spied a small figurine of white porcelain. I stared at it fascinated. It was a Pierrot, juggling a gold ball, while a second one lay at his feet. It was hard to see it clearly through the dirty glass, but I was determined to return the following day when the store would be open to look at him in the daylight. Next day we went back with Maks to check it out. The Pierrot figurine of Viennese porcelain was beautifully modelled: it was delicate and small, maybe 15 centimetres tall. But the price was very high and we did not buy it. I returned several times to look at it, and each time I liked it even better. But then, one December evening as I was passing by that familiar store, I saw that the Pierrot was no longer there. I looked at the empty spot in dismay, and could not hold back my tears. Some nasty person snapped it up from under my nose. I complained bitterly to Maks, snivelled a little, and then life continued on its usual course.

Christmas was approaching. That year winter was very cold, there was more snow than normal and the holiday mood was taking over our lives. We bought a large Christmas tree and decorated it. With Maks helping me whenever he was free, it was to be special for our little girl Eva. When the first star twinkled in the sky and the tree sparkled with myriad lights, her eyes lit up and she stared at it in amazement. A large plush teddy bear, brown with white paws, sat under the tree next to a smiling doll in a pink tulle dress. Beside it lay a small package labelled "For Zosia". I opened it and could not believe my eyes: there in the box lay my Pierrot wrapped in cotton wool. That 'nasty' person who bought it, was my own husband.

I placed the figurine in the cabinet and there was no end to my pleasure. The little Pierrot lived with the three of us through all our joys and troubles. Spring came, then summer, but the clouds on Europe's political horizon were growing ever darker and more menacing, especially over Poland. And then came autumn, the beautiful golden Polish autumn, shattered by the horrors of war. On 1 September 1939 Hitler unleashed his brutal Drang Nach Osten and his iron monsters crashed across the Polish border, attacking from the ground and from the sky the Luftwaffe blitzed the country with incendiary bombs. The Polish army, unable to withstand the impact, retreated eastward when the other criminal, Stalin, attacked the country from the east. Poland was torn apart by the two greatest criminals since Genghis-Khan. In the midst of the tragedy and chaos, my Pierrot, seemingly protected by some magic force, continued to hold the golden ball in his delicate hand, while the other tiny globe lay at his feet. I wrapped him in cotton wool and packed him into a cardboard box, thinking that if he survives, perhaps so shall we. The fragile Pierrot became my talisman."

Pierrrot

Chapter VI

September 1939. The World in Flames

The German invasion of Poland launched on 1 September 1939 was planned in accordance with the Soviet-Nazi Pact made by Stalin and Hitler in August of that year, signed by their respective Ministers Vyacheslav Molotov and Joachim von Ribbentrop on 23 August. Ostensibly touted a non-aggression pact between Soviet Russia and Nazi Germany, it included a secret protocol containing a formula for the dismemberment of Poland by the two signatories. After a coordinated attack on Poland, the USSR and the Third Reich would partition the country between themselves along the line of the River Bug. A two-pronged attack would make Poland's situation indefensible. Accordingly, on 1 September Germany invaded.

Poland's tragic situation, lack of preparedness and of provisions, was painfully obvious from Uncle Zbyszek's recollections. Because of poor health, he had not done military service and so was listed under the so-called category B. *"General mobilisation was announced for 1 September. Those men classified as category B were instructed to go to the regional command post on St. Jacek's Hill. Duly, at eight o'clock I presented myself at that site. The office was closed, a crowd of people was milling around in the street, and a goodly number of them were our familiar street types. Finally, at around 11 o'clock an officer appeared in the window and told everybody to go home. That was when I found out that a military command had been set up at number 5 Boulard Street, so I headed there with some of the other men. A group of lieutenants sat around in an otherwise empty room. 'What do you guys want?' They asked us. We said we were reporting for duty. 'And have you got machine guns?' Came an ironic question. 'No? Then we don't need you.'*

A year earlier I had done training in anti-aircraft patrol with the use of gas masks, so in the end, I was assigned to take command of a street block that encompassed the short side streets of St Nicholas and Romanowicz. I went to the town hall in search of masks, there were none. On the way there, I saw an endless stream of cars from Warsaw, heading for Romania and Hungary, a foretaste of what was to come.

The first German bombs fell on two popular cafés, Roma and Scottish; the latter for years served as a 'home away from home' for a group of mathematicians from the renowned mathematics school of Lwów. They had been meeting there for their daily debates, led by that self-taught mathematical genius, Stefan Banach. The bombs that fell were incendiary and both buildings burnt for days, eerily glowing in the night."

The shock strategy implemented by the Wehrmacht was known as *Schrecklichkeit*, a tactic perfected by the Germans since it was first applied by Bismarck and Graf von Moltke during the Franco-Prussian war of 1870-71. Its aim was to terrorise civilian populations, sow destruction, and spread panic and chaos through unrelenting bombardment. During the siege of Paris,[60] the city was shelled with projectiles from a huge cannon newly designed and manufactured by Alfred Krupp's *Stahlwerke*, and ironically, first demonstrated at the Paris Exhibition of 1867. The random shelling was not directed at military objectives, but at civilian installations. And so this seventy-year-old technique still worked to perfection in 1939. Poland was poorly prepared for such an onslaught having had barely twenty years of independence since the end of the First World War. After two weeks' bloody resistance as the Polish forces were still fighting a desperate battle and not capitulating, the Russians made their move on 17 September, launching an attack from the east. The country was now in a pincer grip.

My father, as captain in the reserves, had been mobilised at the end of August 1939. After Lwów capitulated on 22 September, the regional commander Colonel Władysław Langner issued an order for all officers to present themselves at the regional command centre. According to the terms of the capitulation, common soldiers would be allowed to return to their homes, while officers could depart to any country that would take them. On the way home to say goodbye to mother and me, my father met a young cousin, Czesław Eckhardt, who urged him to discard the uniform. Impossible, my father responded, that would be dishonourable.

---

[60] September 1870-January 1871

Uncle Zbyszek had been waiting with my mother all morning in our apartment. He too urged my father not to report. Years later he described the scene to me: *"Your mother quickly rushed to prepare lunch. Maks ate, and then went alone to the bedroom where you were sleeping. When he came out, he was composed, but broken. I tried to convince him to throw off the uniform and not to report to the command post. He refused. For him, it was a question of honour. He left and that was the end."*

As he was kissing my mother goodbye, father told her: *"During the last war I had a deep conviction that I would return unharmed. Now I don't have it."*

The Soviets did not honour the terms of the capitulation. More than fifteen thousand officers were rounded up, disarmed, and loaded onto cattle trains which two days later departed for three prisoner-of-war camps: Kozielsk in Russia, Starobelsk in Ukraine, and Ostaszkow in Belarus. Colonel Langner managed to escape from Lwów, and after making his way through Romania joined Polish units which by then had fought their way out of the country.

After the war, my Aunt Lusia wrote to me about a relative of ours, Tadeusz Rysiakiewicz, an ichthyologist and graduate of the agricultural school of Dublany who *"during the Soviet occupation was responsible for fisheries in the area of Stanisławów. He saw your father among thousands of Polish officers when the trains with the prisoners-of-war stopped at the local station. He offered to help him escape, but your father would not accept it. He was concerned about putting you and your mother at risk. They did not know, these brave men that they were heading for a horrible death in the Katyń Forest."* Death was the price of love.

As soon as the trains with the prisoners left, all resistance in Lwów was crushed and the Bolsheviks took control of the city. Civic life ground to a halt. All professional activities, except hospitals, were banned; courts, municipal institutions, banks, university, and schools were closed, and the Russians launched massive arrests of prominent citizens. People were being thrown out of their homes, their houses and flats were taken over by Russian officers. The Soviet authorities not only replaced the Polish currency at a one-on-one exchange rate with the Russian rouble, worth one-third of the Polish zloty, but froze all savings deposits exceeding 300 złotys, thus stripping the citizenry of cash.

One day the doorman in our building quietly told my mother of a rumour he picked up through the grapevine 'on the street' that our flat was targeted for a

Soviet colonel, member of the NKVD.[61] One of my mother's traits was, as I discovered later in life, an ability to react fast and remain calm in the face of danger. More than once throughout the war that *sang-froid* would serve her well. As soon as she heard this disastrous piece of news, she acted without delay. No dithering, no handwringing, no waiting for the axe to fall. She immediately decided to move us to granny's house, where Uncle Zbyszek and Aunt Hania were already installed.

My grandfather had now been dead for three years since completing the construction of the votive church, so mercifully, he was spared the sight of devastation visited upon his beloved city.

Basia Yawna, granny's stalwart housekeeper, came to help with the packing. Mr Hartwig, client of my parents' law practice and owner of a moving company, offered transportation. Mother told him she had no money to pay for it. "*Madam,*" Mr Hartwig answered, "*soon none of us may be needing money.*" Barely had the truck left with the furniture and with Basia, when the apartment reverberated with violent banging on the front door and shouts in Russian: "*Open, this is NKVD.*" Quickly picking me up in her arms, mother ran to the back door and down the service staircase, leaving behind the home of her dreams and memories where she had spent the happiest years of her life, a home and a life to which she would never return.

Moscow. March 1940
5 March 1940, note from the chief of NKVD of the USSR, Lavrenti Beria, to Joseph Stalin.

USSR PEOPLES' COMMISSARIAT
P 13 N 144op
FOR INTERIOR AFFAIRS STRICTLY CONFIDENTIAL
5. III. 40
March 1940
No. 794/B
MOSCOW
Central Committee of All-Russia Communist Party for comrade Stalin

---

[61] NKVD, the precursor of KGB and of today's Russian security service, FSB.

In the NKVD USSR camps for prisoners of war and in prisons of the western areas of Ukraine and Byelorussia at the present moment are held large numbers of former officers of the Polish army, former employees of Polish police and intelligence departments, members of Polish nationalist c/r parties, identified members of c/r insurgency organisations, escapees, and others. All of them, determined enemies of the Soviet authorities, are full of hatred for the Soviet system. The prisoners of war, officers, and policemen detained in the camps attempt to continue their c/r activity, maintaining ant-Soviet agitation. Every one of them is just waiting to be liberated, so as to actively join in the fight against the Soviet authority.[62]

NKVD branches in the western area of the Ukraine and Byelorussia have uncovered a number of c/r insurgent organisations. In these entire c/r organisations the part of active leadership has been played by former officers of the former Polish army, former policemen, and gendarmes. Among captured escapees and persons who infringed national borders; a large number of persons have also been uncovered who are members of c/r intelligence and insurgency organisations.

In P.O.W. camps (without counting soldiers and cadres of non-commissioned officers) – 14,736 former officers, landowners, policemen, gendarmes, prison wardens, farmers, and intelligence agents – according to nationality, more than 97% are Poles.

Among them:

Generals, colonels, colonels, lieutenant colonels	*295*
Majors and captains	*2,080*
Lieutenants, second lieutenants, warrant officers, first class	*6,049*
Police officers and junior commanders of border patrol and gendarmes	*1,030*
Policemen, gendarmes, prison guards, and intelligence agents	*5,138*
Civil servants, landowners, priests, and farmers (military)	*144*
Held in prisons in the western areas of the Ukraine and Byelorussia are in total	*18,632*

---

55 c/r: counter-revolutionary

Detainees (among them 10,685 Poles), as follows:

Former officers	*1,207*
Former policemen, intelligence agents and gendarme	*5,141*
Spies and agitators	*347*
Former landowners, industrialists, and civil servants	*465*
Members of various c/r and insurgency organisations and various c/r elements	*5,345*
Escapees	*6,127*

Instructions from NKVD of the USSR: Taking into account that all of them are hardened and unreformable enemies of the Soviet authorities, NKVD of the USSR considers it mandatory to:

1. *Cases of 14,700 persons held in prisoner of war camps, former Polish officers, civil servants, landowners, policemen, intelligence agents, gendarmes, farmers, and prison wardens,*
2. *as also cases of those arrested and held in prisons of western areas of the Ukraine and Byelorussia, 11,000 persons, members of various c/r intelligence and diversionary organisations, former landowners, industrialists, former Polish officers, civil servants, and escapees to be tried under a special procedure, applying maximum punishment – execution [to be shot].*

PEOPLES' COMMISSAR   INTERNAL AFFAIRS

Union SSR
(Signed)   L. Beria
Exec [cute?]   *(Signed: Beria)*

Across the first page of this typewritten document, there are four large signatures: Stalin, Voroshilov, Molotov, and Mikoyan. In the margin, the writer's note: com. Kalinin – for, Kaganovitch – for.

The execution order applied to the POW camps of Kozielsk, Starobelsk, and Ostaszkow.

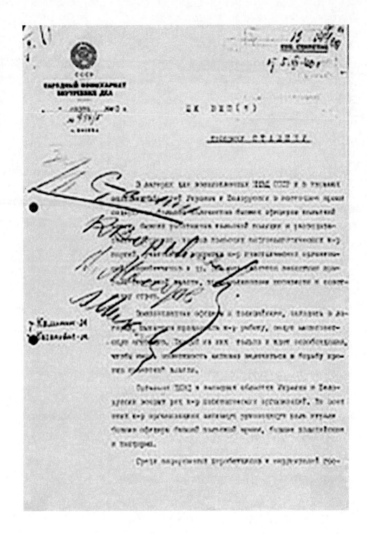

The death warrant Beria's memorandum. [63]

Lwów. April 1940.

After taking control of the city, the Russians plundered it indiscriminately. Food was in short supply, shops got emptier by the day. The old and revered Baczewski establishment, since 1782 dealer in fine liquors and spirits from around the world, and my grandfather's provider of wines, fell victim to spectacular acts of looting by Soviet soldiers. After denuding Baczewski's cellars of their superb contents, the Russians turned their attention to any shop that carried a whiff of alcohol, and perfumeries became their next target. My

---

134

mother's favourite l'Heure Bleu by Guerlain, and my uncle's preferred eau-de-cologne 4711 were consumed with equal glee by Russian soldiers. Soviet women who had tagged along with the troops, paraded around Lwów in silk and lace nightgowns, mistakenly taken for evening dresses. A medieval city ravaged by barbarian hordes from the steppes of Asia.

For the families of the officers taken prisoner, tension grew with each passing week with no word of the men's whereabouts. Finally, shortly before Christmas, my mother received a plain postcard. He was well, my father wrote, he was in the camp of Starobelsk in Ukraine not far from the town of Charkow. He worried about mother and me and begged her not to send him anything. *"Dearest Kacyk, just take care of yourself and Ayka. Don't send me anything, I have all I need. I love you both more than words can say. Maks."* My father's affectionate nickname for mother was *Kacyk – cacique –* Indian chief. What a relief to receive this card. Now at least she knew he was alive and as a prisoner-of-war surely covered by the Geneva Convention.

The world beyond the garden gate could not be held at bay and encroached on daily life. Russian occupational forces brought in Ukrainians from the USSR to run all security and municipal operations, including the police. Polish street names were erased and replaced with Ukrainian ones, even signs on shops and streetcars were changed. National symbols, the Polish eagles on government buildings in particular, were torn down with much fanfare, portraits and statues of Polish heroes and statesmen destroyed with a singular ferocity reserved for those of Marshal Józef Piłsudski, Russia's nemesis in the Russian-Polish war of 1920. The city was smothered in Soviet-style décor with an abundance of red flags and portraits of Lenin. The charming old bourgeois town on seven hills with its ornate façades, baroque churches, streets shaded by chestnut trees, and parks where only recently nannies brought their charges to play, was fast disappearing, engulfed by a tidal wave of *sovietisation*.

Winter months crawled between bouts of nauseating propaganda and of suffocating terror. People were being arrested *en masse* and held in cellars of requisitioned houses. And each day mother waited and hoped for further news from my father, but no second card came. In the meantime, as March snows began to melt, frightening rumours circulated about deportations of the Polish population from Lwów and its environs.

It was Thursday night, 12 April 1940. I was eighteen months old and all that week I had been restless, cranky, running a fever and adding to my mother's worries. Uncle Zbyszek fretted that mother herself would get sick, so by the evening, Aunt Hania convinced her to get some sleep, while she and uncle would take me to their flat for the night. My crib was hauled upstairs and I was bundled off to give mother some respite. It didn't last long. Soon her rest was disrupted by violent banging on our front door and the familiar shouting: *"Open, this is NKVD."*

Aunt Hania ran to the window. On the street below, by our front gate, she could make out the outline of two massive trucks, headlights dimmed, engines running. Behind them, hidden by dense lilac bushes, another truck was barely visible, but clearly audible by the snarling of its motor. In the darkness, she could make out silhouettes of men moving up our garden path. So that was it, there was no doubt; the family was being arrested by the NKVD. Uncle Zbyszek, the most likely target, ran downstairs to join my mother at the front door. Basia in her slippers and nightgown, a brightly coloured shawl wrapped around her shoulders, struggled up the stairs from the basement. There was more shouting outside and banging on the front door as my uncle turned on the lights in the hallway and opened. An NKVD officer pushed his way right into the hallway followed by two armed soldiers. He was holding a sheet of paper. *"Sonia Stefanovichovna?"* He shouted. Uncle Zbyszek froze. They were not calling for him, but for his sister.

Mother stepped forward. *"That's me."* The man looked again at the paper in his hand. *"And Maria Vladimira…?"*

"That's my mother."

"You are both coming with us," he barked. Uncle Zbyszek moved my mother aside.

"I'm the son of Maria Vladimira," he said. *"I will go in her place."*

The officer stared at him. *"Your name isn't here,"* he tapped the piece of paper with his forefinger. *"Your turn will come,"* he added with a snort. Then by way of explanation: *"If I was ordered to shoot my own mother, I would do it"* When uncle still tried to argue, one of the soldiers pushed his machinegun into his face.

"Where are you taking us?" Mother asked. *"To your husband. You have one hour to pack."* Another NKVD soldier who had been patrolling outside walked in. *"There is also a child on the list. Where is she?"*

Uncle Zbyszek turned on him violently. *"You can't take her. The child is very ill."* The man was about to raise his voice, when mother cut in: *"She is*

136

upstairs in another part of the house," she said calmly, *"She is so ill that she would not survive a journey."* He looked at her angrily. *"Show me,"* he ordered. Mother nodded to Aunt Hania. The soldier's heavy boots thumped on the staircase as, machinegun in hand, he followed my aunt upstairs. On the doorstep of the room where I was sleeping Aunt Hania said quietly, *"She is in there"* as she opened the door wider. *"She is very ill,"* she added. The soldier hesitated, and then approached my crib on tiptoe. I was very congested and my breathing was heavy. He watched me for a moment, then turned around and walked out. *"Swear that you will look after he,"* he whispered hoarsely to Aunt Hania. Barely able to hold back her tears, she nodded silently.

Downstairs packing was finished. Mother ran upstairs to look at me for the last time and returned deathly pale but dry-eyed and composed. I would have liked to know what she said to me in this brief farewell, before embarking on a six-year gruelling trek that would take her to the ends of the earth, to Kazakhstan on the border with China, through Persia, Iraq, Palestine, and Egypt, across North Africa, back to Europe, to London into the hell of V-2 rockets.

As they walked towards the door, mother and granny instinctively picked up their handbags and took their black Persian lamb coats from the coat rack in the hallway. Aunt Hania threw her arms around mother's neck. *"We'll take good care of Ayka,"* she whispered, barely stifling her sobs. Then she hugged granny. Uncle Zbyszek, his face ashen, carried two small trunks to the waiting lorry. Basia, hiding her face in her shawl, wailed loudly as the three of them walked down the path and disappeared beyond the garden gate.

It was almost dawn by the time the trucks revved up their engines and moved away, heading for the railroad station through deserted, familiar streets. The city was still asleep. Passing the railroad station Zofia looked up at the glass dome of the edifice that her father had rebuilt after the First World War. Further down trains and more trains stood on the sidings. The bomb, the tank, the rubble, and the freight car packed with people came to symbolise World War Two. From west to east, millions of Polish citizens were taken in freight cars to forced labour in the Soviet Union – to kolkhozes and gulags, to the taiga in the far Siberian north, to Arctic coal mines of Vorkuta, to POW death camps of Kozielsk, Starobelsk, and Ostaszkow. From east to west, millions of Polish citizens were taken in freight cars to forced labour in the factories of the Third Reich, to clear rubble from bombed German cities, and on to die in the death camps of Bergen-Belsen, Dachau, Mauthausen, and Neuengamme.

Under the watchful eye of armed guards, mother and granny were ordered off the truck and onto the waiting train. The step was a metre above the platform, so they had to be helped in. Their two small trunks were tossed in after them. Along the tracks, guards yelled orders, pushed, and shoved people who one by one were swallowed up by the pitch darkness of chilly freight cars. Then, with a metallic clang, the doors were slammed shut from the outside and secured with metal bars.

The indescribable shock, claustrophobia, numbness, were but a fraction of sensations experienced by those dragged out of their homes, forced into metal cages of the cattle cars, without regard for age, gender, or physical condition. How did they react to the violent loss of freedom? To the incredibly crude conditions of lack of basic sanitary facilities, personal hygiene, and a moment of privacy? Did they look out during the day through the small barred windows at unploughed fields, woods, and meadows? At the landscape of their holiday outings and vacation excursions? Did they whisper familiar names of towns and villages along the way? Or did they just freeze within themselves, attempting to grasp the magnitude of their tragedy? At night what other sounds besides the dull rhythmic thumping of wheels invaded the restless sleep? Stifled sobbing, whispers, or the wailing of a child? Was there resignation, apathy, rebellion, or anger? "Where are you taking us?" Mother had asked the NKVD man. "To your husband." The thought that at the end of this nightmarish journey she would be reunited with Maks, may have tempered the pain and longing for the child she left behind.

A few bare wooden planks along the walls served as quasi bunk beds for some. A small iron heater in the middle of the floor was all that provided warmth for the entire car, while early spring temperatures fell below freezing point during the night. Worst of all were the latrines or lack thereof. There was one in each car, an open hole in the floor, with no partitions around it. People tried to provide a modicum of privacy, attaching rags to the roof. What better way to dehumanise than to bring human bodily functions down to the animal level? So began my mother's long trek into the heart of Asia.

To better describe the reality of those years, it is best to give voice to her own recollections, her personal notes written after the liberation of deportees in 1941. Such reports were required as evidence by the Polish army of all servicemen and women who survived the ordeal of Soviet *deportations*. Thousands of records collected at the time are now archived at the Hoover Institute at Stanford

University in California. In her notes written sometime between October 1941 and September 1942 mother wrote:

"My name is Zofia Hoffman, platoon commander; born: 1905; lawyer by profession; wife of Attorney, Captain (in the reserves), Dr Maksymilian Hoffman.

I was taken by the Soviets on the night of 13 April 1940, together with my mother Maria Włodzimiera Neuhoff, from my mother's home in Lwów at Zadwórzańska nr.69. On the list of persons singled out for deportation to the USSR was also my eighteen-month-old daughter, whom I was able to save and entrust to relatives.

Upon my arrest, the reason for the deportation was not given, merely as a comment that I am being taken to join my husband. As a captain in the reserves, my husband had been called up for active duty on 22 August 1939, and had been interned by the Soviets on 22 September in Lwów together with a group of officers and sent to a prisoner-of-war camp in Starobelsk. My mother and I were allowed to pack some things, up to 50 kg in weight for each one of us, and after we packed, the contents of my flat were written up and the apartment door was sealed.

The deportation procedure was executed with a degree of organisational skill and precision that pointed to a highly perfected technique in this type of undertakings.

The conditions in which we travelled were appalling. Under escort, in locked cattle cars into which 30-40 people were crammed without regard for sex or age. Sanitary installations were so primitive, as practically non-existent.

In the cattle car in which I found myself, there were people I knew: Dr Janina Piłat with her mother-in-law, Karolina Zbrożek, Mikołaj Cieński, Mr Nastalski (engineer) with his wife and son, Mr Kujawski (engineer) with his wife, Mrs Kubinowa wife of an air force pilot, with two little daughters aged 2 and 4, Mrs Kuberczyk with her daughter, Mrs Romanowska with her son and son-in-law Dr Góra, Mrs Urzędowska (the sister of Lieutenant Colonel Urzędowski from Lwów), and several other persons whose names I can no longer recall.

The most tragic images were those of trains that we passed at railway stations, crammed with Polish deportees, and the sight of tiny faces of children at the barred windows filled one with a sense of helpless despair. And yet, at that time, even in our worst forebodings, we had no idea of the misery and degradation that awaited us. After two or three days we received our first food rations, once a day, at different times of day and night. Bread, soup, or gruel. We got sugar twice during the entire journey.

On 1 May 1940, we were unloaded at the railroad station of Dzhengistobe in Kazakhstan, in Semipalatinsk Oblast; from where lorries took us inland into villages, kolkhozes, and sovkhozes. With about seventy other people, I was sent to the Burlagasch kolkhoz in Żarminski Oblast. The Kazakh kolkhoz was wretched, but not badly located – only 30 kilometres from the railroad station, some 5 to 6 kilometres from the village of Georgiyevka, and 9 kilometres from another regional settlement Akhzal. The kolkhoz consisted of several clay huts and we were settled – with some difficulty – in some of them, mostly together with the local population, or else in some unused buildings such as stables. My mother, me, Mrs Zbrożek and the Piłat ladies found a place in a shed that housed sheep which were removed from there while we waited. It was no better than a hovel with one tiny window, a mud floor saturated with animal urine and dung, very humid, and crawling with countless vermin, fleas, cockroaches, centipedes, and fleas being the particular bane. On one single bedding, one could crush anywhere between fifty and eighty insects in one single sitting without making a dent in their total numbers. There was no furniture of any sort. We slept on damp ground, our suitcases and trunks served as tables and chairs.

Two days after our arrival, we were assigned to various tasks in the kolkhoz, all of them manual or 'dirty' work, as the Russians called it, (czarnorobocza or griaźnia) in barns, stables, sheds, in fashioning 'kiziak', or brick-shaped logs out of animal dung, to be used as fuel. Other jobs involved digging ditches for watering the crops, layering walls with mud, and working in the fields, weeding, or servicing tractors. Hours of completed workdays and norms achieved were recorded by the kolkhoz leader and we were to be paid at the end of the year. This meant that money that would have paid for our necessities was non-existent. Yet we had to live and provide for ourselves. We were required to pay rent for our sleeping quarters (my mother's and mine came to 40 roubles per month) and we needed to buy food since no rations were supplied. We survived on the provisions we brought from home, on the sale of our meagre possessions, and on money which was sent by families that remained in Poland. The entire standard of living was extremely low, although at that time we still had not experienced the worst of hunger and cold that would come in the winter.

We suffered from a lack of bread. Only flat local Kazakh cakes baked in a most primitive way were to be had. Sheep dung, which was carefully collected on the steppe, served as fuel for cooking, done on two or three stones set together.

Freedom of movement beyond the kolkhoz was very restricted at first and only by permission of the kolkhoz leader (predsiadatel). After a few months, the situation improved somewhat to the extent that it was possible to walk to the regional villages of Georgiyevka and Akhzal, as well as to some of the other kolkhozes nearby. Leaving the kolkhoz for any length of time or beyond a certain radius was almost impossible until the amnesty [in 1941].

The attitude of kolkhoz authorities towards us lacked any trace of consideration and was tainted with mockery and derision. Locals of the younger generation were particularly ill-disposed towards us, at every opportunity mockingly referring to 'aristocratic Poland' and its 'gentlemen and ladies', and boasting of their intellectual superiority in the knowledge of antireligious and communist ideology. Older people, remembering the way things used to be, were well aware of the true state of affairs and looked upon us with a certain degree of sympathy and understanding, but that did not stop them from taking advantage of our situation and in robbing us of the remnants of our possessions. They all acted in concert.

At the end of May, nine persons were sent out to work on a farm and I was one of them. The farm was located in the mountains, a few kilometres away from the kolkhoz, and other than three small mud huts there were no other housing accommodations. We were put up in a ramshackle shed without doors or windows, with handfuls of damp hay for bedding. The work was strenuous, quarrying, and loading stones and making 'kiziak' from animal dung.

Living and working conditions were extremely hard. The tools we were given were quite primitive and awkward and lack of gloves soon turned our palms into a mass of bloody blisters, while the cracked and cut skin made work very difficult. We were not given any food; we had to provide and cook it ourselves in any way we could. It was also very difficult to obtain anything except goat's milk. Poor nutrition and exhausting physical work in extreme heat combined with the dust from the quarry soon began to undercut our strengths. At first, I was assigned to loading stones and boulders on an ox-cart and driving it to the site where a new barn was to be built. Later, while fashioning bricks of 'kiziak', I became infected with brucellosis from sick sheep.

Because of lack of a thermometer, it was not possible to take my temperature, but I began to weaken so rapidly that soon the farm leader sent me back to the kolkhoz where I was put to work in the fields. After two days, exhausted by the physical exertion and the progressing illness, I fainted at work, putting an end to my short career as a kolkhoz labourer, but instead initiating a long period of peregrination through the Soviet hospital system.

The kolkhoz predsiadatel refused to supply a cart to take me to a hospital. Even for a payment it was impossible to get any transportation, he told me, no reason given for the refusal. By pure chance, I managed to get into a passing car that took me to a hospital in Akhzal, where I was treated with unexpected care and kindness by the hospital director, an elderly Tatar physician, himself an exile from Crimea. The only inconvenience was countless bedbugs and infestation with vermin was a real nuisance. There were two likely causes of my illness: malaria or brucellosis. Unfortunately, the hospital lacked any means for running the necessary analyses as well as drugs for treating the fever.

The severe course of my illness, an extremely high temperature causing dizziness and loss of consciousness at night, prompted the physician to refer me to a hospital in Georgiyevka where the necessary means for treating me would be available. In my weakened condition, I had to walk 9 kilometres on foot from Akhzal to the kolkhoz, accompanied only by my mother. Back at the kolkhoz, I spent four weeks lying on straw bedding, first waiting for the return of a nurse specialised in running brucellosis tests, then another two weeks for the injections to arrive. The physician in charge of the Georgiyevka hospital was well known for his open hostility towards Poles and many deportees complained of his brutal and inconsiderate behaviour. For that reason, as well as because of the primitive conditions in the hospital, equally infested with bedbugs as the one in Akhzal, I decided to walk (or ride if possible) there every day to receive injections. A long-term stay in that hospital would have been psychologically devastating.

The medical treatment I got was careless and sporadic. Over two and a half months, I was given three injections. That, coupled with malnutrition, easily explains why my illness dragged on, becoming chronic and debilitating to my entire system. I managed to hang on like this until October [1940]. Autumn rains made the roads impassable on foot, so the NKVD authorities allowed me and my mother to move to Georgiyevka. It was not considered a major concession since it had been made clear to me that I had no chance of recovery and it was merely a matter of waiting for the end.

In Georgiyevka the attitude of the authorities and of the civilian population was as hostile as in the kolkhoz, although there were better living conditions and more food was available. But on the other hand, high prices of foodstuff and housing were catastrophic to our finances, since the value of our remaining possessions, clothing and jewellery, was plummeting."

The report ended here.

Work in the stone quarry was backbreaking. It demanded sheer physical brute force since no tools were available. Apart from extracting the stone, it had to be loaded on carts and taken to the site where a new barn was being built. Zofia did all that work as well. She drove a team of two mild grey oxen and one day the load was so heavy that the animals could not pull the cart uphill and it got stuck at the bottom of a slope. This happened just opposite the hut of the *predsedatel,* a malicious gnome, who supervised the work in the quarries. When she could not get the cart to budge, the man ran out of his cabin with a thick pole, and furiously beat the animals until in a frantic panic they finally tugged at the cart. He then threatened Zofia with his clenched fists, swearing at her. Since early childhood, my mother was very fond of all animals, and now she loved her grey oxen. After their brutal beating, she led them on, crying along the way over their fate, so eerily resembling her own.

Her dry narrative intended for a military file did not do justice to the human drama that played itself out day by day on the steppe of Kazakhstan. Hunger and inhuman living conditions devastated the ranks of Polish deportees. When upon their arrest my mother and grandmother were being led from their house in Lwów, they picked up their handbags, not even thinking of the jewellery that was kept in them for safety. Most of granny's had been tucked into a large armchair that eventually was destroyed when the house was bombed. But the few pieces that were in the bags, a couple of rings, a diamond pendant and earrings, now could be bartered for a meal. During the early months in the kolkhoz, the Kazakhs were willing to swap a pot of goat's milk, a melon, or a handful of flour for a pair of diamond earrings or a gold bracelet. Except that after a while this barter had lost its sheen, because after all, how many strings of pearls could be worn while tending sheep on the steppe or gathering dung for fuel?

In her description of the conditions prevailing in Soviet hospitals, mother remembered the first one in Akhzal, where she was treated with great humanity by the lead physician, an elderly Tatar, from among those whose families were expelled by Catherine the Great from Crimea and exiled to Kazakhstan.

Symptoms of brucellosis spread by infected sheep (Brucellosis Ovis) are similar to those of malaria: high fever in the night, loss of consciousness, then a violent drop to very low body temperature in the morning, causing debilitating weakness. Since mother's symptoms could have been caused by either, the doctor administered quinine, the only drug available and since she did not respond to it, he determined it was brucellosis. For lack of better remedies, it was diagnosis by elimination. Because of the fever Zofia's dark-blonde hair with its touch of copper, which used to be twisted into a chignon at the back of her neck, now started to fall out in handfuls, so her head was shaved almost down to the skin. During Zofia's entire stay in Akhzal, granny walked to the hospital every day, nine kilometres on foot each way.

After she returned to the kolkhoz, mother awaited treatment at the hospital in Georgiyevka, but in the meantime, the weather was growing colder and the shed that housed the deportees offered hardly any shelter. On some nights, temperatures dropped far below zero and people's hair froze to the walls while they were asleep. Walking into town became impossible so the kolkhoz authorities reluctantly decided that Zofia could be written off in the terminal stage of her illness, which she was not expected to survive. She and granny were allowed to move into the town.

In Georgiyevka they rented a spot in the house of a young Kazakh family. The husband, a truck driver, was away from home for weeks on end, and his wife Lena was alone with the baby. The place allotted to mother and granny was a corner in the family's kitchen. The only other room in the house was the couple's bedroom. They were given a mattress filled with hay and the two Persian lamb furs taken hurriedly off the hangers at their departure from the house in Lwów, proved a godsend, just as they did during the bitterly cold nights in the kolkhoz, serving as coats in the daytime and coverings at night.

By October the fierce Russian winter set in and soon the ground was frozen. Contrary to the kolkhoz authorities' expectations, Zofia did not die but slowly began to improve. Not because of any medical treatment which, as she described, was minimal. Mainly her own strong system fought the illness, and the move to the Kazakh cottage away from the cold helped to bolster her recovery. Nutrition still presented a huge problem – prices were sky high and there was a general lack of food. Each time word got around that a shipment of anything was expected, be it salt, sugar in lumps, juicy watermelons, or "bricks" of pressed tea, queues would form the day before outside the local cooperative One time it happened that the delivery of much-prized *chai* was expected. To spare my mother, granny stood all night in line, and finally in the morning the doors opened and the crowd surged forward. Granny, a petite figure squeezed between two huge broad-shouldered Kazakhs could not budge, but then when they moved forward, they swept her off her feet and dragged her along with them, so without touching the ground she landed inside the shop. For the price of a few roubles and a couple of cracked ribs, she got her allotment of tea. Another time mother secured a pot of milk and as she was carrying it home triumphantly, she noticed a flea floating on the surface. Without a second thought, she fished it out with her finger, never mentioning this to granny who, hunger notwithstanding, would not have touched 'flea-infested' milk. And one could only dream of a piece of white bread: the Kazakh cakes proved a poor substitute. Mother remembered this long after she left Russia. White bread was available only for communists.

Apart from the report for her military file, at some later date mother wrote down her personal reflections on the three years spent in Kazakhstan and the USSR, years unlike anything she experienced before or anything that would come later.

"What I am about to relate will be a small fragment of my own life. Those will simply be episodes and images seen along the trail of an unexpectedly long journey from Europe that took me across Asia, Africa, and back to Europe. My story takes place in the East against the oriental background and covers three years of my life.

As a young girl I dreamed of the Orient in the way young girls dream, the land of thousand and one nights. In my mind's eye, I saw boundless expanses of deserts, white cities, domes and graceful minarets of mosques, palaces of alabaster lace hidden by the exuberance of palms, narrow passages under the scorching sun, barred and darkened windows of harems. My imagination recreated the bustle of the eastern street, its dizzying sounds of everyday life, noisy crowds milling around, shrill cries of vendors offering their wares, and the plaintive strains of music of a Persian market. And at sundown, in the air filled with spicy scents of ambergris and sandalwood, the voice of a muezzin from a minaret summoning the faithful to prayer like final chords cooling all the passions of a feverish day. Such did I imagine the Orient to be from the perspective of thousands of miles, a mirage – golden, shimmering, infused with colour.

Then came the year 1939. The world around me collapsed. War swept away all that was dear and familiar. What followed was unknown. My town, its streets, places familiar from childhood became strange and forbidding. My own home ceased to be a home. Beloved faces were disappearing one after another, like pictures erased from the screen of life. Then one night my turn came.

I remember it well. The night was black and ominous, and so quiet that I heard the throbbing of my own heart. Premonition told me to wait. Then it came. The shrill sound of the doorbell tugged at the nerves with a spasm of fear. Then footsteps. A lot of heavy footsteps, closer and closer. Then... I really don't know what happened afterwards. Or rather, no, no, I do know what happened afterwards. Afterwards it was fate.

Uproar, confusion, scattered words, stifled sobbing, and sharp pain around the heart. All the lights in the house blazed in farewell. The dark outline of a freight car, then silence and darkness and the rhythmic, hollow sound of wheels. Then there may have been despair, filth, hunger, lack of water. Or perhaps there was nothing, just a figment of a feverish brain. I don't know, I myself have a hard time believing all that happened, so how can I expect you to believe that it was true?

But it was true that one day the door of the cattle car opened with a violent tug, brilliant sunlight blinded the eyes, cracked lips so greedily gulped the fresh air that it choked the throat, cramped legs unfolded and straightened out. I fell from the darkness of the freight car suddenly into an expanse of space, so boundless and endless, and stretching as far as the eye could see to where the blue sky flowed into the silver earth and where there was nothing else but the immensity of that open space. That was the steppe, and the land is called Asia. I can't speak of all Asia, I got to know just its western fragment, its steppes, silver in the spring with flowering woodworm, burnt yellow in the summer by the scorching sun, and blinding from the whiteness of the snows in the winter.

Thousands of years ago, this land must have been the home of a god of winds. Night and day, they blow without stopping, without respite, and in the winter blustering hurricanes carry mounds of snow that seem to congeal the world into a white shroud. There are days when the sky is cloudless, clear and blue, and the snow shimmers with a million diamonds because a transparent and treacherous veil hangs between the sky and the earth propelled by the wind with incredible speed and ferocity. Small dwellings of the local population sink into the fluffy snow so deep that even the chimneys disappear. Long tunnels are cut out in the snow and people going into the steppe tie themselves with strong and thick ropes so as not to get lost. During those days and nights, white death stalks the steppe awaiting its victims at every turn.

I got to know this Asian winter only later, my initial encounter with Asia took place in the spring, in the full bloom of its monotonous beauty.

The road was sandy and straight as an arrow, without bends, because what need was there for them? There was nothing to avoid or circumvent. Everything was simple and uncomplicated. As simple and uncomplicated was the fact that I, a stranger from faraway Europe found myself suddenly, against my will and desire in the heart of the steppe which in this spot resembled a deep soup plate. Far on the eastern horizon, the rim of the plate rose in gentle slopes into layers. Further to the east, the bulges in the steppe grew into taller and taller hills, ballooning into smooth and gentle shapes. Then the straight sandy road disappeared and ravines determined the trail as the cart pulled by two oxen rolled softly over furrows made in the dense woodworm by wheels of other carts. Those furrows were the only signposts. In this untamed corner of the world forgotten by God and by man days flowed monotonously and were as heavy as that stone that we loaded on the cart and carried from one place to another. The wildness of nature and the primitive life combined into a harmonious whole, numbing the mind and the senses and transforming the human being into a machine.

Finally moving the stone from the quarry was halted. There was sufficient material for the foundations of a new barn. Then came the weeding of fields of millet, digging of ditches for irrigation, working animal dung into fuel. The steppes surrounding our kolkhoz turned reddish-brown. After the sweltering heat of the summer, autumn was approaching fast in a veil of mists and rain. Roads turned into bowls filled with black dough. In October the puddles became covered with a glassy sheet of ice and in the morning the hardened mud resembled furrows of a ploughed field. The steppe turned white with frost until one day thick, heavy snowflakes whirled in the air, dropped down, and blanketed the whole earth. Days followed days, weeks turned into months, spring came and with it the return to work, the trek across the endless steppe overgrown with silvery woodworm, and across the expanse of the landscape, unvarying, monotonous hopelessness."

In Georgiyevka, mother's health slowly improved. The fever brought on by brucellosis which had been ravaging her body for months finally abated and

Lena's kindness may have also contributed to that. Lena was younger than my mother and took a liking to her, perhaps because of the child left behind in faraway Poland. Lena became quite protective of Zofia and called her by the affectionate Russian diminutive – *Sonechka*.

Christmas was approaching, the first Christmas since mother and granny left Lwów. Memories weighed heavily on them with an overwhelming sense of grief and loss. In the years before the war, at home Christmas was all about the bustle and joyful excitement, about wrapping presents, decorating the house, and preparing all manner of delicacies. For days Basia and granny baked feather-light *babas* carefully covered from drafts as soon as they came out of the oven. God forbid that a *baba* should collapse; it was seen as a bad omen for the following year. Poppy seed rolls, almond cakes, chocolate, and walnut tortes, sat in rows on sideboards awaiting *Noël*.

In Polish tradition Christmas Eve is a meatless day and one of abstinence until nightfall. On that day gentlemen would leave their offices early and stop at local pubs or delicatessens for schnapps, a sliver of marinated herring, a chat with friends or colleagues, swapping greetings, and professional gossip with their peers before proceeding home to the very special elaborate evening meal, the *Wigilia* dinner. The table would be set with the best porcelain and silverware, the entire household including the servants would dress up for the occasion. Before sitting down, bits of white wafer were shared by all, with good wishes for health and happiness in the coming year. Beet soup, fish, pasta, followed by compote of dried fruit and desserts, those were staples served with appropriate wines and spirits. In keeping with the old Polish tradition of hospitality, a spare seating at the table was left for an "unexpected guest", since no one should be alone on that evening, and every stranger ought to be welcomed and invited to partake of the meal. Additionally, it was also meant to symbolise those members of the family who for whatever reason were absent. With the country's long history of partitions, uprisings, and deportations, every family had someone to remember.

Live-in servants joined the family at the table and at some point, a tiny bell would tinkle somewhere in the house, the door of the drawing-room would swing open and reveal a brightly lit Christmas tree with presents piled under it. Every year Basia, granny's housekeeper, received yet another shawl in an intricate pattern known as Turkish, which she favoured. Later that night the whole company would make their way to midnight Mass along crowded streets, amid the pealing of church bells, with snow crunching underfoot and one's breath, like a festoon, trailing behind in the frosty air.

All that was now but a distant and painful memory. In the corner of Lena's kitchen, crouching by the small trunk that served them as a table, Zofia fashioned a wafer from a piece of Kazakh cake. She shared it with her mother, in the time-honoured tradition exchanging wishes... to survive and be reunited with their loved ones.

Across the kitchen, Lena watched silently. After a while, she approached them. *"Sonechka,"* she said softly to my mother, *"I want to show you and your matushka something."* Leading them to her bedroom where a large portrait of Lenin prominently hung over the couple's bed, she took it down and turned it over. There was a beautiful icon of a Madonna with Child on the back. She propped up the picture against the wall and silently left the room, closing the door behind her. *Hail Mary, full of grace...*

Chapter VII
The Amnesty

For several months the fierce Siberian winter held Kazakhstan in its grip. Temperatures dropped far below freezing point, hovering at times around minus 50°C, while the *buran*, the powerful savage Siberian wind, raced across the steppes never letting up, never slowing down, burying villages and hamlets in an unforgiving white blanket, carrying with it a deadly, and glittering translucent veil of snow crystals. To leave the house, people had to cut out steps and dig long tunnels in the snow, and when venturing outdoors secure themselves with ropes to avoid sinking in the drifts where many had frozen to death.

Uncle Zbyszek sent as many care packages as he could, some made it through, though many did not. By now cigarettes replaced jewellery as the currency of preference for barter with the Kazakhs, so he sent cigarettes, but by the time they arrived the market got saturated and it was no longer possible to swap them for food. Zofia took up smoking to suppress hunger pangs, but the prospect of survival looked bleak.

After months of mind-numbing cold, the snow and ice began to melt. Mother and granny dreaded the return to the kolkhoz. Their lightweight dresses were in tatters, they had no other clothes except those they were taken in, and the aftermath of my mother's illness lingered. On 13 April, a year in exile since their arrest and deportation came and went. Hard as it was to cope with the cost of living, Zofia clung to the hope that they would be allowed to stay in Georgiyevka where life was less unbearable. As spring advanced into summer, the NKVD made no move to order them back onto the steppes. The monstrous Soviet Moloch ground slowly and for those caught between its gears time remained hopelessly congealed in the relentless monotony of backbreaking labour, cold, hunger, misery that nothing could alleviate.

Yet the unexpected did happen. On Sunday, 22 June 1941 at 3:15 am Hitler launched his offensive against Russia, a massive sweeping attack, *Operation Barbarossa*. The armies of the Wehrmacht that stretched along three thousand kilometres of Russia's western border, crossed into Soviet territory. This should not have been a surprise since Germany had been building up its forces for months, but it was a fact that Stalin obstinately refused to recognise when informed by his own intelligence, clinging to the belief that the *Führer* was his ally whose assurances were genuine and who harboured no evil intentions towards Russia. Thus, the USSR was caught unprepared. Throughout that day news of Nazi invasion raced across eleven time zones of Soviet territory, after Radio Moscow's brief announcement, followed by patriotic calls for revenge. It filtered slowly into kolkhozes, labour camps, and settlements, wherever there were Polish prisoners and deportees. Something overheard here and there, a scrap of a Russian newspaper. Stalin and Hitler at war? It also reached Georgiyevka. Poles huddled, feverishly speculating on the possible outcome of this attack and what it might portend for them. One thing was sure: two monsters of the twentieth century faced each other like furious beasts locked in mortal combat; Poland's greatest enemies were finally at each other's throats. Hated as the Russians were, it was good news that now they had no choice but to turn to the Allied camp to fight the Germans. For Polish deportees, it was like a gift from heaven.

Among the Allied troops fighting on the German front, there were thousands of Polish soldiers who had managed to slip out of the trap created by the Wehrmacht's and USSR's pincer grip in September 1939. Escaping through Romania and Hungary which, though a German ally, was mostly sympathetic to Poland, they reached France, then Britain where the Polish government-in-exile had been set up in London. Stalin now needed allies and the Allies also needed him.

From the moment the Russians occupied Poland's eastern territories, apart from those who were imprisoned in jails and taken to prisoner-of-war camps like my father, the Soviets deported about one and a half million Polish civilians to the Gulag from Eastern Poland to work on railroad tracks, clearing the northern *taiga,* the coal mines of Vorkuta north of the Arctic Circle, and to the kolkhozes of Kazakhstan. By 1941 many deportees were already dead from exhaustion, starvation, illness, and brutal work. Now the survivors became pawns on the war chessboard. Opening their negotiations with the Allies, the Russians proposed to free those deportees who were still alive and form a Polish army in the USSR to be incorporated into the Red Army. Difficult negotiations with the Bolsheviks were carried out by General Władysław Sikorski, the Polish commander-in-chief and prime minister of the government-in-exile.

In the face of the advancing German offensive, after weeks of haggling over the fate of the Soviet-occupied Polish territories and under intense Allied pressure on the Poles to make concessions to the Russians, Sikorski signed an agreement on 30 July with Ivan Maisky, the Russian ambassador in London, to form a Polish army in the USSR that would operate under the orders of the Red Army. General Władysław Anders, who had been himself held in the dreaded Lubyanka Prison in Moscow since his capture in September 1939, was to be given the command of these troops. On 4 August 1941, he was released from prison, still weak from the festering wounds he received in the battles of 1939 and after twenty-two months of incarceration. On 12 August, the Russians issued an *ukase* proclaiming an amnesty for Polish deportees. It took weeks before this announcement filtered through to the remote corners of the Soviet empire; it did not reach everyone, and in many places local authorities ignored it.

On 15 August 1941, Zofia was summoned by the NKVD and escorted to the headquarters in Georgiyevka for questioning. She was led into an office where a burly local NKVD officer sat behind the desk. He motioned her to a chair and lest she be tempted to do him bodily harm, another NKVD operative stood by the door with a *Nagant* aimed at mother's back.[64] In spite of the fear, she found the situation ridiculous. Her cheeks were sunken, her arms bony and as thin as twigs, her collarbone stuck out beneath the tattered neckline of her dress and yet she was deemed to present a threat to this uniformed broad-shouldered bully, whose jacket was tightly stretched across his chest and whose thick neck protruded from the collar like a tree trunk. For a while he said nothing, observing her through narrowed eyes, intimidating, and unsettling. Finally, he spoke:

"Sofia Stefanovichovna, you are accused of spreading anti-Soviet propaganda." Zofia remained silent. He continued: *"Two weeks ago you made*

---

[64] The Nagant (or nagan in Russian) was a seven-shot, gas-seal revolver designed by Belgian industrialist Léon Nagant for the Russian Imperial army. After Russia purchased the manufacturing rights in 1898, production was moved to the Tula Arsenal in Russia. After the Russian Revolution it continued to be used by the Red Army, the Soviet security forces, the Bolshevik secret police, the Cheka, as well as its Soviet successor agencies, the OGPU and NKVD.

statements hostile to the USSR giving out false information with the intent of belittling the Soviet economic achievements"

His words were a snarl as he spat them out. Zofia stared at him in disbelief while her mind raced back trying to recall what meaningless comment might have brought this on. Somebody informed on her, but what and who? Lena?

The NKVD-*ista* watched closely for her reaction to his words and waited for her response. Finally, she shook her head in denial and her answer was quick. *"What do you mean? I did no such thing."* She sounded indignant. By now she was quite proficient in Russian. He consulted a piece of paper on his desk. On 30 July, he told her, she made a statement to the effect that in pre-war Poland it was usual for women to own more than two dresses. Did she say that?

Instant though vague recollection of some trivial comment, but not the details. The absurdity of the accusation caught her off guard, it sounded laughable but it wasn't, as she well knew. She looked the man straight in the eye. *"Well, it was possible to own more than two dresses,"* she answered defiantly.

"Then you admit to denigrating the socialist economic attainments of the USSR by praising a putrid capitalist system?" He raised his voice. *"You rotten bourgeois,"* he yelled, half rising from the chair, leaning towards her, and working himself into a rage to better to intimidate. *"You think you can sow discontent among Soviet citizens?"* His face turned purple, the veins on his bull neck swelled ominously as he pounded his fist on the desk. *"We'll teach you what it is to slander the Soviet system!"* he shouted.

The shrill ringing of the telephone disrupted his diatribe and with an impatient lurch, the spluttering *apparatchik* grabbed the receiver and barked into it. Whoever was at the other end of the line rated as an authority because he instantly sat up and squared his shoulders. His tone became unctuous and servile. He frowned as if trying to understand the faintly audible cackle coming over the wire.

All the while Zofia sat absolutely still, staring straight ahead, conscious of the Nagant pointed at her back. Behind her stillness her mind was buzzing furiously, weighing the odds of this interrogation. She knew that economic "crimes" were punishable with many years in the gulag as she remembered the two women from the kolkhoz who a few times received permission to travel to a small town nearby where in a state gold-purchasing agency they could sell the remnants of their jewellery. After a while this provoked the envy of the local *predsedatel,* perhaps they did not pay him enough, and he denounced them to the

NKVD as parasites. They were put on trial and sentenced to seven years of hard labour in the gulag.

The thought sent shivers down Zofia's spine. She worried about her mother who insisted on coming along to the NKVD building and was waiting outside. If they arrest me now, she thought, mother would not find out for hours. Just keep calm, she told herself, just keep calm. A saying from Russian folk wisdom flashed across her mind: *a man carries his sentence on the tip of his tongue.* Suddenly she felt in control, her deep fear frozen out. Switching her attention to the officer, she caught a change of tone in his responses. As he ended the call, he replaced the receiver slowly, his face still red and angry. But he looked perplexed. A deep frown creased his forehead as he twisted around in the chair with his back to her, silently digesting some unwelcome news, ignoring Zofia's presence. When he finally turned around again, his words surprised her.

"You can go," he said tersely, *"just remember we will check for statements hostile to the USSR and watch for any capitalist propaganda. Next time you try to denigrate the glorious conquests of the Soviet economy, you will not get away with it."* He sounded petulant rather than threatening, but indifferent, as if he had lost the taste for bullying, as he motioned the guard to let her out.

With outward calm belying the quivering nerves, Zofia left the NKVD building. Outside granny restlessly paced up and down. At the sight of my mother, she said nothing, just closed her eyes and for a moment her lips moved silently as if in prayer. *"Zosienko, what did they want from you?"* she finally whispered, unable to disguise the trembling in her voice. By now both mother and daughter looked like pale shadows of their former selves, in dresses that were little better than rags. Yet both were controlled in the face of the averted menace. Zofia took her mother's arm and as they walked away, she noticed a rosary in Maria's clenched fist. *"Mother, please put it away,"* she muttered, jerking her head towards the NKVD building. *"We don't want to be hauled back in there for spreading religious propaganda."*

Although she still felt queasiness in the pit of her stomach, she was now more puzzled than rattled. *"I don't know what they wanted. There is an informer among us who squealed on me, repeating something I said recently. But the NKVD-ista behaved strangely. He started by bullying me, then after he got a telephone call from somewhere, he lost interest and let me go."*

1941. Kazakhstan. Mother and granny at the time of the amnesty

It was important to figure out who might have denounced her. Granny pointed at Lena, mother hoped otherwise since after many months of living under the same roof, Lena displayed sincere attachment to them both. Still, they talked to trusted Polish friends, although, as Zofia told her mother, it was a question: who could or could not be a trusted friend. After some thought, she ruled Lena out, even though she knew only too well that in this land of the terror machine, decency meant little. Children were taught to denounce their parents, siblings their brothers and sisters, husbands and wives spied on each other. And even though granny continued to suspect Lena, my mother relied on her instinct. Lena's relief on seeing her back was all too obvious. Yet somebody close to them did spy for the NKVD and denounced her since her case was not unique. Others had been similarly harassed; all of which undermined mutual trust among the deportees, even though it was preferable to suspect the natives to one's own. After some discrete surveillance over the next several days, the denouncer was uncovered and sadly, it was a young Polish girl who shared a room with a few other women. One of her companions found a scorched piece of paper in the ashes of an open hearth with names and quotes, Zofia's comment about the dresses among them. In the workers' paradise hunger and fear brought out primitive instincts of survival and for a piece of bread weaker human vessels were liable to sell their very souls. But my mother was pleased that it had not been Lena.

All of this got overshadowed when word reached Georgiyevka that Stalin had declared an amnesty for Poles deported to the USSR. For all? For some? Nobody could tell. An unexpected ray of hope in the dark sea of dismal hopelessness, feverish excitement over the news that travelled through towns and villages, camps, and kolkhozes, wherever Poles were to be found. *Amnesty, Stalin decreed an amnesty for Polish citizens deported to the USSR*!

The Kremlin government was preparing to grant amnesty to thousands of Poles from the labour camps and kolkhozes and those held in Soviet prisons in Moscow and elsewhere to organise able-bodied men into Polish military units. The Russians committed to supplying food, uniforms, and weapons. The amnesty protocol was distributed throughout the NKVD network and suddenly the mystery of Zofia's grilling brusquely cut short, became clearer. Most likely at that very moment, the NKVD officer received word of the Soviet government's decision and broke off the interrogation. The fate of deportees, like my mother's, depended on serendipity.

Ten days after the Sikorski-Mayski agreement had been signed, General Władysław Anders, the newly named commander of this to-be army, issued a general order summoning Polish citizens in the USSR to enlist. Soon it would be known that Poles fit for military service – men and women – were to report to one of four recruiting stations in what had been summer training camps of the Red Army: Buzułuk, a remote village on the Volga river, Tatiszczewo, Tockoje, and Kołtubianka. A Polish military mission was organised by General Zygmunt Szyszko-Bohusz who flew in from London; a Polish embassy was set up in Kuybyshev in the Samara region, and Professor Stanisław Kot was named as the first ambassador.

News of the amnesty and of General Anders's summons travelled across the entire USSR, but it was debatable who among the Polish deportees was still physically fit for military service. Men, women, and children – starved, exhausted by inhuman treatment, hard labour conditions, extreme climate, and (like my mother) devastated by diseases – resembled walking skeletons. Yet in spite of that, though barely alive, they desperately tried to reach the Polish outposts. From the gulag, the northern taiga, coal mines, prisons, and kolkhozes scattered across thousands of miles of the steppe, soldiers headed for the recruitment centres any way they could: in barges down the Siberian rivers, by train, even on foot, and they were followed by crowds of civilians, all in the hope of escaping from the land of hopelessness and death. Many would not make it. People died on the way of typhus, cholera, and dysentery; others died after reaching their destination. The military centres were poorly equipped and insufficiently supplied to cope with the influx of patients in conditions of extreme physical exhaustion, suffering acutely from scurvy and pellagra. Hastily mounted primitive sanitary facilities were assembled at the recruitment points and doctors and nurses from among the deportees put in superhuman efforts manning them, often themselves succumbing in the process, infected by the new arrivals. Cemeteries sprouted around the Polish centres.

As soon as the word of the amnesty reached Georgiyevka, my mother initiated a search for my father, hoping to find him in one of the prisoner-of-war camps. She had not heard from Maks since that one card sent to Lwów before her own arrest, neither had Zbyszek. She believed fervently that somewhere in this vast inhuman land he had survived and that she would soon be able to get in touch and join him. She assumed that like other military personnel, he would be heading for one of the recruitment centres and launched a frantic correspondence.

"To Peoples' Commissariat of USSR Relations Archangielsk Oblast, Kotlas, NKVD camp:

Is Hoffman Maksymilian Władysławowicz in this camp? Please inform him of my address Semipalatinsk, Kirova 90. Hoffman Zofia." The answer came back: *"We inform that Hoffman Maksymilian Władysławowicz is not here in Kotlas.* Signed: *Yudnikov."*

To NKVD in Alma Ata: *"I am living at Kirova no. 90, Georgiyevka, Semipalatinsk Oblast, Żarnovski region. Please advise my husband, Hoffman Maksymilian, a Polish citizen.* Signed: *Hoffman, Zofia."*

To Moscow. To Kotlas again. To Kotlas once more. To Alma Ata. To Vorkuta, coal mine no. 3. Pitiful telegram receipts on shoddy little slips of paper multiplied and were pinned together, but all the answers came back negative.

Reluctant to leave Georgiyevka in case Maks should try to contact her there, mother kept putting off the decision on the move towards the Polish recruitment centres. But finally, she and granny would have to go. The unforgiving Russian winter was fast approaching, the roads would be turning impassable and they would end up getting cut off and trapped in that part of Kazakhstan. Her last telegram receipt from Georgiyevka was dated 16 September and the response came back the same as the others: *"Hoffman Maksymilian, not known at this location."* By the middle of September mother and granny had to decide on their next move.

Much of the rail system had been taken over for movement of Russian troops to the front, trains available for public transportation of non-combatants ran irregularly, crammed beyond belief. Rather than heading to a civilian camp, Zofia wanted to reach a military recruitment post. Polish military recruiters sent out by the embassy in Kuybyshev reached remote locations of the USSR in an effort to find as many people as possible and organise transports. When they showed up in Georgiyevka, my mother immediately reported to them and was assigned to a train heading to Buzułuk. But she was told that only one place was available. Maria at sixty-one was not a candidate for the draft, while Zofia at thirty-six was so her mother would have to stay behind and wait for another train. Priority was given to military personnel vital to the war effort. *"Impossible,"* mother said, *"we cannot be separated."* In that case, they would have to wait for the next opportunity and then head to the south of Kazakhstan to the centres set up for civilians. When? Nobody knew.

Mother returned home deeply disappointed. Transports to Tockoje passed through that very Buzułuk which she was so desperate to reach, but in these feverish days waiting for a train had become a nerve-wracking guessing game. Just as the chance seemed lost, a recruiting officer came to tell Zofia that there would be room for two. In a mad rush, scooping up the remnants of their few belongings, hugging a tearful Lena standing in the door of her little house, mother and granny dragged their bundles to the railroad station and boarded the train for Buzułuk.

Those, at least, were not the freight trains that hauled a million and a half people from Poland to forced labour in Kazakhstan and Siberia; they were passenger trains with compartments, though some did have barred windows. The cars were packed to capacity. Whenever the train stopped at a station people raced to reach the *kipiatok*, the rudimentary canteen that sold hot water for tea, warm watery soup with bits of fat floating in it, and *pierogis* (dough pockets filled with ground meat). A few tables and chairs were set up for the lucky ones who got to the food counter first and then could sit down to eat; however, soon a circle formed behind them, and sometimes those waiting prodded the sitters in the ribs, urging them to eat faster. There were also those who could no longer walk on their own to the canteen, or were unable to swallow the food. Zofia noticed one man whose sick wife, a tiny woman little better than a skeleton covered in rags, lay curled up on a piece of a blanket in the corner of the carriage. At the first stop, the husband rushed out to get something and mother saw him waiting in line for a *pierog,* which he stuffed into his breast pocket, then returned to the end of the queue for a second one. Back on the train, he tried to feed his wife, coaxing bits of dough into her mouth, to no avail. The woman died before they reached the next station. After that, the bereaved husband didn't bother to get off the train. But the available victuals themselves presented many dangers. Months of starvation left people vulnerable and incapable of digesting the greasy food and often the canned preserves were spoiled. Among the passengers, dysentery and fatal food poisonings were rife.

As the train chugged along, wherever it stopped stations were crammed with emaciated Polish soldiers in tattered military uniforms, wearing weird headgear and remnants of boots held together with bits of string. Some had their feet wrapped in pieces of rubber tires. All were desperate to reach the Polish recruitment centres. Eventually, on the way, food became scarce since much of it was being redirected to feed the Soviet army. Local Russians grumbled that it was ever so much better under the tsars and that now white bread was for party members only.

In the aftermath of the German attack on the Soviet Union, the mood among ordinary people turned openly hostile towards the communists. Common folk were unafraid to speak out and perceived the German invader as a saviour. My mother heard words of hatred directed at the Soviet regime. She would later say that *"Hitler had victory over Russia within his grasp. Ordinary Russians welcomed the advancing German army as liberators and covered their tanks with flowers. But rather than taking advantage of this hostility towards the Bolsheviks, the Wehrmacht proceeded into the terrain like a bulldozer, burning villages, destroying crops, leaving scorched earth, terrorising local populations into submission with executions and hangings of the despised Slavic 'Untermensch.'. So, Hitler succeeded in turning the tide of anti-Bolshevik sentiment into a tidal wave of heroic resistance against the Nazi invader."*

Towards the end of September, mother and granny finally reached Buzułuk, a small town of muddy streets and miserable dwellings in the Orenburg Oblast in the Southern Ural on the Samara River, a tributary of the mighty Volga. New arrivals were assigned places on the outskirts, in tents or in mud huts. The staff headquarters of the army was located in Buzułuk itself. The camp commander, Colonel Leopold Okulicki,[65] had been only recently released from Russian prison where all his teeth were knocked out during brutal interrogations by the NKVD. Okulicki was now facing a prodigious challenge of how to fashion an operational army from legions of emaciated beggars. The Fifth Infantry Division was formed in Tatiszczevo, the Sixth Infantry Division and the Supply Centre in Tockoje. Alongside these units, both in Buzułuk, and in Tatiszczevo and Tockoje, the army organised women's units known as Auxiliary Women's Services, *Pomocnicza Służba Kobiet*, abbreviated to PSK.

After completing the identity checks, my mother was drafted as a private into the PSK. The army made a huge effort to save as many people as possible from the Russian inferno and my grandmother, in spite of her age, was enlisted as a 'senior private.' Both received the priceless gift of uniforms: thick skirts and heavy quilted jackets which earned the women the sobriquet of 'penguins.' Mother and granny were lodged in one of the mud huts inside the camp. Zofia was assigned to work in the kitchen. *"I started my military career from peeling rotten carrots,"* she would later say.

In this miserable little town, the Polish command occupied the only impressive building, which offered a jarring contrast with the surroundings. It was known as *Dworianskoje Sobrania* or *Assembly Hall for the Gentry* in its previous existence. Over several decades it housed a variety of users. Before the October Revolution, it was a meeting place for local landowners. After the revolution, it was taken over by the local *soviet* and now, undoubtedly densely crammed with bugging equipment installed by the Russians, it served as the headquarters of the newly minted Polish army's general staff. A Polish flag fluttered from the roof and Polish sentries guarded the entrance. For those like my mother, arriving from the horrors of mines and kolkhozes, the pristine white hall stacked along the walls with boxes of files, bags of mail, where smartly uniformed Polish officers sent over from England officiated in the midst of the clatter of typewriters and crackling of radio apparatus, this must have seemed a

---

[65] Okulicki (promoted to General May 1944) was parachuted into Poland in August 1944 to take charge of the Warsaw Uprising. At the end of the war. he was 'invited' by the Russians to Moscow with the 'group of sixteen' Polish politicians "to discuss" plans for a new Polish government. He was then imprisoned in the Lubyanka and eventually murdered by the NKVD in Butyrki prison. His son died in the Battle for Monte Cassino, January- May 1944.

scene from Dante's Paradise. Here endless queues of spectres in rags and remnants of footwear, straight from the hell of the Russian gulag, shuffled across the floor, giving evidence, obtaining documents, and searching for news of missing loved ones. A chapel had been set up in a small side room where Fr. Władysław Cieński, erstwhile pastor of the church of St. Mary Magdalene in Lwów, celebrated Mass.

1941. Buzułuk. Zofia Hoffman and friend Ama Mager

The Russians did their utmost to obstruct recruiting with absurd rules. Polish Jews, Ukrainians, and Byelorussians who were former citizens of the Second Polish Republic were no longer recognised as Polish citizens, though some managed to evade the Soviet trap with the help of the army. One couple, Karol and Amalia (Ama) Mager, were lucky enough to slip through the net and my mother and granny struck up a warm, long-lasting friendship with them. Back in Lwów Ama, a pretty brunette with large dark eyes had been a theatre actress.

Mother's main concern was to keep track of all the information about the officers from the POW camp of Starobelsk. Captain Józef Czapski was assigned to search for the prisoners from the three camps of Kozielsk, Starobelsk, and

Ostaszkow. He had been interned in Starobelsk himself, but at some point, inexplicably was moved to another camp in Griazov. As of that moment, there was no sign of his missing comrades, while in the meantime General Anders counted on the experienced officer corps. Pressed by the Poles, the Bolsheviks gave evasive answers, claiming that the Polish officers were released and most likely escaped through Manchuria. Apart from the missing men and in spite of the declared amnesty, there were still many Poles languishing in Soviet prisons. Bronisława Wysłouchowa, who served as Colonel Okulicki's code breaker, was arrested with him in Lwów and had been sentenced to death by the Russians and was awaiting execution in the Lubyanka prison when the amnesty was declared. She was released only after General Anders's forceful intervention.

The winter of 1941 was one of the fiercest in living memory. In December the temperatures fell below minus 60 degrees Centigrade and unprecedented snowfalls buried the tents and the mud huts. The Soviets committed to supplying equipment, uniforms, heaters for the tents, and food, but as yet the deliveries were minimal, while the number of new recruits grew exponentially. During the early training, soldiers used wooden imitation weapons, and many had no boots. The Polish authorities wanted to transfer their troops to Persia under British command, but Stalin violently opposed such a scheme, even though he would not or could not equip the Polish divisions, insisting instead on despatching unarmed Polish units to the German-Russian front.

In the end. the first substantial supplies of *matériel* to reach the Polish army came not from the Russians but from the British, ferried by Polish seamen serving in the Royal Navy. Shipments for the USSR were delivered at great risk as part of Arctic convoys organised by Britain. These convoys succeeded in running the gauntlet of German U-boats and bombers stationed in occupied Norway and by way of Kola Peninsula delivered, among other supplies, much-needed uniforms and underwear for Polish soldiers. Each convoy consisted of five or six small or medium merchant craft, escorted by Royal Navy warships, cruisers, destroyers, and minesweepers. In the beginning, they sailed from Hvalfjörður or Reykjavik in Iceland, but later most were organised to sail from Scotland, with some departing also from Liverpool.[66] The ships sailed along

---

[66] Between 1941-1945, the British Royal Navy, Royal Canadian Navy, and US Navy took part in 78 convoys, mostly assembled in Scotland. It was a highly successful operation which lasted from August 1941 until May 1945 when the last convoy sailed from the Clyde.

northern sea lanes so perilous that they were known as the trails of death. The first convoy left on 29 August 1941 under the code name *Dervish* and headed for the northern port of Archangelsk. Subsequent transports, code-named PQ and QP were scheduled to run simultaneously with clockwork precision, two a month – one going towards and one returning from Archangelsk – while their escorts at mid-point switched their coverage of the outbound and the homebound groups. The merchant vessels were also guarded by heavy surface units since this route was exposed to the German Luftwaffe and U-boats deployed in occupied Norway from where the convoys were in danger of attacks in the daylight. The first convoy to include an aircraft carrier, HMS Avenger, sailed from Loch Ewe in Scotland on 2 September 1942. By 1943, the convoys became larger and changed the code name to JW. Rather than leaving from Iceland, as previously, they were mostly assembled in Loch Ewe, Oban, or the Clyde in Scotland, or Liverpool, and sailed with a substantial destroyer escort to guard against surface attacks which proved so very effective with the series PQ.

At night, cohesion was hard to maintain under cover of darkness in waters plagued by ice-drifts and frequent fog. As long as milder weather allowed, the supply transports headed for Arkhangelsk, but when severe winter weather set in increasing the danger of ice-packs, their destination shifted further south. With the onset of the northern winter, the North Sea froze and Murmansk became the port of entry for the deliveries. The first British uniforms and *matériel* for the Polish troops in Buzułuk arrived on 10 November 1941 by way of Arkhangelsk. Complete uniforms consisted of a side cap with the Polish eagle, a fabric greatcoat, a battle-dress jacket, fabric trousers, shoes, and other accessories. Women received a similar set up modelled on the British ATS uniforms: a greatcoat, skirt, battledress jacket, warm underwear, and laced leather service shoes, somewhat inadequate for the extreme Siberian climate.

Organising the PSK women's service and incorporating it into the regular army formation was the one and only way to rescue hundreds of women and girls from certain extermination in Soviet kolkhozes and labour camps. During his negotiations with the Soviets, General Anders insisted that the word 'citizen' applied to both women and men, eventually winning the argument. The women took over many operations initially performed by men in offices, kitchens, laundries, canteens, storerooms, and in particular in hospitals, where there was a growing demand for additional nursing staff due to a constant increase of seriously ill patients.

After arriving in Buzułuk, my mother ran into a schoolmate from her days at the school of The Sacred Heart. Krystyna Ujejska came from a family of landowners with a large estate in the vicinity of Lwów. When her father developed heart problems, she moved to the countryside to take care of him and to manage the estate, but before she did that, she took a nursing course. Deported to Kazakhstan on 13 April 1940, she now reported to the hospital.

Krystyna was quickly promoted to nursing supervisor in Tockoje, serving with the 6th Infantry Division. Of the difficulties with which the hospital grappled in those early days, as the head nurse, she had this to say: the local hospital which comprised of 3 barracks, lacking equipment, instruments, and medicines, served the entire garrison, i.e. several thousand people. It was located in wooden shacks without heating, with thin walls full of cracks. Many patients were originally tended by Soviet physicians and nurses. Polish doctors and nurses took over in October 1941. Very sick people were arriving daily, emaciated beggars, living skeletons in rags, dragging themselves so as to reach the Polish centres, often only to be felled by diseases, the most serious being pellagra and scurvy. The hospital lacked basic drugs and supplies, even primitive syringes and heaters. Everything had to be forced out of the Soviet authorities with wile and cunning. Patients lay on the floors, there was no bed linen or clothing, straw mattresses, blankets, and patients' coats – these were the hospital furnishings in the early days. The most tender care, improved nutrition, and blood transfusions supplied by the nurses saved lives.

In spite of these superhuman efforts, many died. Extremely low temperatures impeded hospital work, while the number of patients grew daily. In spite of the freezing temperatures, there was an outbreak of typhus fever, complicated by kidney problems, pneumonia, and severe frostbite. Each sister took care of 30 patients. The nurses did between 16 and 24-hour tours of duty. What was involved in night duty? The nurse, wrapped in any warm clothing she had, with a smoking lamp in her hand that kept blowing out, moved around the sick whose blankets often froze to the walls, while the snow blowing through the cracks fell on them. When injection was needed, the one and only available syringe was frozen in the sterilizer while the medicine in the bottle turned to ice. Multiple cases of frostbite required surgery. In December, an operating room was finally organised where Lt Col Dr Adam Sołtysik frequently operated by candlelight with freezing hands. The sense of helplessness, coupled with bad living conditions, where temperatures hovered around -15°C in the sisters' quarters, started to destroy the nurses' health, already fragile and undermined by years of forced labour. Yet when illness overtook them, they would only resort to bed rest when overwhelmed by extremely high fever, forcing themselves to remain with the patients in the face of all odds. One nurse died a few hours after completing her night duty. Similar conditions prevailed in other hospitals. The division hospital of the 5th Division of Infantry, was overflowing with patients. The nurses did 36-hour tours of duty in an unheated building. They lived in quarters built of cardboard planks cobbled together, and with no heaters.[67]

The women serving in the PSK units were jokingly called '*pestki*' from the play on words in Polish meaning fruit pips. In time, someone composed a ditty:

Your grandpa served in Tobruk,
Your grandma in Buzuluk,
And don't forget my honey,
That your granny was a Pip in the army.[68]

On 1 December 1941 Private Zofia Hoffman left her post in the kitchens and was transferred to the military legal services department of the *Polish Army Command in the USSR*. That same day Dr Stanisława Duczymińska, mother's gynaecologist who was at my birth and had been also deported from Lwów, joined the hospital in Buzuluk.

In December General Sikorski, commander-in-chief of Polish troops within the Allied forces, flew from London to Kuybyshev. At issue was the situation of Polish civilians that needed to be resolved, and to that end, a conference was arranged with Soviet authorities in Moscow. Sikorski travelled in the company of Colonel Okulicki and General Szyszko-Bohusz. During the meeting with Stalin, it was agreed that the Polish units would be moved to a milder climate in Central Asia. The Soviets also promised significant financial aid to relocate and provide for the civilian population. At that point, the Polish Army in the USSR stood at around 66,000 men, but it was estimated that this number would increase to 96,000, which was enough for six divisions. Twenty-seven thousand men were to be evacuated to England to replenish the losses in the Polish Independent

---

[67] Anna Bobińska. *Pomocnicza Wojskowa Służba Kobiet 2 Korpusu. 1941-1945.* p. 29, 30. Warszawa. Wydawnictwo Krupski i S-ka. 1999.
[68] Polish original: *Pamiętaj o tym wnuku, że dziadzio był w Tobruku, a babcia w Buzuluku. Pamiętaj wnuczko miła, że babcia Pestką była.* Author anonymous. Trans. into English by Eva Hoffman Jedruch)

Carpathian Rifle Brigade fighting in Africa under British command. After Sikorski's discussions in the Kremlin, four embryonic divisions were organised in Buzułuk and the Women's Auxiliary Services were launched alongside these units.

Christmas was approaching, the second one since mother and granny had been taken from Lwów. Mother's anxiety over lack of news of my father, compounded by concern about me, memories, longing, all combined with the sense of regained freedom. This Christmas was different from that of a year earlier. A Christmas tree in the hall of the staff headquarters and garlands of tiny lights strung between the columns created a festive atmosphere. During Midnight Mass on Christmas Eve, as she received the Holy Communion, mother's thoughts turned to Lena's bedroom and the icon on the back of Lenin's portrait: *Hail Mary full of grace…*

Chapter VIII

1942. On the Silk Road

At the beginning of January 1942, the Polish command issued its first order for the organisation of PSK, fundamentally changing the women's status. The PSK Inspectorate was established under Władysława Piechowska as the Inspector General, and a regular draft commission was set up. Piechowska's deputy was Kazimiera Jaworska, and Bronisława Wysłouchowa became the PSK Secretary, as part of the army's general staff. With both of them, my mother struck up a lifelong friendship. As a result of Sikorski's negotiations with Stalin in Moscow, the Polish units were to relocate south to a milder climate and this also applied to PSK. By mid-February, the command was transferred from Buzułuk to Jangi-Jul in Tashkent, in the middle of an oasis, site of ancient settlements. The PSK Inspectorate travelled with the general staff, and that included all the women who served in positions directly reporting to the senior command. The rest of the army was spread over three southern republics: Uzbekistan, Kyrgyzstan, and Kazakhstan camping in tents and mud huts among sparsely scattered villages, on desert steppes where except for stunted dwarfish trees nothing else grew.

1941. Buzułuk. At the military judiciary services

The Polish civilian population released from the camps and kolkhozes was directed by the NKVD to these same southern republics, under the pretence that the Polish government had received substantial financial aid to facilitate the relocation, which as it turned out was an outright lie. As a result, thousands of deportees without any means of subsistence camped out on these desert lands in appalling conditions. Had it not been for the miraculous appearance of one additional seat on the train in Georgiyevka, mother and granny would have ended here as well.

Jangi-Jul sits on the legendary Silk Road, some 20 kilometres to the south of Tashkent, the capital of Uzbekistan, on a fertile plain to the west of the Altai mountain chain at the foot of the Tian Shan Mountains on the Chirciq River between Shymkent and Samarkand. The Silk Road, one of the oldest trading routes of antiquity, was travelled for centuries by caravans carrying silks and spices from the Orient to Europe. And suddenly, lo and behold, my mother found herself in the land of a thousand and one nights, the same that enriched her girlish musings about Asia, but under circumstances that even the most fertile imagination could not have envisioned. Zofia was always curious to see the world and courageous by nature, so this land, in which she found herself unwillingly, fascinated her with its overwhelming desert expanses, its ancient cultures, and its civilisations that went back several millennia. Alma Ata, Dzhambul, Samarkand, Bukhara – names that evoked a mysterious past, carried a whiff of exotic perfumes, and the lure of distant horizons enveloped in mists – all fruit of her youthful imagination, unexpectedly were within her grasp.

Granny did not share my mother's sentiments. In contrast to her daughter, the exotic nature of these lands impressed her not at all. This *par excellence* Victorian matron, so polite in her manner of speech, in one case could never restrain herself and never speak otherwise than *damned Russia*. Tragically, for many deportees, the sites on the Silk Road merely marked the cemeteries where they buried their loved ones. Polish hospitals overflowed with patients while lacked medicines and instruments, so civilians camping across these hostile regions died in their thousands of malaria and malnutrition.

The general staff headquarters in Jangi-Jul were once a gardening school in tsarist times, with a small river that surrounded a large orchard and irrigated it. A processing facility alongside the orchard made compotes and jams that were distributed all over the Russian Empire. The owners of this enterprise were two wealthy Uzbeks, murdered during the October Revolution; their orchard and the rest of their property confiscated by the Soviet state. Not surprisingly, the building intended for the Polish army, as the one in Buzułuk, was densely packed with bugging equipment. Before the command could start functioning, Polish technicians worked around the clock ripping out cables, detaching small boxes from lamps, unhooking tiny microphones installed in the ceilings by the NKVD.

Members of the general staff were housed in small huts surrounding the building, the rest of the personnel camped in tents on the verge of the orchard, on the other side of the river. Each morning, on her way to the office, my mother walked across a small bridge, passed a sentinel in his booth, and cut across the orchard under a canopy of white and pink blossoms of flowering cherry, apple, and apricot trees. The short walk gave her a chance for a moment's solitude, prayer, and reflection, but not much time for lengthy dwelling on her own concerns. Her identity card from Jangi-Jul dated 21-2-1942, and signed by Colonel Okulicki, listed her particulars: rank: "private recorder, military court"; physical description: height: "tall"; eyes: "green"; hair: "blonde".

The army administration and the military legal services department were flooded with thousands of cases involving new arrivals; in particular, the number of Polish orphans posed a gigantic organisational problem. The army set up orphanages where they placed children rescued from the Soviet orphanages or *dietdoms,* although in searching for them they often ran into stiff resistance from local administrators. The children were in an appalling physical condition: dirty, lice-infested, starving little skeletons with sticking ribs, staring with glassy eyes, and no sign of life, at the people who came to fetch them. Many were gravely ill and were taken straight to the hospitals, but in spite of superhuman efforts by Polish doctors and nurses, mortality among the youngsters was exceedingly high.

There were many stories of near-miraculous escapes to freedom by children, one in particular made the rounds, of an eight-year-old boy whose parents died in the kolkhoz, leaving him with his eighteen-month-old sister. The boy somehow heard of Poles in the area looking for Polish children, but this kolkhoz was quite isolated, twelve kilometres from Samarkand, surrounded by muddy, almost impassable roads, and the *predsedatel* had not the slightest intention of helping him. Afraid to miss the chance, in desperation, the boy set off across snow-covered fields and marshes, with the little girl on his back, and eventually reached one of the Polish army outposts.

From every corner of the USSR, wherever news of the amnesty spread, swarms of Poles took off in an attempt to reach the recruitment centres, but many died on the way. Starved people greedily ate what food they could find, raw fruits and vegetables, and in the heat of the Siberian summer drank contaminated water from lakes and rivers, succumbing to dysentery, diarrhoea, and dehydration. Because of acute food shortages, soldiers shared their skimpy rations with the civilians. In Guzar, Uzbekistan, the army set up an organisational and supply centre, and established schools for young male and female cadets, an absolute priority in my mother's mind because she feared that the traumatic experiences suffered by these adolescents were liable to cause long lasting scars, both mental and emotional. In her opinion any delay in countering the noxious effects of the damage done carried a grave risk, she argued. Among the deportees in the army, there was an abundance of teachers, professors, and educators, more than enough to set up educational programmes at various levels.

By March 1942 the Polish army stood at around seventy thousand men and three thousand women, but Stalin's plan to incorporate the Polish units into the Red Army ran into stiff opposition. Survivors of the Siberian gulag, Arctic mines and Kazakh kolkhozes, were mostly deportees from south-eastern Poland, taken after the treacherous Russian attack on 17 September 1939. Their steely resolve not to fight alongside the Soviets, their open hostility towards the USSR created a flashpoint in the Allies' discussions with Stalin. In this situation, the Russians refused to supply equipment, uniforms, and most importantly food, and blocked further recruitment. Stalin ordered that rations for the Polish army be halved. Yet, in the face of determined resistance and the arrival of British supplies in the meantime, and after General Anders's stormy sessions in Moscow, he finally agreed on 18 May 1942 to the transfer of forty-four thousand Polish soldiers to Persia under British command. Knowing the dictator's fickle moods, the Polish authorities launched feverish preparations for the evacuation and the *exodus* commenced immediately.

Before leaving the USSR, mother attempted to renew her disrupted contact with Uncle Zbyszek. She sent her first message on 14 February 1942 through the Polish diplomatic mission in Kuybyshev, via the International Red Cross, addressing it to Aunt Hania and writing it in German since Lwów was now under German occupation:

"Neuhoff Anna Zadwórzańska 69; Lemberg, Galizien; General-gouvernement: Zofia Hoffman mit ihrer Mutter ist gesund und bittet Nachrichten."[69]

The answer reached her three months later in Teheran, typed on the reverse of the original message:

"Comité International de la Croix Rouge, Genève. Reponse a votre telegramme du 14.2.42: Polmission Kouibychev: Zbigniew Neuhoff, Anna, und Eva gesund und in guten Lebensverhältnissen. Eva entwickelt sich ausgerechnet. Zbigniew als Advokat tätig. Weitere Familie befindet sich wohl. Lwów. 9.5.42."[70]

Her next message went also through the Red Cross, this time in Polish, from Iraq on my birthday, 9 October 1942: *"Hoffmanowa Zofia...jeteśmy zdrowe. Bardzo tęsknimy za Wami. Bożenna-Maria."*[71] She avoided writing to Uncle Zbyszek directly, so the message was addressed to Basia Yawna, granny's

---

[69] Zofia Hoffman and her mother are well and are asking for news.
[70] Zbigniew Neuhoff, Anna, and Eva are well and in good condition. Eva is developing as expected. Zbigniew works as lawyer. The rest of the family are well.
[71] Hoffman Zofia... we are well. We miss you very much.

housekeeper. This time the answer took five months: *"Jesteśmy zdrowi. Ewa rozwija się doskonale, jest bardzo mądra, chodzi do szkółki i zapytuje często o Was. Zbigniew. 1.3.43."*[72] Red Cross seal: 25 Mars 1943.

My mother's road led from Jangi-Jul in Tashkent to the port of Krasnovodsk in Turkmenistan, then across the Caspian Sea to Pahlevi in Iran, present-day Bandar-e Anzali.[73] The Russians supplied the ships, the British stationed in Persia were to receive the Polish units from the USSR. An order was dispatched from London to evacuate only military personnel, no civilians, supposedly because of insufficient supplies. General Anders ignored it, ordering the evacuation of a maximum number of civilians languishing around the military encampments, mainly women and children. The Soviets allowed barely two weeks for the transfer of forty-four thousand undernourished, exhausted, and sick people. Before the first transport could leave, bases in Krasnovodsk and Ashkhabad had to be prepared to receive those from the camps in Kazakhstan, and then relocate them from Pahlevi to Teheran. Polish drivers were dispatched to Iran to secure enough jeeps, lorries, and uniforms. An Evacuation Base was set up in Teheran and transition camps were organised for the arrival of soldiers who needed medical care since the general health of the evacuees continued to be exceedingly precarious.

My mother was totally absorbed by the preparations for the move to Persia. With granny, they boarded the train from Jangi-Jul on Saturday, 28 March 1942. This time it was a very different trip. Smiling soldiers and civilians leaned out of windows and waved, an army band on the platform played the Polish national anthem, the locomotive jerked forward spewing steam and a million golden sparks. This moment on the road to freedom was engraved in my mother's memory forever and the next day, Palm Sunday, acquired the symbolism of approaching resurrection.

The rail line built in the nineteenth century stretched for one thousand eight hundred kilometres and ran parallel to the Silk Road. On the way to Krasnovodsk, the train stopped in Samarkand and Bukhara picking up fresh contingents of soldiers, circumvented the Kara-Kum Desert with its boundless

---

[72] We are in good health. Eva is developing very well. She goes to kindergarten and often asks about you.

[73] After the 1979 Islamic Revolution that toppled the regime of Shah Mohammad Reza Pahlavi, all places bearing his dynasty's name had been renamed.

expanse of grey sands, sparse burnt-out vegetation, and small clusters of huts with not a scrap of greenery for shade against the scorching sun. The legendary Amu Darya river which the Greeks called Oxus, the longest waterway in central Asia, cuts across the desert in a wide swath, spilling its waters far beyond the riverbed and was so shallow in places that my mother could see the stones on the bottom. The river's source lies amid the snows of Pamir from where it flows through the Hindu Kush, along the frontier of Afghanistan, cuts across Turkmenistan and on to the Sea of Aral. The four-day trip offered a priceless image of exotic Asia, and from the strategic bridge above the Amu-Darya, my mother could appreciate the river's immensity. As soon as the train left the station of Ashkhabad, snow-covered peaks of the Elburz Mountains emerged in all their majesty. Stretching along the southern coast of the Caspian Sea, they form a natural bridge between the Caucasus and Afghanistan, ending in Hindu Kush. On the southern side of the Kara-Kum Desert, the mountains create a buffer; the frontier between Iran and Turkmenistan runs along the peaks. That land route was taken by groups of Polish orphans transported from Ashkhabad in American trucks driven by Polish drivers.

On 1 April, Wednesday of the Holy Week, mother and granny arrived in Krasnovodsk, their final stop in the USSR. Russian ships were moored at the pier; the NKVD strictly checked the passenger list. In the meantime, people camped at the pier on their beat-up luggage and shabby bundles. By late afternoon, the boarding began. Two ships were to leave that night, one with PSK women volunteers, the other one with soldiers. A Polish officer took the roubles from the passengers and issued receipts for the equivalent which was to be paid out in Iran in British pounds sterling. A Soviet officer confiscated all the identity cards which had been issued after the amnesty, which had allowed the deportees to move around the territory of the USSR. They were stamped in various locations of forced labour and the Bolsheviks were not keen on that information to leak out, particularly since it pinpointed the sites of mines, kolkhozes, and camps throughout the gulag. In spite of that precaution, a great number of identity cards did get smuggled out.[74] Yet people who managed to get out of Russia left behind thousands of unmarked graves of their loved ones, cemeteries stretching from the coal mines of Kolyma and Vorkuta in the Arctic Circle to the

---

[74] The identity cards called *udostowierenia* in Russian, in time found their way into the archives of the Hoover Institute in California, as material proof of the gulag's existence. They were used by the Americans to draft a map of forced labour networks in the USSR.

Siberian taiga, and the kolkhozes across the steppes of Kazakhstan and Uzbekistan.

The first evacuation of March 1942 included forty-four thousand people, of these thirty thousand soldiers, one thousand one hundred PSK volunteers, one thousand nine hundred male and female cadets, and eleven thousand civilians, mostly from military families. When the ship's engines revved up, the siren roared, the decks vibrated, and as the vessel began to move away from the pier, my mother was overcome by two conflicting emotions: relief that she was finally

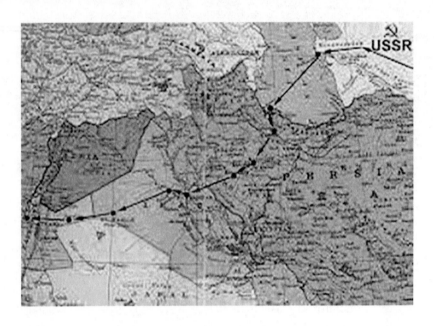

1942. Polish Army's Trajectory: from USSR to Palestine, present-day Israel

escaping from Russia and despair that my father still remained somewhere in this inhuman land of hopelessness and death. Working in close proximity to the general staff, she had followed anxiously every scrap of news on the search for the missing fifteen thousand Polish officers, but up to that moment Captain Józef Czapski's efforts to track them down had proved futile. Now standing at the railing, she embraced her mother, and tears flowed abundantly. Through the thick fabric of her jacket, she fingered the round cover of Maks's watch which she carried at all times in the breast pocket of her jacket. It was a gold pocket watch in a hunter case with a short chain and the monogram MH engraved on a small square pendant. My father had left it at home when he went to report after the capitulation of Lwów and when she opened the back cover, she found her

174

own picture as a nine-year in a winter coat and a cute beret. She never knew Maks had it. He must have taken it on the sly from her parent's home during their short courtship.

Maks's watch and Zosia's picture

The crossing of the Caspian Sea took two days, mother tolerated it well, granny stayed below deck throughout. On Good Friday 3 April, the ships docked at Pahlevi. After two years, almost to the day of their arrest and deportation, my mother and grandmother finally felt truly free. They could surely repeat after Dante: "*E quindi uscimmo a riveder le stelle.*" Indeed, emerging from the bowels of hell, they saw the stars again.

An impeccably uniformed British officer in a cap, shoes polished to perfection, awaited the arrival of the ships at the pier. My mother watched him and admired his impassive demeanour: not a single muscle in his face betrayed the sense of shock that he must have felt at the sight of the arriving Poles, whose appearance surely exceeded all imagination. At this moment the Englishman was probably asking himself, how in God's name could this ragged crowd of beggars trailing down the ramps, dragging their bundles, ever be remade into a regular army? The exceedingly short time allowed by the Soviets for the evacuation of

175

forty-four thousand people created difficulties for the British command as well as for local Persian authorities. About three thousand disembarked every twenty-four hours, sometimes more, many were sick and required immediate hospitalisation in Pahlevi, where the Polish authorities improvised a sanitary centre. Healthy people were picked up by Polish drivers and taken over to a neighbouring beach where tents and a camp kitchen had been set up. The kitchen served hot soup, but there were insufficient tents and bedding, so some had to sleep on bare ground but nobody cared. The soothing murmur of the sea, the waves spreading themselves gently on the sands, their white crests leaving a fragile line of foam on the beach, these were moments to savour, the first whiff of true freedom. The camp attracted local hawkers eager to buy or sell anything and since the Poles had no money, a lively barter began right away although it had been strictly forbidden. On Easter Sunday, a chaplain said Mass on the sands of Pahlevi.

The next stretch of the way from the port to Teheran was covered in trucks driven by Iranian drivers. But before that, Poles arriving from the USSR had to be "de-liced", because the dreadful lice infestation throughout the entire USSR brought with it a risk of fresh outbreaks of typhus. All items had to be disinfected; the most essential ones could be kept, but only as much as a single person could carry. The rest was to be burnt for fear of spreading the infection. As soon as the order was posted, people anxiously began to untie their bundles, pulling out their most precious possessions. It was hard to part with what had been the underpinnings of one's daily existence. Soon huge piles of stuff grew on the side, rags full of holes and memories. Every scrap carried a meaning. British military personnel oversaw the operation from a discreet distance. During two years of starvation, my mother was unable to sell hers and granny's jewellery which had been stowed in their handbags at the outbreak of the war and remained there at the moment of their arrest. Now safely tucked away in a khaki sewing kit together with needles, thread, and buttons, it would criss-cross the entire Middle East.

Away from the camp, the British authorities had installed large tents with showers and distributed soap and towels. It was my mother's first real bath since leaving Lwów. The entire operation lasted about an hour, after which civilians were given back their clothing that had been disinfected with steam, while the military was issued fresh uniforms. English style uniform worn by the British women's Auxiliary Territorial Service (ATS) was assigned to members of PSK, now referred to as the Polish ATS.

After showering, the bathers were instructed to exit through the opposite end of the tent and directed to another part of the beach. Nobody was allowed to return to the "dirty" side of the camp. For mother the shower meant more than just a bath, it was *katharsis*, a return to life. *"I feel again like a human being,"* she confessed to my grandmother and meant it literally too. The dehumanising effects of the Soviet system dissolved in the overpowering smell of disinfectant Lysol with which the shower waters were generously treated. Around the site huge bonfires burned brightly, consuming bits and bobs, pillows, blankets, and scraps of food that had been carefully stashed away throughout months of hunger and cold. All this was generously sprayed with naphtha and went up in smoke.

A long line of American military Dodge trucks stood ready to transport the army personnel to Teheran, their olive-coloured tarpaulins rolled down, powerful engines humming in unison. Iranian drivers were assigned to this task because crossing the Elburz Mountains was perilous. Their forbidding lofty majesty was softened by the rose tint of the rocks and the green slopes, at this time in spring covered by patches of red and yellow tulips. The serpentine roads climbed steeply, taking dizzyingly sharp turns and at moments the lorries seemed to teeter on the edge of a precipice. The drivers knew their roads well, racing at breakneck speed through deep canyons and valleys. At one point, as they passed a small group of mud huts, a little child ran out into the road and was hit by a lorry. My grandmother witnessed this but to her horror, nobody stopped. The convoy sped on.

Teheran, the sprawling heart of modern Iran at the foot of the Elburz Mountains. The Polish Army Evacuation Base headquarters were located in the city, as was the *Delegature* for handling civilians, and the Army Command Judiciary to which my mother was assigned, while the camp itself was set up outside Teheran. Zofia was fascinated by the millennia-old Persian culture, the noise and bustle of colourful bazaars, superb rugs thrown nonchalantly by carpet merchants onto the streets where vehicles ran over them to compact the weave. She was equally charmed by the easy civility of the people, in stark contrast to the brutish Russian roughness. In her contacts with local officialdom, she dealt with individuals from the social upper crust: officers from the Shah's army and highly educated civil servants. But even merchants tending the bazaar stalls behaved with a friendliness born of freedom. She found herself in her dreamland of the Arabian nights.

Soon mother realised that camp conditions were undermining granny's health, so she petitioned for permission to take lodgings in town. Iran was under virtual British control and accommodations requisitioned in private homes were available for the officer corps. By chance, one owner requested specifically that only women be lodged in his house. A few days later, mother and granny moved to their private quarters in Sephasalar Alley, into a spacious room with piles of soft pillows and carpets in lieu of beds. On the first evening the master of the house, a distinguished civil servant fluent in French, invited them for coffee in the family's elegant drawing-room furnished with magnificent rugs and exuberant plants. Soon his wife joined them, a young woman many years her husband's junior. She wore European clothes with a large, fragrant rose at the neckline. She was very beautiful. Since she did not speak French, her husband carried on the conversation with my mother throughout that entire evening. This first pleasant experience came to be repeated daily for as long as mother and granny lodged there. Invariably, the lady of the house appeared exquisitely dressed in European fashion, each time a magnificent rose pinned to her bodice. My mother silently called her *Scheherazade*. There were other, older women in the house, subservient to the young wife and granny's curiosity was piqued. *"Who are they?"* She asked. Since her daughter seemed indifferent to the mystery, granny drew her own grim conclusion and declared darkly: *"I think they are his other, older wives who had been discarded."*

By now mother had fully recovered from the effects of the brucellosis, and months of backbreaking work and starvation in Kazakhstan. A photograph from those early army days shows her face restored to its oval shape, short hair tucked under the military cap jauntily sitting on her head at an angle. In her relaxed smile, who would have recognised the haggard creature in tattered dress staring bleakly ahead, expressionless, as in the picture taken upon her release from the kolkhoz?

She was beautiful again, but not exotic, she never was. A subtle Northern European type, but she tanned easily and in the sun her complexion took on a light golden-peach colour. When she spoke, she looked people straight in the eyes – a friendly and steady gaze; when she was angry, her green eyes narrowed slightly with their colour deepening. Intellectual, perceptive, analytical, but though not sanctimonious, still holding deeply ingrained ideas of right and wrong, which served her well in times of tough decisions. In crises, she displayed amazing *sang-froid*. Her razor-sharp mind would match any man's who valued intelligence in a woman, yet at the same time, she was warm, feminine, and supremely tactful. Evening conversations with her host over coffee proved charming and animated, never trite, never boring. Two cultures in search of common ground over trays of pressed figs, dates, and almonds. In June, mother was officially confirmed as a member of the legal service team of the Polish Army.

Following the initial evacuation of some fifty percent of Polish troops from the USSR to Iran in March 1942, by July Stalin was forced to release the remainder of the army which was being threatened by the German juggernaut as the *Wehrmacht* in a pincer manoeuvre penetrated ever deeper into Russia. On 8 July 1942, the Polish High Command in Jangi-Jul was authorised by a telegram from Moscow to start the next wave of evacuation. It began on 9 August and ended with the last convoy crossing the Caspian Sea on 1 September. In total around seventy-seven thousand soldiers and thirty-seven thousand civilians departed the USSR, leaving behind almost half a million unidentified graves, over four hundred thousand missing persons, and nearly seven hundred thousand persons who were prevented by the Russian authorities from leaving the Soviet Union. After the second evacuation, the Soviet authorities forbade further recruitment, deprived those still remaining of their Polish citizenship, forcibly imposing on them Russian citizenship, and thus killing all further chance of escape. Thousands remained and perished in the inhumane conditions of the Soviet gulag. The second evacuation took place in the nick of time because Stalin's relations with the Polish government-in-exile in London were deteriorating rapidly. Unable to break the Poles' resistance to becoming part of the Red Army, the Soviets launched a new draft effort to form a separate "red" Polish army, giving men the option of joining or remaining in the gulag. For most, it was not a hard choice. These units were indeed incorporated into the Russian army under the nominal command of a Pole, Colonel Zygmunt Berling, a man considerably more accommodating to the Russians than General Anders. By July 1943, sixteen thousand Poles, mainly exiles forcibly taken in 1940 from

Eastern Poland, enlisted. In the absence of a professional Polish officer corps, training and leadership were entrusted to the Soviet military.[75]

In the meantime, Bronisława Wysłouchowa who had been appointed as the new Inspector General of PSK arrived in Teheran and on 9 August 1942, the PSK Inspectorate began to operate formally. At the same time, as the second evacuation to Persia was underway, the army prepared to move on to Iraq to join Polish units that fought in North Africa against Rommel's Afrika Korps. The combined troops became the Polish army's Second Corps, part of the British Eighth Army.

Civilian survivors from the gulag who were fortunate enough to make it to Persia were being dispatched to India, South Africa, Kenya, Uganda, and Lebanon where the British set up facilities for the civilian population. After leaving the USSR, in spite of improved living conditions, many continued dying of diseases brought from the Soviet labour camps. Among them was Zofia Teliczkowa, the owner of the delicatessen on Akademicka Street where my parents enjoyed stopping on their way home from the court hearings. Departing from Teheran, the Poles left behind 2800 graves.

As the huge Dodge trucks ferried the soldiers towards Iraq, one group crossing the mountains somewhere between Hamadan and Kangwar came upon a young Iranian boy walking by the roadside, carrying a bulky sack on his back. The soldiers stopped for a cigarette and since the kid looked frail and malnourished, they offered him a few tins of preserves when suddenly the head of a bear cub popped out of the sack. The men didn't speak Farsi, but using clumsy sign-language they made out that a hunter killed the mother bear and the boy found the cub in a cave. For a few pennies, a can of corned beef, and a penknife, they bought the little bear. Since he was in a bad shape the soldiers quickly filled an empty whisky bottle with condensed milk, inserted a twisted handkerchief and so fed the cub. The bear was named Wojtek and became not so much an army mascot as the soldiers' companion and the army's favourite.[76] Wojtek also acquired some animal companionship, because while still a cub, he was befriended by a Dalmatian belonging to a Scottish liaison officer.

---

[75] This became the First Polish Army on the eastern front, under Russian command. It participated in the liberation of Polish territories. In 1944, it was combined with the underground Communist People's Army, creating a Polish People's Army, which was employed by the Russians to gain control of Poland at the end of the war.
[76] Wojtek accompanied the army throughout the entire campaign, He came with the Second Corps to Britain and died at the age of 21 in the Edinburgh zoo.

After a few months in Teheran, as the time drew near for the army to move on to Iraq, mother's Iranian host surprised her one evening with an unexpected suggestion: *"Madame Sophie, there is a war on in Europe and who knows how it will end. Would it not be better for you and Madame Marie to stay in Teheran?"* For a moment this probing question caught Zofia off guard, though its meaning was clear. She was deeply grateful to the couple for their hospitality, for inviting her and her mother into their world of culture and refined manners, for the daily respite from the unsettling reality beyond the garden walls, and she did not wish to hurt his feelings. But she knew, of course, what her answer would be: *"I have a daughter there."*

Wojtek the Soldier Bear member of the Polish 2nd Corps

"Perhaps we could help you bring her out of Poland?" An offer that Zofia sidestepped diplomatically: *"I belong to the army."* In her leisure moments, my mother may have been a dreamer but in real life, she was a tough lawyer, a dedicated member of the armed forces, and a loving wife. Shuttered harem windows of her youthful fantasies were best left to Scheherazade.

In June 1942, mother left Teheran with the department of legal services and during the summer and early autumn the entire army moved on to Iraq. In the process of reorganising on 12 September, the name *Polish Army in the USSR* was officially changed to *Command of the Polish Army in the Middle East*. The troops arriving from the Soviet Union were joined by regular units fresh from the African campaign, where they fought bloody battles. In a furious assault, the Polish Independent Carpathian Rifle Brigade, under General Stanisław Kopański, broke through the German lines to relieve the British Eighth Army that was being besieged in Tobruk for ten weeks by General Rommel's Afrika Korps, a feat that earned them the name of *Tobruk Rats*, bestowed by their Australian comrades-in-arms and a well-deserved R&R. They had been on the campaign trail across North Africa non-stop since September 1940. The Carpathian Rifle Brigade was combined with General Anders's forces and became the 3rd Carpathian Rifle Division.

The general headquarters were located in Quizil Ribat, and the army was deployed in the Khanequin region in the vicinity of Kirkuk. The camp was pitched on the desert sands, a sea of white tents stretched over a couple of square kilometres under a blazing sun in blistering daytime temperatures that exceeded 50°C, and on occasion even reached 70°C. There was no shade because neither trees nor shrubs could grow there. Tropical uniforms were in order. Although the camp lay on a canal, parallel to River Diyala, the waters were heavily polluted and required extensive purification to make them potable. As soon as the sun went down, the temperature dropped sharply. At night the air around the camp resounded with the fiendish laughter of hyenas and the barking of jackals. Scorpions abounded and dropped down from the roof of the tent, so soldiers were taught how to shake them off without leaving the predator's legs imbedded in the flesh. Not everyone heeded these lessons and the medical personnel were kept busy cleaning up nasty festering ulcerations. Periodically the camp was blasted by the *hamsin*, a ferocious dry and hot wind blowing from the Saharan desert at 140 kilometres an hour, carrying sand that penetrated into every corner and crevice of human body and abode, even into tightly locked suitcases. People blinded by dust, choked and coughed, while the temperature of the air instantly rose by several degrees. The oppressive wind blew for days and the sun appeared hazy and blood-red through the mist of fine particles. In the old days, the populations inhabiting these desert lands perceived the *hamsin* as a messenger of approaching plague.

And yet, in spite of the oppressive climate, these were hot and heady days in Iraq for the men and women who left the Russian nightmare behind. Free people again, soldiers in uniforms, under arms with restored human dignity. It was that trampled dignity, the enslavement, the bare survival under the Russian whip that killed even more than hunger and cold. After a year and a half in existence, the Polish army, built of physically devastated men and women, was coalescing into a structured military society, a strong and disciplined fighting machine.

In Habbaniya, on the lake to the west of Baghdad, the British air force set up a base. The waters of the lake were so warm as to seem heated, so when my mother got a chance to go there, she gladly accepted, hoping for a swim. But the brucellosis contracted in Russia left its mark and after the initial dip in the warm waters of the lake, Zofia developed an acute inflammation of joints that put an end to further swimming. A souvenir from the USSR.

Three months later, on 1 September, mother was dispatched to the British base in Palestine, Training Depot ATS, south of Haifa, for English leadership cadres. ATS units were scattered across the entire Middle East, their principal base was in Sarafand. The month-long course was run by Lieutenant Colonel Kathleen Gaudin Stocker with a contingent of English non-commissioned officers.

1942. Sarafand. Palestine. End of course at Training Depot ATS

1942. Iraq. Platoon Commander Zofia Hoffman

The programme was broadly designed covering all disciplines within the ATS structure, military law, organisation of the army, command, disciplinary regulations, uniform requirements, hygiene, muster, with particular emphasis on the English language, which mother was eager to learn. Zofia had a good ear for languages, she already spoke three: Polish, German, and French so the fourth one came to her quite easily. In October mother returned to Iraq and was promoted to platoon commander with the function of unit adjutant.

By order of the Ministry of War dated 18 December 1942, the Auxiliary Women's Service (PSK) was transformed into Auxiliary Military Women's Service (PWSK) and given full military status. Members were no longer volunteers, but soldiers on active duty, including wages, service levels, and military rank. They received general training in muster, military regulations, and handling of weapons. What followed was individual training as drivers of military lorries and jeeps, as car and airplane mechanics, and radio and telegraph operators. They drove heavy army trucks and Jeeps, staffed army ordinance depots, led convoys, and managed switchboards. Women's units were formed along with the army model into companies, platoons, and troops. Specific functions were established for commanders, inspectors, and clerks. The uniform was the same as for the British ATS's: jacket, skirt, stockings (all in khaki), low-heel brown laced shoes, cross belt for the officers and battle-dress as 'casual' jacket. This uniform included the addition of Polish badges: cap with an eagle, and buttons with an eagle; a red badge on the sleeve with the word *Poland* in white letters, and the insignia on the epaulettes indicating the rank.

My mother did not bond with other women easily, as many women do. She was perceptive and a keen judge of character and anything that smacked of phoniness turned her off. The army with its rank structure was a fertile ground for undue self-aggrandisement, so while friendly and polite, mother shied away from excessive familiarity and tended to be somewhat reserved. But over time, one woman among her fellow officers gained her unreserved admiration and sincere devotion. In due course, she and Bronisława (Bronka) Wysłouchowa, the Inspector General of PWSK, became intimate friends and their friendship lasted throughout the war and beyond.

By all accounts, Bronka Wysłouchowa was an exceptional human being. She was courageous without being pompous, deeply patriotic, since her youth engaged in social work, compassionate, and very caring towards her subordinates. When the war broke out, she joined the resistance movement, served as a courier for Colonel Okulicki, got arrested by the Soviets in Lwów, and imprisoned in Moscow where the Russians hoped to extract information from her. She spent several months locked up in cells with common female criminals, tortured, never disclosed any names of co-conspirators, and eventually was put on trial and sentenced to death. She was saved by the amnesty.

Friendship with Bronka was a palliative for my mother, who after taking charge of her platoon was forced into a world of human *realpolitik*. It was not easy to deal with women of diverse backgrounds, some ladies – some less so – with their woes, losses, and grievances. Problems arose with the younger lot, much restored to health and vigour after the hellish life in the USSR. They were prone to enter into forbidden liaisons with male officers, many of whom had wives and families in Poland. Dramas resulted that placed my mother in various roles: of commander, counsellor, and disciplinarian. Highly protective of her own reputation, she struggled at times to understand any lack of concern in the younger generation. Occasionally she would turn for advice to her commanding officer, although more often to Fr Lucjan Królikowski, the army chaplain.

At the end of January 1943, mother was transferred to become the Clerk of the Base Command (*referentka*). The army headquarters were in Baghdad, but the Military Justice Department was out in the desert, a few kilometres from the camp. Each day rows of jeeps picked up the personnel and took them to various posts. Zofia threw herself body and soul, into her work, a therapy of sorts that kept her thoughts at bay. It blocked her fears for Maks and Ayka.

One late afternoon in the suffocating heat of the small office in a short-sleeve khaki shirt, she was poring over files making notes in the margins in her even slanted script, meticulous and compact. Maks's gold watch lay on the table in front of her and smoke curled gently upward from the ashtray. Since Kazakhstan, she had been smoking heavily and her signature accessory was an azure cigarette holder. She buried herself so completely in her work that day, that she lost track of time and when she looked up from her paperwork, the last jeep for the return trip to the camp had left. Somehow her absence at the boarding post went unnoticed; she was stuck in the building with no transportation. The building was empty except for two guards who remained overnight. They offered to radio for a driver, but Zofia refused. It was her fault she insisted, *"It's not that far, I'll be able to make it on foot,"* and set off across the desert sands, following the deep furrows carved out by military vehicles. It was daylight and what were a few kilometres of the beaten track for one who walked for miles with raging fever across the steppes of Asia?

But in these regions, there is no dusk, night falls abruptly and halfway to the camp it was suddenly pitch dark. The moon had not yet risen, the tire tracks dissolved in the shadows and though she continued in what she believed to be the right direction, she soon realised that she had lost her way. Camp lights should have been visible by now but were not, there was nothing within sight on the horizon. Unexpectedly a light appeared further off to the right and she turned towards it. It was not the camp but an abandoned construction site and the light she noticed seeped from under the door of a small shack at the rear. A guard's cabin, perhaps? She headed towards the hut and pushed the wooden door. It creaked as it swung open and three bearded Arabs inside turned around like on command. They surely recognised her British uniform, khaki from head to toe. Perhaps for a split second they wondered if there were more soldiers behind her, they were startled at first, but not for long. It was a hideout and Zofia instantly became aware of the danger but it was too late to turn back. Sounding matter-of-fact, she spoke to them very fast in French, asking for directions to the military camp. They stared at her in silence. The short gold chain of Maks's watch which she had shoved hurriedly before leaving the office into her breast pocket, hung over her khaki jacket and three pairs of eyes zeroed in on it. Imperceptibly Zofia moved back towards the open doorway, but one of the men already slipped behind her and with his outstretched arm across the entrance blocked her way. She turned slowly, facing him as if undecided what to do, then with a sudden knife-like thrust of her hand she hit his arm. It dropped and she rushed out.

The moon had risen by now and she could clearly make out the ramshackle walls. In the commotion behind her, she heard the men's angry voices, as if arguing. Dashing into the construction site and running along the wall, she saw ahead a pit filled with water, probably for mixing lime. It was barely visible in the deep shadow cast by the wall and without a moment's hesitation Zofia dove waist-deep into the slimy trough gluing herself flat against the pile of bricks. Hardly breathing, she heard the men's excited jabber, their footsteps running back and forth on the other side of the wall, but eventually, all grew quiet. She waited for a long while before crawling out of the sludge. Keeping well within the shadow of the protective wall, her skirt heavy with water and caked with mud, she crept to the end of the building site. In the moonlight ahead of her she could make out the beaten track. At that instant, to her relief, a pair of headlights appeared in the distance, fast approaching. As quickly as her heavy skirt allowed, she ran across the sand towards them, furiously waving her arms. It was not a military jeep but a private car with two passengers and a chauffeur. It slowed down and stopped. Breathless, in French, she blurted out her predicament. *"Madame, quelle chance vous avez eu!"* One of the men exclaimed, aghast. They offered to take her to the camp.

"Chance, indeed," mother ruefully admitted to my shaken granny. *"Tomorrow I would have shown up somewhere as a body stripped down to my khaki underwear. And perhaps not even that."* Many years later my mother recalled the incident: *"They were so very gracious,"* she said of her two Iraqi saviours, *"they didn't even say how foolish I had been; and I was lucky they even stopped, because coming from that hole filled with sludge, I was surely quite a sight. I must have really messed up the seat of the car with all the mud on my skirt,"* she added wistfully.

Jackals and hyenas were not the only dwellers of that animal desert kingdom. One day a large turtle waddled into the tent and over granny's strenuous objections, took up residence. Mother named him Pawełek – Little Paul. She felt compassion for all living creatures, whether grey oxen, emaciated donkeys, or ungainly turtles – all found a spot in her heart, scorpions excepted. So Pawełek remained in the tent for the duration.

Just as she was enthralled with Persia, in spite of her near misadventure, she became fascinated by the 'land between rivers'. To be on the site of ancient civilisations of Babylonians and Assyrians in itself exceeded anything her fantasy had ever conjured up. Whenever she got a chance, she visited the city, bewitched by the din of the bazaars, the stalls, and the copperware. Military luggage was restricted so she resisted the temptation to buy trinkets, except for a little copper plate engraved with the Assyrian bull. She brought from Iraq one other item that she cherished all her life, a small prayer book published by the Polish army. Hers was inscribed by the army chaplain: *"May this little book be a comfort in your ascent towards the heights of spiritual excellence. I am offering it as a memento of our stay in Mesopotamia to Magistra Zofia Hoffman. Signed: Fr. Królikowski. 1942."*

Soon my mother's faith was to be sorely tested and she would need more comfort of prayer than ever before, as the news of the massacre by the Russians of Polish officers from the prisoner-of-war camps of Katyn, Starobelsk, Ostaszków, became public knowledge.

Chapter IX

The Near East

On 1 March 1943, German forces encamped deep in the Russian territory made a grisly discovery in a forest on the edge of a village called Gniezdovo, uncovering pits with bodies of thousands of Polish officers. The Germans brought in the International Red Cross and conducted exhumations. It was soon established that the murdered men found in the Katyń graves, around five thousand, were from the prisoner-of-war camp of Kozielsk. Personal documents found on the victims' frozen bodies indicated by the last entries in several diaries that the executions were carried out between March and April of 1940. The news of the tragedy soon reached the Polish troops in Iraq and there was no doubt in the Poles' minds that a similar fate befell the remaining ten thousand men from the other two POW camps, Ostaszków in Byelorussia and Starobelsk in Ukraine.

My mother's reaction to the news was terrifying. She now knew beyond doubt that Maks was dead. *"Your mother locked herself up in a small room in the camp that day,"* my grandmother told me, *"I heard her hitting her head against the wall. I was so afraid for her... I begged her to come out; I don't think she even heard me. When she finally came out, she didn't utter a single word, she was deathly pale, her eyes were dry, but ever since I have not heard her laugh as she used to. That day something had died up inside her forever."*

Up to that moment, my mother had still been searching for traces of my father. Earlier on she had received puzzling information that in January 1941 he had been seen in the coal mine number 3 in Vorkuta in the Gulag above the Arctic Circle. Following up on that bit of news, she launched another appeal through the Polish embassy in the USSR. An excerpt from the official report of the diplomatic note read: *"Once more in connection with the cases of Capt. Maksymilian Hoffman and Lt. Włodzimierz Pawlukiewicz, prisoners of the Starobelsk camp, who had been taken away in an unspecified direction, and who have now been traced, the Embassy by note D-2092/42 is renewing the issue of prisoners from camps Kozielsk, Starobelsk, and Ostaszkow, as a follow-up to previous attempts, underscoring the fact that 10 months have elapsed since the publication of the legal decision by which they should have been set free. As for HOFFMAN, in view of the information received by his wife in December 1942 that at the beginning of October 1941 he was at the Kargopollag NKVD [camp], Jercewo, Mostowica/Archangielsk Oblast... The Embassy requested that the Decree dated 12.8.41, be applied and that a reply be given... LKSZ by note nr 200 dated 30.9.42 replied that Capt. M. Hoffman had not been found."* [77]

The Katyń Forest tragedy played itself out on many fronts as combatants on both sides used it for their own propaganda purposes. A report dated 1 March 1943 prepared by the Wehrmacht, remained a closely guarded secret for several weeks until April when it was sprung as anti-Russian propaganda and made public. On 13 April 1943, loudspeakers in Kraków and in all Polish cities under German occupation blared out news of the massacre. The Soviet response followed swiftly: two days later the Russians claimed that the mass murder of Polish officers was perpetrated by the Nazis during their advance into the USSR in 1941. Polish demands for investigation were met with vitriolic and absurd accusations that the Poles, locked in deadly combat with the Germans on every front, were actually in league with the Nazis and stoking anti-Soviet propaganda. Calling them *Hitler's Nazi collaborators*, Stalin, whose far-reaching plans involved post-war designs on parts of Polish territory, used this argument as a convenient pretext to break off diplomatic relations with the Polish government-in-exile in London, while the American and British press dismissed the reports of Soviet culpability as another piece of Nazi propaganda. Józef Mackiewicz, the Polish member of the commission sent to exhume the Katyń graves, said that *"I personally haven't the slightest doubt, absolutely no doubt that they were murdered by the Bolsheviks."* Franklin Roosevelt and Winston Churchill chose not to confront Stalin on this issue.

The war machine continued to grind on relentlessly, regardless of personal tragedies. In May, my mother was promoted to company commander and in

---

[77] Although my mother was convinced that my father died in the Starobelsk massacre, his supposed presence in Archangelsk remained a mystery until 1994 when NKVD records became accessible. Another Captain Maksymilian Hoffman, born in the same year, whose wife's name was also Zofia, was sent to the Vorkuta coal mine number 3 close to the Arctic Circle where he died. When the Polish army gathered evidence, the information on both men was conflated into a single entry.

June, General Sikorski visited the camp. His arrival had been delayed from April by the discovery of the Katyń graves and now the Inspector General Wysłouchowa hoped to secure the resolution of several pressing issues concerning the PSK during his visit. The inspection went smoothly and Sikorski returned to London on 17 June. It was to be his last encounter with the women of the Polish ATS in the Middle East. Three weeks later, on the night of 4 July 1943, he died together with his daughter, his Chief-of-Staff, General Klimecki and several other members of his entourage in an airplane disaster in Gibraltar. The tragedy occurred immediately after take-off. The bomber plane, type Liberator II AL523 operated by RAF 511 Squadron took off from the runway but plunged into the harbour 400 metres from the control post. Only the Czech-born pilot, Eduard Prchal, survived.

Air Marshal Sir John Slessor ordered an inquiry into the crash. The report presented to the British Parliament read: *"The findings of the Court of Inquiry and the observations of the officers whose duty it is to review and comment on them reveal that this most regrettable accident was due to jamming of the elevator controls shortly after take-off, with the result that the aircraft became uncontrollable. After careful examination of all the available evidence, including that of the pilot, it has not been possible to determine how the jamming occurred, but it has been established that there was no sabotage. It is also clear that the captain of the aircraft, who is a pilot of great experience and exceptional ability, was in no way to blame. An officer of the Polish Air Force attended throughout the proceedings."*[78] Sikorski's body was collected by the Polish Navy destroyer ORP *Orkan* and transported to Britain, but doubts concerning his death lingered and conspiracy theories persisted. Sikorski had become something of a liability to the Allies, a thorn in their dealings with Stalin, since he kept demanding an investigation into the Katyń murders, thus incensing the Soviet dictator.

Throughout the oppressive summer months on the Iraqi desert in the sweltering heat, the soldiers' health was deteriorating rapidly, mortality was high caused by sun-stroke with the recurrence of tuberculosis and malaria, so news

---

[78] General Sikorski's death remained a *cause célèbre* over the years, surrounded by many conspiracy theories of sabotage, particularly after it became known that at the time of the catastrophe Harold Adrian Russell "Kim" Philby was in Gibraltar. Philby was a high-ranking British intelligence agent who turned out to be a Russian spy, one of the "Cambridge Five". He fled to Moscow in 1963. There were suspicions that Sikorski had been murdered on Stalin's orders and his body was exhumed in 2008. It was confirmed that he died of injuries consistent with the crash, but the causes of the malfunctioning in the plane were never fully determined.

that the army was to move on to Palestine was welcome. Finally, in August 1943, in the midst of blinding sand storms, while the savage *hamsin* was raging, long columns of army jeeps and lorries crossed the desert, mostly driven by women. Military hospitals, packed with sick soldiers, followed immediately. The Polish army's official name now became *Polish Armed Forces in the East*.

Palestine offered an improved climate and better overall conditions and life became more bearable. The army set up the camp in Rehoboth, with the same white tents from Iraq, but this time not in a pitiless desert. Although temperatures were also high, there was vegetation, and the camp was surrounded by citrus groves that saturated the air with the delightful aroma of orange blossom. Nearness to the sea provided a refreshing breeze and assured cooler nights. A bushy linden tree at the entrance to the camp served as a favourite spot for hitching rides into town.

In an article for the Polish newspaper Dziennik Żołnierza, *The Soldier's Daily,* [79]Mr W. Jagiello wrote: *"A year ago we left Palestine because that was the order. We had to add to the Polish Books of Pilgrimage a new trail, through Iraq, this time burning us with hot hamsins and choking with soft desert dust. A year later we returned... Palestinian black asphalt roads roar under the thundering wheels of lorries with symbols of Pines, Bisons, Lions, and Sirens.*[80]

I'm standing by the roadside hoping to catch a ride. My lungs, burned by the Iraqi sun, greedily inhale the humid scents of orange groves... Ah, here it comes, a huge Dodge with three black circles against a white-and-red background... I raise my hand, it stops. A small face surrounded by curls leans from behind the steering wheel and a bright energetic soprano voice calls out: "Are you heading for M? That's good, that's where I'm going. Just hop in quickly, I can't be late'. I get in. We pass other vehicles on the way, some single, some entire columns, and in most of them the same thing, black berets and curls. I knew there were women drivers in the army because they were already present in Iraq, but I didn't expect that many."

When in 1941 Stalin decreed the so-called amnesty for Polish deportees in the USSR, the Russians had put up many stumbling blocks to the eligibility for release, race being one of them. Barred from enlisting in the army were Polish Jews, defined as 'Polish citizens of Mosaic faith'. It was hard to tell what drove

---

[79] Dziennik Żołnierza. London.19. IX.43.
[80] Coat of arms of Polish cities were used as regimental symbols, such as Warsaw's Siren and Lwów's Lion.

this discrimination, but Polish military authorities did what they could to get around the restrictions and smuggled through the Russian screening process many Jews who were Polish citizens. Among those who evaded the control net was a Warsaw lawyer by the name of Menachem Begin. As the troops moved on to Palestine Begin who was a Zionist, found himself where he had always wanted to be. With a group of other Jewish soldiers, he left the army *awol* and joined the *Haganah.* The Polish command, sympathetic to their liberation aspirations, did little to deter the deserters and in spite of British pressure and frustration, General Anders refused to prosecute them.

Best spot for hitching a ride into town…

… for a decent cup of coffee

The Polish army pitched camp and launched extensive operations in Rehoboth. Along with intensive military training, schools run by Polish educators were set up for male and female cadets, with formal high school curricula that allowed them to complete their secondary education disrupted by the years spent in the USSR. A printing press produced textbooks, works of Polish literature, calendars, pocket agendas, and newspapers.

When the Russians set out to deport one and a half million people, members of the Polish *intelligentia*, intellectuals, professionals and artists were their particular targets. Now there was no shortage of good material for the theatre. Actors, some well-known from before the war, organised a theatre ensemble, *The Polish Soldiers' Theatre,* that toured army units entertaining the troops. Artist and poet Feliks Konarski, whose stage name was Ref-Ren, and his wife, comedienne Nina Oleńska, the indomitable Private Helenka in her beret, oversize coat, and clunky shoes, were an instant hit. The army could count on actors, composers, and writers to produce high-quality literary stuff for the soldiers' entertainment.

The theatre ensemble spread its wings well beyond the camp. In Baghdad, it received an enthusiastic review from the English language press after a performance in the King Feisal II theatre, at which the commander of the British tenth Army was present. Sir Henry Maitland Wilson had been regent of Iraq ever since the British restored the monarchy after the coup of 1941. There were further tours, as far as Cairo and at several other Allied camps. The theatre launched its first show on the sands of Quizil Ribat. As the army press duly reported, *"The first campfire celebrated the joining of two brigades, the Lwów and the Vilnius brigades, into the Fifth Frontier Infantry Division. Several hundred men and women took part in the performance: actors, choir, brigade orchestras, and one entire army regiment. The second show to be put on was a Christmas pageant, set up against the backdrop of the desert, under a starlit sky. In the glare of searchlights, shepherds hurried to the manger, while the star of Bethlehem pointed the way and a beautiful chorus of angels accompanied them. From a little further off, the three Kings on camels came bearing gifts. The performance charmed by its realism."*[81] Both my mother and my granny retained the same unforgettable impression of the desert, its boundless expanse, pitiless heat, the night sky suspended lower than anywhere else along their journey, and a million stars scattered across a deep midnight-blue blackness. It was like the mystery of oceans and high mountains, the power of nature not to be harnessed, which made man aware of his insignificance.

In the midst of constant changes, moves, daily chores, and soldiering, mother attempted to come to terms with her personal loss. Camp life left no time for mourning, little chance of solitude that was so necessary for coping with grief. Personal tragedies were secondary to the requirements of the moment and military discipline. Added to her longing for me, the loss of my father heightened a sense of responsibility. From now on there would be no sharing, all was left to her alone. Small comforting moments helped, as when on a visit to the Church of the Nativity in Bethlehem, she donated a gold coin as a votive offering in the intention of recovering me. And even with her life so totally blighted, her irrepressible curiosity of people and places took over.

Driving through the countryside in an army jeep she was bewitched by the multi-coloured trees in bloom lining the roads, and by the citrus groves that scattered an exhilarating scent. One day she met an old Jew from the small town of Rawa Ruska in Poland. Now he was a wealthy owner of *pardes*. As they chatted, mother told him how enchanting she found his orange grove. But the man just shook his head sadly. *"Oy, madam, if you saw what I left behind there,*

---

[81] Idem. Anna Bobińska. p.194.

in *Rawa Ruska. The horse-chestnut trees in the market square, the little benches, and the cool breeze in the summer."* He wiped a tear. *"And what have I here? Just look around: heat, sun, sand…and more sand,"* he sounded downcast. Mother recalled that encounter many years later: *"I passed through Rawa Ruska once,"* she told me, *"a sad dump, puddles, poverty, and dirt. And yet, this rich man, owner of perfumed orange groves, with a nice home, what did he mourn? Horse-chestnut trees on the little muddy common? Rickety benches? Wretched streets? Memories of his youth no doubt."* When she said this, I remember how her green eyes narrowed as they always did whenever her gaze wandered far away. Then she murmured, *"Home is where you leave your heart."* Who was she speaking to?

My mother experienced the Holy Land as a tangled skein of the ordinary with the extraordinary. Land of perfumed *pardes*es, silver olive groves, and roads lined with flowering trees, the holy of holies where three religions converged in the midst of a strange, multicultural world and where the Polish army became a visible presence. On Good Friday, uniformed members of the Polish ATS carried a wooden cross in a procession on Via Crucis, winding their way through the old town of Jerusalem. In Nazareth, women-cadets deposited a marble plaque with an invocation reading: "Restore Freedom to our Homeland…" For my mother, while at times it might have felt enormously stressful, it was still deeply enriching.

Plaque placed by female cadets at the Church of St Joseph in Nazareth

Not everyone felt that way of course. When it came to her subordinates, the cultural level varied. Before the war some were simple farmers' wives, some were teachers, some were office workers, while others held doctorates. Mother, whose daily life up to the war was permeated with the sense of 'culture', precious to the Central European intelligentsia, tried to inject a touch of it into the military routine, arranging trips to the most significant sites in Egypt.

The results were not always satisfactory. One of her underlings stubbornly resisted any attempts at enlightenment, cutting short all explanations with, *"well, but back in my home town of Nowy Sącz…"* On a trip to the pyramids of Giza and the Great Sphinx, in frustration, mother forewarned her: *"Please, don't say there were pyramids in Nowy Sącz as well."*

Visiting the Sphinx

The temple   and the Great Pyramid of Giza

Among her close associates, she had no such complaints. Two poets in her inner circle often did poetry readings, others pitched in with short lectures, or with stories and reminiscences, but all bonded as only women knew how to bond in times of crisis. One of the best storytellers was their commanding officer, Bronka Wysłouchowa.

Inspector General Bronisława Wysłouchowa

Commanders: Zofia Hoffman and Irena Wachlowska

When she was held in the Lubyanka prison in Moscow after her arrest, Bronka shared the cell with Russian and Ukrainian women, mostly petty thieves and prostitutes who often sang and recited Russian street ballads and *dumkas*. Now with her prodigious memory and a natural gift for comic imitation, the Inspector General delighted her friends with realistic renditions from that rich repertoire during long and tedious evenings in the desert.

Waiting for a briefing in the desert sun

The Temporary Organisational Ordinance published in January 1943 by the Polish Ministry of Defence in London, imposed certain regulations on the Polish ATS, now labelled PWSK, which provoked serious dissent in the ranks. It confirmed the women's status as soldiers on active duty, subject to the general military discipline, but introduced inequality in officers' grades between men and women in certain categories, such as that of physicians. As a result, with General Anders's full support, the command of the PWSK was to prepare a list of proposed organisational structures to be presented to the minister of defence in London. A nine-member committee was set up, consisting of the following officers: Z. Hoffman and J. Scheinkönig (attorneys), M. Trojanowska, K. Jaworska, I. Wachlowska, J. Piłat, H. Naglerowa, M. Olechowicz, and Inspector General B. Wysłouchowa. The actual drafting of the proposal was assigned to the lawyers. But soon my mother's colleague, Platoon Commander Scheinkönig, sailed away to England with a group delegated to the RAF and the Royal Navy, and mother was left alone to handle the committee's task. It was her sort of work, she relished it. Once the report was finished, it was submitted to General Józef Wiatr, commander of Base Planning and Support, who decided that it would be most effective if Inspector General Wysłouchowa flew to London and personally discussed the proposed organisational changes with the powers that be.

The battle of El Alamein in 1942 drove the Germans out of Africa, saving the strategically important access to the Suez Canal for the Allies. As the winds of war blew variably, in favour and against, Cairo became a chessboard, a hotbed of espionage and counterespionage, and the prevailing atmosphere was as sizzling as the Egyptian sun. In the midst of preparations for further war action, the British government recalled military commanders, nominated new ones, diplomats of all stripes roamed among members of the armed forces, spies snooped, journalists jostled for hottest scoops – it was a heyday for gossip, intrigue, and eavesdropping. Britain held a mandate over Egypt, although theoretically there existed an Egyptian government under a prime minister nominated by King Farouk, whose politics were truly Byzantine. Formally pro-British, how could he be otherwise with British troops stationed in Egypt, but on the sly he attempted to remain neutral and dealt with the enemy, for who knew how the dice would fall? Earlier on, in 1940, Prime Minister Ali Maher in a surprise move declared Egypt's neutrality, proclaiming Cairo "an open city"; but since Britain betrayed no intention of pulling out its armed forces, either then or later, it left the city's status in limbo.

From Palestine, the army moved on to Egypt and the Polish Army East became the Second Polish Corps joining the British Eighth Army in preparation for translocation to Italy. On 15 September 1943, my mother became chief of the Office of the PWSK Inspectorate, as an integral part of the Polish Army's general command. Her promotion was celebrated by her colleagues with a gift of a small white ivory scarab on a blue-black velvet cushion and a dedication that read:

"To Madam Adjutant:
A scarab is a bug most sacred
Like an adjutant, remains untainted
So please accept without reservation
This symbol of your authority and our admiration."

Even though she was working intensively, she still tried to carve out time to explore this incredible world of cultures accumulated over millennia. Together with my grandmother, they made two visits to Cairo's City of the Dead, one at night by moonlight, and a second one in the daytime. Such excursions could only be made safely by jeep with an army escort. *"In daylight, under the blazing sun, it made a much greater impression on us than at night,"* Granny Włodzia recalled many years later, *"you would have thought it would be the other way around."* The City of the Dead was a huge cemetery, where the poorest of the poor of Cairo camped out. The mausoleums were open, people lived there, slept there, and relatives picnicked at their family tombs on certain feast days. My grandmother especially remembered a dried wedding bouquet lying on a bridal veil in a mausoleum. Why, she did not elaborate. Was death, love, and marriage, a reminder of her own daughter's tragedy?

One day an Egyptian showed up at the Polish headquarters with an urgent problem. He had already spoken to the British authorities, got nowhere, rather was given short shrift by all. Indignant at such a lack of respect, he happened upon my mother and poured out his complaints in refined French. She was sympathetic and also embarrassed by the shoddy treatment he received in his own land from a bunch of arrogant foreigners. The matter was simple and could be promptly resolved. The man was deeply grateful. Who he was, mother did not know. He returned the following day and said he wanted to thank her by taking her and my grandmother to Al-Azhar, the famous thousand-year-old school of theology, the oldest Moslem University, where infidels were not usually admitted and women even less so. The magnificent courtyard of the mosque was surrounded by slender pillars that supported pointed arches, and a roof topped by delicate almost lace-like stone ornamentation. At each of the alabaster columns in the *madrasa,* students sat on the ground surrounding a teacher who conducted his class in a barely audible whisper. In the tumultuous and noisy city beyond its walls, this seemed to my mother an oasis of peace and quiet.

In response to the report prepared by the organisational committee of PWSK, Inspector General Wysłouchowa was summoned to London by the Polish Ministry of Defence together with my mother. Preparing for the trip, mother spent a few days in Cairo at the Continental Savoy Hotel. In the evening from the terrace on the edge of the desert, she watched spectacular sunsets and caravans slowly moving along the opposite bank of the Nile. This was her farewell to Egypt.

Good-bye to Egypt

She and Bronka flew off to London on a RAF plane, accompanied by a British liaison officer. A special visa stamped into mother's passport by the British authorities, read: *"Bearer is travelling to the United Kingdom on an official mission to H.M.Govt."* They left on my birthday, 9 October 1943.

Even though the Germans had been forced out of Africa, the Mediterranean continued to be a fierce battleground and a major theatre of operations with the enemy entrenched in Italy. The route from Cairo to London was roundabout, and led over the British and French African colonies, over the Sahara Desert, and over jungles. Each day the plane landed for refuelling and for the night. In the French Congo, the stopover was a convent in the heart of the jungle. Mother and Bronka were lodged with the nuns for the night, the pilot and the liaison officer were put up by the priest in the parish house. Early in the morning, Mass was said in the chapel, black barefoot altar boys served. Mother was particularly touched by the sight of their pink soles showing from under the lace trimming of the white surplices.

Memento from Africa

After Mass, the mother superior invited everyone for breakfast in the refectory. Exuberant tropical vegetation was peering inside through the open windows, and the loud chatter of birds poured from the surrounding trees. Before boarding the plane, a nun brought out a small ivory cross and an ivory statuette of the Virgin made by local artists. Mary's face had African features. The nun turned to the two women: *"Ladies, please pick, which one of you will take the cross, which the statuette of the Madonna, as a memento of your stay here with us."* Bronka turned to my mother: *"You have a child back in Poland. You take the one of Our Lady,"* she said as she took the cross for herself.

On the west coast of Africa, they landed in Bathurst. Their reservations were in an elegant hotel, comfortable rooms with beds under mosquito nets, and large bathrooms. Mother looked forward to a relaxing bath, but to her dismay, she found the tub full of frogs. The chamber-maid, urgently summoned, was apologetic. *"I'm so sorry, madam, we had a very heavy rainfall recently, the frogs always come out then."*

Chapter X
Finally Europe

Lisbon, 19 October 1943. Three and a half years, almost to the date, since she had been carted off to hard labour in the USSR, Zofia set foot back on European soil. There was a time when it seemed impossible that she would ever see Europe again. Neutral Portugal had cosy arrangements with His British Majesty's government and the RAF plane landed without a problem, albeit the passengers were required to change into civilian clothes before disembarking. Rooms had been reserved at the Grande Hotel Borges, and there were no frogs. Mother took advantage of the twenty-four-hour layover to visit the International Red Cross hoping to resume the disrupted contact with Uncle Zbyszek in Lwów which continued under German occupation.

No frogs in this hotel

Shannon, Ireland. The last stop before London. After long months of deserts and blazing sun, the emerald green of Irish vegetation, visible from the air was like a magic balm. Then, one short hop across the Irish Sea, and it was England. From Cairo to London the flight took eleven days.

Talks on the reorganisation project at the Ministry of Defence lasted for several days. In a letter to General Anders, Marian Kukiel, the minister of defence, thanked him for delegating Inspector General Wysłouchowa and Company Commander Hoffman to Great Britain. *"I believe,"* he wrote, *"that their immediate contact with our people and cooperation will create new bases for the Women's Military Services, greatly enhancing our cause in this matter... For the purpose of continuity in completing this task, I am requesting your permission to retain in London Mrs Hoffman, whose legal erudition and familiarity with the structures of PWSK in the Middle East would be an invaluable asset in the general headquarters."* In the same letter, General Kukiel proposed Bronka Wysłouchowa as the ideal person to fill the vacant position of Commander General of PWSK in London. *"We are all most impressed by her gravity, intelligence, and charming personality."* However, when this promotion was offered to her, Wysłouchowa declined, requesting that she be left in her current post. She wished to remain close to the women she led, mindful of the bonds of the shared ordeal in the USSR. In the demanding military camp environment, she was enormously protective of her subordinates, as my mother herself experienced on more than one occasion.

If Zofia was to remain in England, what about granny? Would it mean separation? That would have been a serious problem for my mother. She raised the question outright. General Kukiel assured her that within six months her mother would be brought over to Great Britain. The army took good care of their own.

Of all the Allied officers stationed in London, Poles seemed to enjoy a singularly privileged standing with the elitist English upper classes. Many, like General Kukiel, were highly educated men of impeccable manners. Old-school charm didn't hurt. One society hostess regularly invited five Polish officers to high tea and bridge, while refusing to admit Canadians into her house, deeming them "too rustic". Never mind that at that time the traditional English high tea was no guarantee of gastronomic delights, everybody suffered food shortages, but Scotch was often to be found in these upper-crust homes, while many young ladies perceived future husbands in the gallant, hand-kissing young Poles.

Mother was promoted to Inspector and on 1 December became Deputy Commander-General of PWSK, under Colonel Maria Leśniak. In London, the general staff headquarters were located on the top floors of the Rubens Hotel on Buckingham Palace Road, a few steps away from Victoria station. At first, she took up lodgings in the ATS officers' club where she struck up an acquaintance with a young Englishwoman, Junior Commander Elizabeth Connors. Soon it turned into a warm friendship. Christmas was approaching, the first one that Zosia would have to spend by herself since granny was still in Palestine; but Elizabeth took care of that, by inviting her to her parents' home for Christmas. This was to be the first of many intimate contacts my mother had with English people outside of her military sphere. War was raging on but the holiday spirit was relaxed with a Christmas tree, mistletoe, crackers, and the traditional somewhat indigestible plum pudding. Zosia found the childlike simplicity of these small pleasures charming and enormously appealing. After it became known that Poland had been ceded by the Allies to Stalin, Elizabeth Connors offered my mother a miniature edition of Alfred Lord Tennyson's poetry with a dedication: *"To Lt. Col. Zofia Hoffman, with affection and very best wishes – to note particularly page 18 of this little book. From Elizabeth Connors. Christmas 1947."*

How long, O God, shall men be ridden down,
And trampled under by the last and least
Of men? The heart of Poland hath not ceased
To quiver, though her sacred blood doth drown
The fields; and out of every smouldering town
Cries to Thee, lest brute Power be increased,
Till that o'ergrown Barbarian in the East
Transgress his ample bound to some new crown:
"Lord, how long shall these things be?
How long this icy-hearted Muscovite
Oppress the region?"

Tennyson wrote this sonnet, one of two entitled "Poland", after receiving news that the Russians had crushed the Polish Insurrection in November 1830. One hundred fifteen years later history repeated itself and the poem acquired fresh poignancy.

After spending a few weeks in the ATS officers' club, mother rented a room in a boarding house at 36 Belgrave Road in preparation for granny's arrival. Soon she was visited by another lodger, a small mouse that came for daily offerings of bread crumbs left on the window sill. In spite of the wintery weather and fog saturated with coal dust and smoke from fireplaces, the legendary smog, so dense that people became disoriented and lost, my mother loved London. She admired the English self-control as well as the public's discipline and honesty. Though the food was rationed, a pint of milk left by the milkman in the morning on the doorstep of a bombed house remained there until its owner came to pick it up. Compared to Poles, my mother may have found the British short on emotionality, but big on dry humour and self-deprecation, all of which suited her fine.

In the midst of the rubble and destruction, time rolled by in a strangely routine way, and in her reflections on those years, my mother retained many vignettes of ordinary life in London. Passing by Victoria Station she discovered a small delicatessen, a poor version of Mrs Teliczkowa's breakfast room albeit without her exquisite snacks, but offering an abundance of pickled herring fillets and the rollmops. The rationing system strictly controlled sugar, butter, meat, milk, jam, and margarine, allowing two eggs per person per week. All inhabitants had ration books and registered at the shops of their choice which, in turn, were allocated the amount of produce based on the number of registered customers. But fish was excluded from rationing, so consumption of fish-and-chips available in newspaper wrappers in kiosks around town rose dramatically. Luckily my mother loved herring, so on her way home, she stopped regularly at the delicatessen at Victoria Station.

Underground tube stations served as air-raid shelters with camp beds and bedding set up along the walls. In the evening people came down and took up their assigned spots. As she got off the train, each day my mother saw the same hat with a lilac flower, typically worn by elderly English women, lying on the bunk bed, although its owner was never there. She imagined her as a pensioner sitting somewhere with a friend finishing her "cuppa", the balm for all stress, before the night bombing raids began. To my mother tea seemed to be an integral component of English psyche. One day on a bus a small girl threw a panic attack on hearing explosions and her mother tried to calm her down with a promise of a cup of tea as soon as they get home. Not a lollipop, mind you as would have done for a continental child, not ice cream just "a nice cup of tea". True to its word, within three months the army sent granny to England.

In the meantime, mother was dispatched to the north of Scotland, to the officers' training camp in Aberdeen, the first officer course for Polish ATS (PWSK). In the time of war, the army ran a double rank system for career military and for contract officers. My mother returned from Aberdeen with a dual-rank of a regular army lieutenant and contract lieutenant colonel. The following year she was promoted to the rank of regular army captain, but as contract lieutenant colonel she wore two stars and two stripes on her epaulettes.

1944. Aberdeen, Scotland. Officer Training Course.

In addition to the stars and the stripes, mother brought back from Aberdeen a small silver cup won in the shooting competition at the closing of the course. She was near-sighted from childhood, and as she herself said, when it came to shooting from a rifle, the bullets flew all over the place. But shooting from a revolver at her hip was another matter. Into the target, a cardboard figure holding a heart, my mother packed eight bullets forming a neat, compact wreath in the heart. This achievement was celebrated with a long ballad composed by another member of that course, who described the final stages of the competition at the shooting range:

"The cadets take aim, but shots go astray
too often, too far, and out of the way.
The youthful instructor with holy indignation
tugs at his moustache in sheer exasperation.
While the cadets to everyone's surprise,
display murderous instincts in their ladylike guise.
As their shots misfire all over the range,
they scare the little rabbits from the nearby grange.
The cadets go crazy, bullets whizz and fly,
instructors take cover in a shed nearby.
Now a senior officer finally makes her way
to the firing point. Can she save the day?
Her dignified posture, though not quite as prescribed,
speaks volumes of resolve and battle-hardened pride.
Slowly she takes aim at the target station
and fires eight shots with cool determination.
Eight bullets lodge in a tight little wreath
in the target's heart, the range explodes in cheers.
In the quiet Scottish town at the end of the world,
Our shooting exertions bore fruit in the end."[82]

Cadets on Parade

---

[82] Translated from Polish by Eva Hoffman Jedruch

Mother's shooting trophy

After the early bombardment of England in the first years of the war, life "under the bombs" became quite routine. In London rubble was removed, damaged buildings were secured; shelters were set up as well as canteens for the homeless. As the war on the Continent rumbled on, increasingly there was talk of new intensive air raids on Great Britain. Rumours circulated of secret weapons developed by the Germans on the Island of Peenemünde, that Hitler intended to use against England. As before an approaching storm, there was an eerie silence for six months until D-day. Allied forces landed on the beaches of Normandy on 6 June 1944 and on 13 June the first flying bombs V1, the *Vergeltungswaffe* – weapons of retribution, fell on England. The name was intended to sow panic, the number 1 indicated that it was the first in a series of such weapons in Hitler's secret armoury and there were more to follow. On that day only a few bombs reached the Island, but two days later, one-third of the V1s hit their target. Of 244 bombs launched on 15 and 16 June, 73 fell on London.

To avoid giving intelligence to the enemy, the British government ordered total press blackout, so the rest of the country was unaware that London was under heavy bombardment. Early attempts to bring the V1s down with small anti-aircraft cannons proved useless. The roar of the cannonade across the city was deafening, but the falling bombs only exacerbated the damage. The cannons were moved to the southern coast of England so that part of the bombs could be intercepted before they reached the populated areas. However large swathes of London were burning. The characteristic buzzing sound of the approaching V1s earned them the name of buzz bombs or doodlebugs, the Germans called them hell hounds or fire dragons.

The flying V1s were more lethal than ordinary bombs, although occasionally they didn't explode. It was more frequent during the first "great" Blitz of 1940 that a bomb would not explode, but got buried deep into the ground or lay on a lawn. Then UXB – *unexploded bombs* – teams were then called to disarm them. In November 1940, London papers gave extensive coverage to the case of Frederic Leighton-Morris who carried a 50-kilogram unexploded bomb out of his flat on Jermyn Street, fearing that it would explode and destroy the house. He intended to take it to St James's park to be disarmed. On the way there, he ran into a policeman who arrested him for entering an "evacuated zone". Leighton-Morris appeared in court before a judge and was told that it was unacceptable for a private citizen to be carrying bombs around town. He was sentenced to a fine of one hundred pounds or three months in jail. Leighton-Morris replied that even if he had one hundred thousand pounds in the bank, he would not pay the fine and preferred to go to prison. The story hit the headlines, Prime Minister Churchill was quizzed in parliament over the whole affair and the hero's neighbours collected one hundred pounds for the fine, but in the meantime, Home Secretary Herbert Morrison intervened and reduced the fine to five pounds. Mr Leighton-Morris announced that he would frame the neighbours' cheque as a memento and the entire neighbourhood celebrated with a block party.

Four years on since Mr Leighton-Morris's act of defiance, and with the massive destruction wreaked by flying bombs, nobody thought of partying. My grandmother suffered from claustrophobia and refused to go into a shelter, neither did she want to die under the rubble. Fire-watchers patrolled the city from roofs and at street corners, so as soon as the air-raid alarm was sounded, granny went out and planted herself next to the nearest fire-watcher. Mother had no choice but to go out with her. One of her colleagues saw them standing on the corner one evening and was shocked since neither of them wore protective headgear. *"For God's sake, Sophie, at least cover your mother's head with a helmet!"* He pleaded. From that time on, mother and granny wore hard hats during air raids. After a while granny got tired of standing on the street, so the next step was to board a double-decker bus and ride around London.

It was not only granny who treated German air raids with nonchalance, most Londoners did. Approaching flying bombs were shrugged off with disdain and a general sense of apathy prevailed. Rumours abounded of yet another secret weapon readied in Hitler's arsenal, although it was not much of a secret since the information had been already leaked by German prisoners-of-war. Open discussion on the topic was forbidden, so speculation, feeding on imagination, was rife. The biggest fear stemmed from air raids where the flying bombs and rockets would be launched together. But as the V1 attacks grew less frequent and no rockets had fallen on London, Duncan Sandys (minister of Works in Churchill's cabinet and chairman of the "defence committee against German flying bombs and rockets") announced at a press conference on 7 September that the worst was over and anxiety over V2 rockets was greatly exaggerated. The next day, 8 September at 6:40 am, the first V2 rocket *Vergeltungswaffe* 2 (technical name *Aggregat 4)* fell on London, followed by a second explosion a short while later. Again, total press blackout was imposed by the government. At first, people assumed that the explosions and the huge holes they left were caused by gas lines or weapons depots that had been hit. The government encouraged these speculations. But as the attacks increased to four a day, nobody doubted that a new wave of Blitz had been unleashed and Londoners began referring to the V2s sardonically as the "flying gas pipes". My grandmother described the effect as incredibly frightening: *"You heard the swishing roar of the rushing air after the rocket had already fallen."*

Mother and Granny- Boarding-house on Belgrave Road.

The V2s contained 1000 kilograms of explosives, covered a maximum range of 220 miles, a ceiling of 50-60 miles, and flew at a speed of 5,600 kph (3,400 mph). From a portable rocket launcher in Holland, the missile reached its target in a few seconds, and it was impossible to intercept it because it dropped perpendicularly from the stratosphere. Two months after the first attack on 8 November, the Germans broke the silence, and on 10 November Prime Minister Winston Churchill announced in Parliament that *"Great Britain has been under attack for the last few weeks"* and disclosed the nature of the projectiles.

Huge damage was done by V2s. The rockets tore out enormous craters that swallowed multi-storey buildings. During seven months of relentless bombardment, some 500 V2s fell on London. Just before Christmas, a rocket hit Woolworth's department store during holiday shopping hours, around two hundred people died on the spot and some bodies were never found. Each time the V2 hit a busy market or a crowded building, destruction was total and the death toll massive. Because there were not enough deep public shelters, the government ordered mass production of Anderson type shelters which were placed in parks and gardens. But those living close to the Underground stations preferred the tube to any other type. London was sinking into a pervasive mood of war-weariness.

On the other side of Europe, Lwów was still under German occupation. On 1 May 1944, the Soviets launched a surprise air raid, unexpected since it was the International Workers' Day, a Soviet patriotic holiday. At around nine at night, alarm sirens sent us scurrying down to the basement. In the heavy bombardment of the city, two Russian bombs tethered with chains fell on our house destroying most of it. Contact between mother and Uncle Zbyszek was now severed.

Chapter XI

Lwów. 1944. And the Bombs Keep Falling

Recollections of the early years following my mother's and granny's deportation from Lwów on 13 April 1940 filtered through my memory as disconnected fragments, blurry photographs pulled out of a drawer, and loosely scattered on a table. In time they became fixed and combined into a single narrative in the flickering light of a candle, of a cellar filled with people, of a house reduced to rubble, of a staircase suspended in the air like a garland, of a wild rose bush crushed under a black grand piano.

The first images and seasons were mere sketches, interchangeable and hazy. Listopadowa Street at dusk, my nanny holding me by the hand as I trotted beside her. How did I know this was Listopadowa? I just did. Trolley tracks wet and shiny from the rain ran down the middle and disappeared in the distance. A streetcar approached sounding a warning bell and stopped with the screechy noise of brakes. Uncle Zbyszek told me once, *"Your mummy took this trolley to school,"* and from that moment the tramway, the tracks, the autumn mist became a part of my mother's image. My mind stirred and sponge-like began to absorb the world around me.

A wire fence, painted rusty orange and a thicket of white and purple lilacs concealed our garden from the street, a walkway led from the garden gate to the front door. There was a small orchard behind the house surrounded by a tall wooden fence, a golden reinette apple tree and a couple of cherry trees took up most of the space, and bushes of gooseberries and raspberries grew along the periphery. In the sun the branches of the trees sagged under the weight of fruit. Throughout the summer, a large crystal bowl standing on uncle's grand piano overflowed with sweet cherries, but in a show of defiance, I nibbled the green and sour gooseberries straight off the bush. *"You'll have tummy ache,"* Aunt Hania never tired of warning me.

After I recovered from whooping cough, the doctor recommended fresh air and every day we walked up to the top of the hill called High Castle.[83] We sat on a bench, Aunt Hania and me, and looked out at the vast panorama of the city below. Uncle Zbyszek, always armed with a camera once snapped my picture just as I turned to my aunt saying *"I feel sick."* The camera recorded that historic moment.

With auntie on Wysoki Zamek in Lwów

Motion sickness was my recurring problem and nowhere more so than on a streetcar. My teeth were my other weakness, so Uncle Zbyszek maintained strict control and regular visits to the dentist were *de rigueur*. Doctor Salmoński, tall, with greying hair, was a family friend and a frequent visitor in our house and I liked him because he played with me. Once he tossed me up in the air a mite too high and I grazed the bronze ball of the chandelier with my head. Pandemonium broke out, I howled, my uncle and aunt rushed off to the kitchen for wet compresses, Doctor Salmoński yelled for Basia to bring a cold knife to apply to the spot on my head. It was just a slight bump. Our dentist was an old bachelor.

---

[83] High Castle: a tall hill in Lwów where the king of Poland, Casimir the Great, built a castle in the second half of the fourteenth century.

He had a little dog that went with him everywhere, and a pretty dental assistant at the office. He was a firm believer in the curative powers of garlic, so every day after work his assistant prepared three portions of crushed garlic in buttermilk, for the doctor, for herself, and for the terrier. Supposedly sour milk killed the stink of garlic and since the office never smelled of it, there may have been some truth to it.

Each morning my Nanny Basia, walked me down to the kindergarten run by nuns. One day we received a visitor, a very tall man in a black coat so long that only the tips of his black shoes showed from under it. We children were lined up to greet him in a shaky unison with a *"Good morning, your eminence,"* and he answered *"Good morning, children,"* and smiled at us. A sister took me by the hand and led me up to him. *"This is Mr Neuhoff's granddaughter,"* she murmured. The black coat seemed to reach from the floor all the way up to the ceiling, but it bent down a little and a pair of piercing eyes looked into my face in silence. The man put his hand on my head and made the sign of a cross on my forehead. It was Bolesław Twardowski, archbishop of Lwów, my grandfather's friend, expelled by the Soviets from his residence, who now lived in a small room in a convent. At the time of this visit, he was already suffering from advanced heart disease. In a year he would die of pneumonia, after catching a cold at the funeral of Metropolitan Archbishop Andrzej Szeptycki. In one single month, Lwów lost its two outstanding churchmen: one the leader of the Roman Catholic, the other of the Greek Catholic church.

In some people smells revive memories, in others it may be the sounds. I'm of the latter kind. As I lay awake in bed almost every night, I heard the distant whistle of a locomotive that filled me with indescribable longing, a yearning for I wouldn't know what. In the morning I would go out onto the balcony where red geraniums grew in wooden boxes, I held onto the railing and looked over the wide panorama of roofs covered with green patina, scanning the horizon for traces of the night train. Perhaps in the hope that it would bring my mother back? Uncle Zbyszek kept her memory constantly alive with pictures and stories of the sort *"when we were little your mummy had very long hair."* Another image that clearly etched itself on my brain was that of a Soviet tank crunching its way down our street. Its tracks tore at the edge of the curb, crushed the flagstones, carved out chunks of pavement, and splinters of cobblestones scattered to either side. Russian soldiers sat on the tank. I was about three; I stood with Basia by the garden gate and watched the slowly moving iron monster rumble by.

At the garden gate with Basia Jawna.

We lived, my uncle, my aunt, and me, on the top floor of granny's house. Uncle's black grand piano which had been hoisted upstairs through the balcony occupied a goodly portion of the sitting room where I slept. The piano stood directly across from my bed. One summer evening the balcony door was slightly ajar, a soft breeze gently swayed the muslin curtains, a metronome, which I liked to set in motion, clicked rhythmically on the piano next to the music rack. Uncle Zbyszek was playing. The light from a small lamp shone on his hands and his profile was sharply etched against a large carpet covering the wall. Whatever that music was, at that moment it sunk deep into my memory. Years later and up to this day, whenever I hear Beethoven's Moonlight Sonata, I see my uncle's head lightly bent forward over the keyboard.

A single long room now served as a combination of the library and dining area. A portrait of a canon in a purple scarf hung above the sofa, a small coffee table stood in front of it. Across the room, the entire length of the wall was lined with bookcases stacked with volumes almost to the ceiling. At this end of the house, the balcony overlooked the orchard. A large rectangular table and six chairs occupied the centre of the room which connected to the next one where uncle's grand piano now stood. Here the balcony gave onto the front garden and the street. A large glass case next to the balcony door held a valuable collection of antique watches. There were paintings on the walls and a large grandfather clock in the corner. One afternoon, while we were having lunch in the dining room, a thief climbed up the outside drain pipe and cleared out the watches from the glass case. The theft was not discovered until later, even though we had a dog in the house, a schnauzer called Kuba. Earlier there was a second dog, my mother's small mongrel terrier, Smyk, a stray she picked up from the street. But Smyk now was gone. After mother was arrested and taken away by the Russians, he refused food, spent entire days lying by the garden fence, and got so thin that one day he slipped under the gate and never returned.

Since September 1939, Lwów had been occupied by the Russians, but as soon as Hitler launched his offensive against the USSR in June 1941, they began feverish preparations for a withdrawal. Their priority was to massacre thousands of Poles held in the Brygidki Prison and in other makeshift prisons scattered across the city. An incessant roar of lorry engines muffled the sound of gunfire as the NKVD supervised executions of prisoners in cellars and courtyards all over town until June 30, when at 2:00 am the last Soviet unit pulled out. Around 7,000 prisoners were massacred; those that could not be shot were bayoneted and left in basements stacked to the ceiling with bleeding bodies. A few hours later, German tanks rolled in to find a good deal of the "wet job" already done for them by their erstwhile ally, the present enemy.

Repressions by the Gestapo now followed: arrests and executions. A Polish committee allowed by the Germans and known as the Polish Protection Committee[84] (shortened to Pol.K.O), was set up by the citizens, made up of members recruited from all walks of life and social strata. Ostensibly, the Committee's official goal was to assist people deprived of any means of livelihood. But an even more important unofficial role was to rescue as many

---

[84] Polish Protection Committee: Polski Komitet Opiekuńczy, (PKO or Pol.K.O), part of Central Protection Council RGO – Rada Główna Opiekuńcza.

prisoners as possible from the hands of the Gestapo. During the Russian occupation, Uncle Zbyszek was fictitiously employed as a technician in Professor Steusinger's laboratory to avoid being shipped off to the USSR as a "social parasite". As soon as the Soviets retreated and he found out about the newly created Committee, *"from your mother's colleague,"* he told me, *"Attorney Antoni Kozłowski, whom I met on the street by chance,"* he immediately reported to the headquarters at number 5 Kopernik Street and was accepted as a member of the Pol.K.O. The composition of the Committee pretty closely reflected the cross-section of society and in his recollections, my uncle listed some of his fellow members: *"Tadeusz Kapko, the oilman, who became the managing director, Professor Doctor Adam Gruca, one of Lwów's best surgeons,, Father Michał Rękas, Countess Aleksandra Dębska, the merchant Mr Leon Matwiejski, Mr Błądziński, the owner of the pharmacy on St Anthony's Square, Attorney Doctor Leopold Teszner, Wanda Rudnicka, neé Countess Scazighino, wife of General Klemens Rudnicki and Zosia's schoolmate from her days at the School of Sacred Heart.*

Pol.K.O's function was to help those most vulnerable among the Polish population. Soup kitchens were set up to feed those persons who, because of their professions, were deprived by the occupant of all means: actors, judges, lawyers, professors. Twenty-six soup kitchens were set up around the city. German authorities, which sanctioned Pol.K.O's official activities, as well as the International Red Cross, supplied blankets and clothing for distribution to the needy. The Committee also took care of political prisoners held by the Gestapo, who were permitted special food packages and underwear three times a week. Many fictional certificates were issued that allowed people to obtain a 'kennkarte,' the basic identity document without which one was liable to be shipped off to forced labour in Germany.

After a while, Pol.K.O moved from the original cramped location to a larger one on Sobieski Street and greatly expanded its activities. A medical department dispensed medicines and first aid to the extent it was possible. At that time, Ukrainian nationalist bands named after Stepan Bandera were roaming across Eastern Galicia with impunity, conducting ethnic cleansing throughout Polish villages. Polish farmers were being expelled and massacred, and those who could escape took refuge in Lwów. Hundreds were being treated and cared for by the Pol.K.O.

The Committee was organised on the lines of specific functions. The economics department made all the purchases needed for the soup kitchens: sugar, flour, and other supplies. Its chief was Roman Świeykowski, who at the same time held a high position in the Home Army (AK – Armia Krajowa) which was the Polish military underground resistance organisation. The group had a truck and its driver, Jurewicz, was also a member of AK. Władysław Kuta, a major and former deputy director of the Municipal Savings Bank in Lwów, ran the accounting; the care department was managed by Jadwiga Sawracka and one of her co-workers Zosia Witkowska, widow of an officer killed in the first weeks of the war.

Many members of the Committee were heavily involved in the underground activities of AK, the Home Army. Jasia Milczanowska, a young woman, daughter of a tailor, had been planted by AK as a cleaner in the Gestapo offices. When a shipment of blank 'kennkarte' was delivered to the office, one package disappeared. A man carrying it was caught, but from the very first the Germans suspected the cleaners. Jasia was interrogated and tortured by the Gestapo, red irons were applied to her arms, but she gave away no names, and in the end, she was released for lack of evidence.

Often people came to the Committee's office straight from prison as was the case of Dr Zygmunt Hahn, the Appellate Court judge in Lwów, as well as of the actor and theatre director Edward Żytecki. As soon as they were released, the Committee fitted them out, procured clothing, and helped them disappear from the area."

In May 1943 the Gestapo arrested Roman Niewiarowicz, the son of Uncle Zbyszek's beloved diva, Helena Miłoska[85]. Since 1940 Niewiarowicz had been openly active in Warsaw running the theatre, at the same time as he headed the counterespionage commando of the AK, the Home Army. In 1941 he directed the execution of Igo Sym – an actor, traitor, and collaborator of the Gestapo who was responsible for arrests and executions of many of his colleagues. Since the Gestapo could not find any perpetrators of Sym's execution, immediately twenty-one Poles were executed as a reprisal and several outstanding rtists were arrested, among them the great dramatic actor Stefan Jaracz and the theatre Director Leon Schiller, (full name was Leon Schiller de Schildenfeld), both of whom were sent to Auschwitz. Schiller was ransomed by his sister, Anna

---

[85] Helena Miłoska Niewiarowicz was executed by the Germans on 8 September 1944 during the Warsaw Uprising.

Jackowska, with money she got from the sale of her jewellery and Jaracz was released from Auschwitz after numerous interventions. Two years later Niewiarowicz was himself arrested. First, he was held in the notorious Pawiak Prison, then transferred to Lwów and sentenced to death. It was possible, however, to get his sentence commuted and he was sent to the concentration camp of Gross-Rosen.[86]

Uncle Zbyszek usually arrived in his office early and not infrequently he found little bundles on the doorstep, with Jewish babies dropped off by desperate mothers during the night. Sometimes there were older children as well. Zbyszek worked closely with the nuns of the Order of the Sisters of the Most Sacred Heart of Jesus, in Polish Siostry Sercanki, which ran an orphanage in Lwów and the children were quickly taken away. The superior of the convent, Sister Janina Wirbal from Poznań, was a woman of great heart and equally great courage, whom Uncle Zbyszek called *"an extraordinary human being"*. As can be imagined, the convent sheltered many Jewish children. Those that had black curly hair had to have their heads shaved immediately, they were also taught the Lord's prayer since the Germans often conducted unannounced raids and the children were ordered to recite it. On 17 March, uncle's Saint's Day of St. Zbigniew, the nuns prepared a reception and offered him a large cardboard heart with sixty-seven little hearts inside, painted by Polish and Jewish children rescued by Pol. K. O.

Thursdays were Uncle Zbyszek's visit days to the Gestapo with letters and parcels for prisoners. Some instructions that he had to carry out were harder and riskier than others, like *springing* somebody from prison by bribing a Nazi officer. He spoke German fluently and a German surname helped, though not always. As soon as the Wehrmacht occupied Lwów in 1941, recognising his German roots, Zbyszek was offered the citizenship of the German Reich as Reichsdeutsche,[87] a singular honour which he declined – a fact no doubt duly noted in the Gestapo files for possible future use. Similarly, Professor Rudolf Stefan Weigl – the eminent scientist and inventor of the vaccine against typhus

---

[86] Roman Niewiarowicz survived the concentration camp, but after war during Stalinist years he was persecuted by the communist regime. He died in 1972.

[87] Citizen of the German Reich, was different from Volksdeutsche, which referred to ethnically Germans citizens of another country, an inferior category of citizenship, like a colonial. Poles who accepted either of these two citizenships were deemed traitors, cowards, and social pariahs.

– born to Austrian-German parents, who became an ardent Polish patriot, also refused to give up his Polish citizenship.

"Springing" somebody free from the Gestapo jail by means of a bribe was a risky proposition which, when clumsily executed, could lead to dangerous consequences as happened to Aleksandra (Lesia) Countess Dębska, my uncle's colleague from Pol. K.O, who was also once a week entrusted with parcels for the prisoners. Unexpectedly, one day she was arrested, and Uncle Zbyszek was summoned to the Gestapo. *"It was 5 December 1943,"* he remembered. *"I got a telephone summons to come immediately to the central headquarters of the SS. I barely walked through the door of Sturmoberführer's office, when he leaped from his chair yelling at me that somebody wanted to bribe one of his guards."*

Hermann Neuhoff, one of the Luftwaffe's flying aces, son of a university professor in Berlin, was our distant cousin. Uncle Zbyszek had never met him, but the Gestapo knew all the family connections of close and distant relatives. It was useful information. During one Thursday visit, the SS officer accepting the packages for the prisoners, on seeing my uncle rose from his chair saying: *"Ich gratuliere Ihnen, Herr Doktor. Your cousin, Hermann Neuhoff has just been decorated with the Ritterkreuz des Eisernen Kreuzes mit Eichenlaub."* the Knight's Cross of the Iron Cross with Oak Leaves, the highest award in the military forces of Nazi Germany. By a twist of fate two men, distantly related stood on the opposite ends of a tragic conflict.

The year 1943 was memorable in our family for the death of three members. Uncle Karol (Lolo) Düring, Aunt Lusia's husband and my father's brother-in-law, followed by Michał Tapkowski, granny's brother, and finally Czesław Eckhardt, granny's brother-in-law, husband of her youngest sister, Helena. These last two men had worked as "lice-feeders" in Professor Weigl's laboratory for producing the vaccine against typhus and even though supposedly the lice were not infected, both contracted the disease and died of typhus. Uncle Zbyszek gave permission to bury all three in my grandfather's mausoleum at the Łyczakowski Cemetery, but there was no time to engrave their names on the stone. They were eventually added in 2001.

My grandparents' house where we continued to live stood on the edge of the residential part of town which had some of the most elegant private villas, many of which had been requisitioned for Nazi officers when the Germans moved in. Ours was not very grand, so for the time being, it had been spared. On 1 May, this being the Soviet International Workers' Day, the Germans didn't expect any action from the Russians, so they were relaxed, unprepared for an attack which caught them off guard when it came. It was already dark when the protracted howl of the air raid sirens ripped through the night air. All the inhabitants of our house rushed into the basement, Uncle Zbyszek carried me downstairs and sat me in a large armchair, on top of my grandfather's greatcoat lined with brown fur. I spent every air raid in this chair, sometimes a couple of nights in a row, and I hated that fur which was rough and scratched my neck. The coat was black and heavy and my grandfather wore it in his younger days, when as a railway engineer, he rode in a sleigh in the winter, inspecting the tracks. A stack of potatoes lay in one corner of the cellar, a heap of coal glistened in the other. That night our residential area was targeted, the bombs fell all around us and the walls shook, sending loose potatoes rolling into the middle of the floor. Basia picked them up each time and threw them back on the pile. The narrow window of the cellar was covered with a black cloth, a small naphtha lamp swung on a hook, barely dispersing the darkness, and in the middle of the floor, a candle in a jar spread a tiny bit of light, its flame flickering with each explosion casting dancing shadows on the ceiling. At one point, auntie said, *"Our neighbour's house has been hit."*

The raid lasted through the night; the all-clear was sounded at dawn. Aunt Hania was the first to step outside and we heard her shouting. It was not the neighbour's house that had been hit, but ours. No balcony, no second floor, the first floor was almost destroyed, the ground floor still partly intact. Uncle's grand Bechstein piano lay smashed on the grass, its legs up in the air. A single twig of a wild rose protruded from the heap of wooden splinters and of tangled keyboard chords, the rest of the bush was crushed under the lid. Among the bits and pieces of furniture, the canon in his lavender scarf survived in his shattered picture frame, another painting from my mother's flat still hung on a piece of wall, except that the blast of air from the explosion wiped the paint clear off the canvas.

As Uncle Zbyszek and Aunt Hania shuffled through the debris, he picked up a small stuffed bulldog, my one surviving toy. In the meantime, I crawled around the piano, slid my fingers over the keys and the ripped chords gave a mournful groan. *"Don't do that,"* Uncle Zbyszek said sharply. As I continued my peregrination over the wreckage, I spied a cardboard box on the grass, so I picked it up and brought it over to my uncle. He opened it carefully and stared in silence at whatever was inside. Then he called out to my aunt: When she came over, he said very softly *"Zosia's Pierrot."* He lowered the box to show me and there wrapped in cotton wool was a white porcelain figurine, intact, of a clown holding a golden globe in one hand. Another one lay at his feet. At that moment Aunt Lusia arrived, Uncle Zbyszek put down the box and left it there[88].

We stayed with our neighbours for the next few days, but uncle decided that Aunt Hania and I should move to Jarosław, some 120 kilometres west of Lwów. With the help of his Committee colleagues, he travelled there and found us a small flat. We took some stuff salvaged from the wreckage of our house, a few pieces of furniture from mother's apartment which was not totally destroyed, pillows, comforters, blankets from the cellar, and a suitcase of my grandparents' tableware, twenty-five kilos of solid silver. Hefty soup spoons, forks, and knives, gigantic soup ladles, cute small sauce ladles, serving sets, all part of a massive silver service purchased by my grandfather in Vienna after he and granny were married. It was used only on special occasions, banquets, at Christmas, and at Easter. There was also a hot chocolate set in a case lined with cream-coloured satin, each white and cobalt-blue demitasse cup in delicate silver basket holder, a dainty coffee pot with an ivory handle, sugar bowl and creamer to match, the obligatory furnishings of any respectable upper-class nineteenth century establishment. Apart from the tableware, there were other items: my grandfather's silver cigar box engraved with the words: *"To Stefan Neuhoff, may God reward you, Jesuit fathers, Tarnopol. 1908,"* my mother's sugar bowl with her initials "ZH," part of her dowry, a silver candle wick-trimmer on a tray, that belonged to my great-great-grandmother Leszczyńska, and a silver bread basket that was my great- grandmother's wedding gift to my parents. My father's silver cigarette case, as well as uncle's antique Tula snuff box that he used for cigarettes, made up the rest. Carefully preserved from generation to generation, tenuous symbols of bygone times amid the wreckage of a world crushed by the cataclysm of war.

The Committee offered us their truck for the move. We departed for Jarosław on 8 May, Aunt Hania with me in the driver's cabin next to Mr Jurewicz, Uncle Zbyszek in the back with the suitcases and the few surviving pieces of furniture. On the pavement by the garden gate, we left Basia in tears, another tragedy of separation this time from me, her beloved "Hayusia".

After settling us in, Zbyszek returned with the truck to Lwów. Soon afterwards going through some correspondence, he found a puzzling card in his

---

[88] Aunt Lusia picked up the Pierrot figurine and kept it; in 1963 she sent it to my mother in Buenos Aires where we were living after the war.

office mail, scribbled in pencil, nothing but doodles with no obvious meaning. *"I showed the card to my colleague, Jadwiga Sawracka,"* he told me, recounting the incident many years later. *"She examined it carefully, then asked, 'When did you get it?' I said that just a while ago. She pointed to a word disguised in the curlicues: Smert. 'It's a death sentence pronounced against you by the Ukrainian underground.' I was stunned."*

Shortly before this incident, the Polish underground had executed a Ukrainian nationalist, professor of botany, and as retribution, the Ukrainians decided to assassinate Professor Adam Gruca, head of the Lwów Pol.K.O. But Gruca was away, so the sentence fell on my uncle, his deputy. He described what followed: *"Mrs Sawracka disappeared in her office, then returned with Zosia Witkowska and told me that within an hour I will have bodyguards from the Home Army. I then realised that both ladies were part of the Polish armed underground and as I found out, Zosia was a member of the AK Executive. Six AK men were assigned to me wherever I went. I was allowed to take only certain streets."* At all times in the midst of war, such was life on knife edge.

By the beginning of 1944, the Nazi-Soviet front shifted decidedly westwards and the Germans began preparations for abandoning the city where, however, they fully expected to return soon. In that expectation, my uncle was summoned by Frey, head of Gestapo's Political Department in Lwów, who proposed a weird scheme. He tried to pressure my uncle to form an "ears-and-eyes" group, made up of twenty or thirty working-class men who would remain in Lwów after the German withdrawal, and for a substantial sum of money, he said, would gather intelligence for the Germans, awaiting their return. When Zbyszek assured him that he lacked appropriate contacts for such an enterprise, Frey ordered him to maintain their conversation secret, but to be ready for further meetings. The absurd idea of forming such a clandestine information service made up of Poles bordered on political fiction and to uncle's great relief no further encounters with Frey ever took place. As was duly noted by the Polish underground, *"Neuhoff reported the entire incident to the Home Army, requesting further instructions."*[89]

Many years later Uncle Zbyszek described this incident in more detail because there was a personal twist to it. While he was in his office, he received a call from the Gestapo instructing him to show up at six o'clock on Kadecka

---

[89] Bogdan Kroll. Rada Główna Opiekuńcza. 1939-1945. Warszawa. Książka i Wiedza 1985. p. 256.

Street at number 12 where he was to see the Obersturmführer. It happened to be the apartment building where my parents had lived after they were married, in a flat my grandfather had rented for them. *"It was a warm summer evening. I showed up on Kadecka just before six. I was thinking about your parents. The low wall, the familiar gate now guarded by an SS man. I was let in and directed to the first floor, the flat where Zosia and Max had lived. The Obersturmführer met me at the door and chatted of trivial things. The door opened and a big brute of an SS guard came in carrying a tray of wine glasses, poured the wine, and served canapés. Only then did the subject of a Polish intelligence gathering group come up."* As Uncle Zbyszek left the building, the German accompanied him out into the street. With his hand, he swept aside some branches of ivy creeping on a telephone pole and pointed to a hidden bell. *"If you are ever in danger, Herr Doktor,"* he said, *"please press this bell."* Uncle Zbyszek never availed himself of this offer.

Throughout that entire spring, the eastern front continued advancing and by early July, the Germans decided to retreat. As the Russians were closing in, Pol.K.O. ordered my uncle to leave town. Just before his departure, Zbyszek went to say goodbye to a few familiar places, parks, squares, and buildings. *"During the war, there was no time for old prints and manuscripts, but for one last time, I went to Batory Street where Klaper and Igel had their bookstores. They stood empty. Behind the Grand Theatre lay that strange world of second-hand stuff that hid unexpected treasures, that world had also vanished on 1 September 1939, when German planes darkened the sky over Lwów and the roar of their engines forever stifled young Ritel's friendly exclamation: 'Dr Neuhoff, you were lucky!'"*

Jadwiga Sawracka and Jasia Milczanowska, the fresh scars on her arms bearing witness to the Gestapo interrogation, and two of uncle's bodyguards accompanied him to the train station. *"It was a balmy summer evening; in the distance the sky was glowing red where Bandera's Ukrainian gangs were torching Polish villages. We walked around the station that my father had built; now empty except for a sea of tracks. And then we saw the locomotive, the last German locomotive ready to depart. For a bribe, the engine-driver agreed to take me."*

Lwów, the beloved city of his childhood bade him farewell with signal lights of the semaphores against the setting sun. In the Łyczaków cemetery-books, an entry of his father's record reads: *"Neuhoff, Stefan (1864-1936), eminent builder of churches, among them the church of Our Lady of Ostra Brama in Lwów and of the parish church in Tarnopol."* Next to it, somebody's hand added a note: *"Father of Zbigniew Neuhoff, eminent lvovian attorney, who during the Hitler occupation held the difficult and responsible position as deputy RGO director, saving jointly with Father Michał Rękas, hundreds of people from deportation to the concentration camps."*

Chapter XII

For Whom Are the Bells of Victory Tolling?

Throughout that entire journey from Lwów, by way of Drohobycz and the bombed Borysław, Uncle Zbyszek had been shovelling coal into the boiler. By the time they reached Jarosław in the morning, after the sleepless night, he was exhausted and very dirty, covered in coal dust and soot. As he stepped outside the train station, he was instantly swept up by a German street raid and forced to the end of a long column marched under guard towards waiting lorries. The line snaked down the middle of the street in the direction of the parish church, with armed Germans at the head and on the sides and a *navy-blue policeman* closing the rear.[90]

A relative of ours, Marysia Tapkowska, the wife of uncle's cousin who moved to Jarosław earlier, lived across from the station. From her window she watched the men being taken to the lorries and caught the moment when Zbyszek was grabbed by the German guards. She raced across town in her bedroom slippers and dressing gown to let Aunt Hania know. We were just sitting down to breakfast when the banging on our door startled us and Marysia rushed in crying that there was a street raid and they got Zbyszek.

Aunt Hania turned white and silently slid onto a chair, Marysia grabbed a glass of water trying to revive her, I was sobbing hysterically when the door opened and Uncle Zbyszek walked in; the pandemonium turned in sobs of relief. Washed and shaved in fresh clothes over a cup of coffee and a cigarette, he told us what happened next after he was nabbed. He was the last man in line followed only by the *navy-blue policeman* when somebody behind him said: *"When we get to the church, sir, as we pass it..."* He didn't turn to look back he was still in

---

[90] Known as *Granatowa policja* or *Navy-Blue Police* these were Poles incorporated by the Germans into auxiliary police force in the *Generalgouvernement* In German: *Polnische Polizei im Generalgouvernement.*

a daze and hadn't realised this was meant for him. But as the file stepped onto the pavement and passed a hedgerow in front of the church, he felt a powerful shove, lost his footing and stumbled into the bushes. His hat rolled on the pavement and by the time he struggled to his feet and picked it up most of the column disappeared around the bend, only the policeman lingered, then turned around and gave him an imperceptible nod. My uncle recognised one of the doormen from the Lwów courthouse.

In this strange atmosphere, our daily life slowly drifted into a routine. One day, this was still before Uncle Zbyszek arrived, on a warm sunny morning Aunt Hania announced that we are going to have a picnic on the beach. It was a very tiny beach, just a sandy patch overgrown by some bushes on the River San. We put on our bathing suits, auntie packed a basket with two hard-boiled eggs, two slices of bread and a couple of ears of corn, my favourite, and we took off for the river. It was a gorgeous day, barely a white puff of a cloud crossed the sky, we found a secluded spot, spread our towels, and opened our basket. Then auntie stretched out on the towel while I dug around in the sand. She was a beautiful woman, Aunt Hania, not very tall but with a lovely figure, black hair and dark eyes with something mysterious about them. It was hard to read her moods, except when she got angry, then dangerous little sparks appeared. Ever since I could remember, her jet-black hair had a strand of white just above her forehead and people thought she dyed it that way. She would laugh when they asked her. *"There's a war on,"* she would say, *"who on earth can think of dyeing hair?"*

Aunt Hania was a true sun-worshipper and a day such as this was a rarity. After a while, I got bored with my spade and bucket, and started bugging her to let me get into the water. Finally, she got up with a sigh, took me by the hand and we waded into the shallow waters of the river. Neither of us could swim so we moved slowly along the gently falling bottom. Suddenly I lost the ground under my feet and started sinking into a deep and invisible crater. My head was already under the water, Aunt Hania desperately tugged at my arm, but I was quite heavy, so instead, I began to pull her down with me. We were both drowning. A fisherman sitting nearby saw us and reached us with one leap, grabbed my aunt's arm and dragged both of us out and back onto the bank. We sat shivering and spitting mud as the man helped us get back to our towels. *"It's those damned Soviets, ma'am,"* he said to my aunt. *"When their troops were camping here, the soldiers threw hand grenades into the river to stun the fish and scoop them up that way when they surfaced. Those grenades tore out huge craters in the river bed and already quite a few people drowned.* " This adventure put an end to our excursions to the sandy patch.

Once Uncle Zbyszek was with us, we would take long walks in the park on Sundays. Little girls ran around chasing large wooden hoops, propelling them and keeping them straight with small rods. Looking back on those memories from my childhood, I think of a Renoir painting, of sunny summer days in parks with small figures in flounced dresses with wide sashes, strolling along the paths through the greenery, joyous and carefree. Perhaps we, the little wartime girls also provided our elders with a fleeting moment of respite from the nightmarish reality beyond the park.

Playing with hoops in the park

On weekdays, I played with other children in the inner courtyard of the house where we lived. The main entrance from the street was a *porte-cochère* paved with cobblestones, with stairs on either side leading to the upper floor flats. A second gate in the back opened directly onto a large courtyard, with an orchard on one side, a stable and a barn on the other, and a large horse-chestnut tree in one corner; with the chestnuts and matchsticks we fashioned toy animals. The flats on the first floor ran along a wooden balcony overlooking the courtyard. They were small, perhaps at one time, the entire building served to house domestics and animals belonging to a large estate. At the time we lived there, the owner was Zygmunt Kijowski, supposedly a high school teacher before the war. Tall and elegant, he lived on the ground floor with his pretty plump wife. He had two magnificent stallions in the stable, one black, the other light chestnut colour, which he managed to hide from the Germans and the Soviets. He never rode out of the courtyard, but once in a while he let the horses run on a *longe* line and then we, children, were ordered to stay away. From the first-floor gallery, I watched the two magnificent stallions gallop around and I would get goose bumps at the thrilling thought that I could fall down over the bannister into the courtyard straight under their hooves. Sometimes Mr Zygmunt led them quietly, one at a time, putting them through various paces. Out in the courtyard when he exercised them, he wore tall riding boots. There were times when he disappeared for weeks on end and Uncle Zbyszek once whispered to Aunt Hania that it had to do with the Home Army, something of course, I did not understand.

Apart from the horses, there was an old mean-tempered goat called Baśka that also lived in the stable. In the daytime, she was tethered to a tree. She was sneaky, that one, and when an unsuspecting human got close, she hid behind the stable door, then jumped out and from the back rammed her victim's backside. It took a while before I learned to give her a wide berth. Zygmunt's wife milked the goat and made butter in a tall wooden churn, a rare commodity in those days. Hay was stored in the barn for the goat and for the horses and there was a hay cutter. One evening Mrs Kijowska, dressed in a flowery dressing-gown, tumbled into our flat wailing loudly with blood pouring from her hand. She blurted out that her husband was away and she was shredding hay for the animals and slashed her finger on the hay cutter. Aunt Hania grabbed a towel and made a tourniquet to stop the bleeding, while Uncle Zbyszek ran out in search of medical help. I stared at the blood dripping all over our floor and tried not to puke. Finally, a doctor was found and he patched up her hand. Though her finger was saved, it remained stiff because she severed a tendon. After this incident, I developed a fear of sharp blades.

On another occasion, I myself provided a bit of gory excitement. In the old days, which meant before the war, the gate that opened directly into the back courtyard from the side street was used for bringing in carts from the fields, perhaps with hay or straw bedding for the horses that would have been stabled there, but now it remained closed, secured with a heavy bolt. Fooling around with other kids I smacked my forehead just below the hairline against a sharp spiky end of a nail sticking out from the bolt. Blood spurted out streaming down my face, my little friends stared, then screamed in panic. I crawled back up the stairs and Aunt Hania almost fainted at the sight of me when I showed up like a vampire's victim. Luckily the wound proved superficial.

On more than one occasion I added spice to my aunt's life, though mostly in less dramatic ways. On a warm summer afternoon as the rain was gently falling, the children were running around the courtyard screeching happily, so I begged my aunt to let me go out and play. In her innocence, she said yes because she had no idea what this fun was all about. Potholes and cracks in the yard filled up with tepid rainwater turning them into huge puddles. We kneaded the soft mud with our bare feet, we splashed each other screaming and laughing, we were in seventh heaven. Soon our legs were caked in mud up to our knees. After an hour or so Aunt Hania called me to come home. Barefoot I flew upstairs and bounded into the flat, covered with mud from the waist down, and ran across the floor which she had just finished washing, dropping thick blobs of mud with every step. A verbal storm broke out, Aunt Hania furiously dragged out the dual-function wooden tub we used for bathing and for washing laundry, heated the water and hosed me down. The water turned chocolate in colour, I was blubbering loudly when told there would be no more playing outdoors that day. Unfair, I snivelled, after all, she said it was alright for me to go. In the meantime, the kids were still horsing around and calling for me to come down. It was too embarrassing to tell them I had been grounded by my aunt's selfish sentence; I desperately needed to save face. Scrubbed clean, with my hair neatly combed, I stepped out onto the balcony and gravely informed the little upturned faces below that I was being quarantined because my baby brother had just come down with whooping cough. It was the only illness I knew. Standing behind the kitchen door, Aunt Hania was choking with laughter. When my uncle came home, she told him that not for nothing I was the daughter of two lawyers and a niece of a third one. Nobody ever enquired after my little brother's health.

It was July 1944. The Soviets arrived in Jarosław, the Red Army soldiers, toting their guns roamed the streets hunting for watches. It was a standard procedure to stop a passer-by and ask for time. As soon as the victim pulled up his sleeve to check the hour, the Russian would yell *davai chasy.* [91] Some soldiers wore several watches on each wrist. People meekly handed over their timepieces, afraid of getting a bullet through the head. But one man in Jarosław successfully resisted the robbery. It was our parish priest, Father Opaliński, a big broad-shouldered man with a slight limp, who talked straight and carried a hefty walking stick. Early on he discovered that my uncle was not only a lawyer but also a pianist, so he asked him to play the organ at Mass. They struck up a friendship and Uncle Zbyszek, starved for music, readily agreed. Since then, the church filled to capacity on Sundays, when adaptations of Chopin's etudes, ballads, polonaises, and scherzos accompanied the liturgy.

One day Uncle Zbyszek saw Father Opaliński across the street on the opposite pavement and was about to cross over to greet him, when a Soviet soldier caught up with the priest, yelling at him in Russian:

"Got a watch?"

"Yes, I do." Father Opaliński replied quietly.

"Davai!"

"You want my watch?" The parson asked meekly. He waited for a fraction of a second then set his walking cane in motion. *"Here it is, and here, and here,"* he raised his voice as the blows rained down on the assailant. Shielding his head with his arms, the *"czerwonoarmiejec"*[92] took off. Zbyszek ran over to the priest.

"We won this round, doctor," Father Opaliński said, smiling. *"Come, let's go to the parish-house and have a drink to celebrate."*

As the Soviet troops advanced west, General Berling's Polish First Army came with them. The soldiers were referred to as *berlingowcy.* On a warm summer afternoon, I was out playing with my best friend Basia who lived with her mother across the yard. Basia was very timid, she followed me around like a puppy, and took part in all the games I invented. Her daddy went to the war, like mine, and just like mine had not returned, so I figured out a way to send kisses to our absent parents. We picked leaves from the tree, kissed them, and placed them behind a pile of wood by the fence. The next day we checked, if the leaves were gone, we knew the message had been delivered. On that particular day, we

---

[91] Давай Часы: Russian for "Give me the watch"
[92] Russian for a red army soldier. Could be loosely translated as *red-armyist.*

were preparing our next leaf post when three officers in uniforms and tall boots walked into the yard. In Polish, they asked a boy who was just crossing about Doctor Neuhoff's flat. The boy pointed to the balcony; I felt like screaming that we didn't live there, but I couldn't get a word out. Instead, I jumped up and flew upstairs, ahead of the three men, dashed into our flat and grabbed my uncle's arm, shouting, *"run, run, they came for you."*

Uncle Zbyszek turned white: *"Who?"*

"NKVD. Three men in uniforms."

Just then we heard the knocking, Zbyszek took a deep breath, straightened his shoulders and walked over to the door, Aunt Hania moved away and put her arm around me. Then we heard my uncle's voice: *"I don't believe it! Doctor Salmoński!"* It was our dentist from Lwów, now an officer in Berling's army, who somehow found out that we were living in Jarosław and came with his two colleagues. Their large frames filled our small flat; there were not enough chairs so one of them sat on the edge of the bed. Aunt Hania made chicory coffee – the only kind available. Over coffee and cigarette, they told us that their unit was on the way to liberate Warsaw from the Germans. They laughed at my panic and Doctor Salmoński remembered how once in Lwów he picked me up and I smacked my head on the chandelier.

"I wouldn't be able to toss you up like that now," he joked, *"you're a grown-up young lady."*

So many memories and a tearful goodbye. They didn't know, neither did we, that two weeks later as they reached Warsaw on the banks of the River Vistula, they would be blocked by their Soviet allies from aiding the Polish underground uprising that had just broken out. They were forced to stand helplessly and watch as Hitler was turning Warsaw into a heap of rubble and ashes, a graveyard, a burnt-out husk of a once beautiful city. We never saw Doctor Salmoński again.

That year I turned six and my awareness of the world grew sharper with each day. We, the wartime children, matured faster in the warped mirror of our times. Tanks, sirens, Soviets, Nazis, bombs, street raids, camping and decamping from place to place, these were our daily fare, we knew no other reality. Instinctively we guessed who to trust and who not to. We borrowed our vocabulary from our elders, and in the daily talk we gave it our own twist, communicating with each other in a *sui generis* code language. *"Where's your mummy?"* One little buddy would ask. *"She was deported,"* I would say. *"So was my daddy,"* he would answer. In this telegraphic style, no explanation was needed.

The Warsaw Uprising – *Warschauer Aufstand* in German – a major operation by the Polish Home Army coordinated with and encouraged by the Allies, broke out at *hour W,* on 1 August and lasted for 63 days.[93] Throughout that entire heroic and tragic struggle, the Red Army stood by on the opposite banks of the Vistula blocking the Allies, by refusing to allow the allied planes to land and refuel, as the insurgents battled the Germans across every scrap of the city, in the streets, in houses, churches, sewers, and parks. Only a few of the air drops coordinated with the RAF eventually were carried out. In London Arthur Koestler in a letter to the Tribune magazine dated 15 September 1944, called it *"one of the major infamies of this war which will rank for the future historian on the same ethical level with Lidice."*[94] The Uprising was crushed and on 2 October Warsaw capitulated. As a reprisal, Hitler ordered the destruction of the city. German sappers moved from building to building, drilling holes in the walls, and systematically dynamiting the structures. Some 150,000 Poles and 26,000 Germans died during sixty-three days of bloody battles. Thousands of Poles were taken to concentration camps.

There was still a handful of people left living among the rubble, mostly in the basements of the destroyed buildings. My husband Jacek recalled walking through the deserted streets in search of relatives who had lived on the other side of town. *"It was winter and by then heavy snow had fallen. As I walked along the silent deserted snow-covered streets of this ghost town, I occasionally saw the flickering light of a candle from a cellar among the ruins."*[95]

After the destruction, the Germans were not done with Warsaw. It was the last major city on the road to the frontier of the Third Reich. Hitler's plan was to turn it into *Festung Warschau* – Fortress Warsaw, blocking the Red Army's advance. But by then Berling's Polish First Army, now commanded by a Russian officer, standing with the Red Army on the other side of the River Vistula, began infiltrating the area. By 18 January 1945, as the Germans retreated, the Red Army and the Polish First Army entered the ruins of the deserted town. By 31 January

---

[93] "Hour W" was the encrypted code for launching the Uprising. 17:00 hours on 1 August 1944. The Uprising was fought for 63 days with little outside support. It was the single largest military effort taken by any European resistance movement during World War II. The Uprising began on 1 August 1944 as part of a nationwide Operation Tempest (Akcja "Burza").

[94] Lidice, Czech village razed to the ground by the Germans on 10 June 1942 in reprisal for an assassination of Reich Protector Reinhard Heydrich all 173 men over 15 years of age from the village were executed; women and children sent to extermination camp.

[95] Jacek was a native of Warsaw. He was 16 when he joined the Home Army (AK).

the Red Army was standing on the banks of the River Oder, 90 kilometers from Berlin.

While the war was raging across Europe, it was now distant from Jarosław, although the ubiquitous presence of Soviet troops still made it very close. We continued to live in our cramped flat without a kitchen, so Aunt Hania cooked our meals on a small round metal camp stove that sat on the floor in the entrance area. She had to kneel by it and there were ashes everywhere from the charcoal that was burnt. Food was in very short supply so our menu was skimpy. Potatoes were the basis of our diet and could be readily bought, as were the onions, so one of auntie's "specialties" was delicate cookies made with flour and onions that we called *onionettes*. The unassuming multifunctional "spud" tasted differently in every guise: as mashed, boiled and served with a bit of butter when available, or fried gold as a crunchy pancake, so good when eaten with cold yoghurt-like sour milk that had been de-creamed long before it hit the market. No buttermilk, for sure. The watery stuff that was available miraculously acquired a consistency of sour cream after a couple of days in a jar on the window sill. Occasionally we got bits of crisp bacon, whenever Aunt Hania could lay her hands on a piece of lard. Uncle Zbyszek jokingly called my beloved thick potato-and-carrot soup *"the dishtowel soup"* because of its unappealing grey colour, and that greatly annoyed my aunt. *"What am I supposed to feed you?"* She would exclaim exasperated, her dark eyes flashing with indignation. Then my uncle would laugh and kiss her hand, *"don't be angry, dearest,"* he would say.

Christmas was approaching. Each night before I fell asleep, I watched my uncle as he sat at a small table by the window, intent on doing something that I couldn't quite make out. He would open up two rolls of paper, one red and one silver, cut out small pieces of cardboard, glue them to the paper, knot a bow of thread, and carefully lay down whatever it was he was making in neat rows on a rolling board. He didn't know I was peeking from under the comforter, he thought I was fast asleep. Uncle Zbyszek's hair which was an ash brown colour, shone under the light of the table lamp. His cigarette in a short amber holder always lay on the edge of the ashtray, bluish smoke curling up, and from time to time he took a puff. I didn't know how late he stayed up because I would drift off to sleep before the light was out. In the morning I couldn't find any trace of his handiwork, snoop around as I might. Now, many years later, I know that he was making cardboard decorations for our Christmas tree and that this was his way of keeping at bay the despair as he saw his world disintegrate before his eyes forever.

239

That year there were just three of us for Christmas Eve. Auntie spread the brocade tablecloth salvaged from the rubble of our house and laid the table with the coarse faience plates we used, alongside my grandparents' finest silver tableware. *"Look,"* she said pointing to the embroidered letters on the tablecloth, *"these are your grandmother's initials, a monogram."* I touched the fabric with the tip of my nose, it still held a familiar smell and I was instantly transported back to Basia's basement room where she did the ironing; I was sitting on the edge of her bed, my feet dangling in the air; I inhaled the smell of starch in the steam as it rose from under the hot metal. Basia was meticulous, monogrammed pillowcases, sheets, tablecloths emerged from under her hand smooth as a sheet of paper. She sprayed water, and as the iron hissed between sprinklings, she spun an endless story of a wolf. *"And you know, Hayusiu,"* she would begin, *"the wolf went into the wood, and the wood was very dark, 'i tyvo'..."* Basia ended each sentence with the mysterious *I tyvo*, her version of *etcetera, etcetera,* in Ruthenian folk-speak. We never got past the wood, and I never found out what the wolf did there, even though I tugged at her sleeve demanding more. Had I been older, I might have suggested that he met the Red Riding Hood there? As it was, the scope of Basia's tale did not reach such levels of sophistication in story-telling, but it was good enough for me. When we were leaving our destroyed home, she packed my grandmother's great monogrammed tablecloth, part of granny's dowry, which she had kept under her own bed when the war broke out, laundered, ironed, and folded, awaiting better days.

Now as I sniffed the starched fabric, memories washed over me and I began to snivel. I longed for my old nanny. *"Where is Basia?"* I whimpered, *"Why isn't she with us?"* Aunt Hania quickly grabbed my coat and scarf and told me to put on my gloves. *"Come, we are going to see if we can spot the first star."* Holding hands, we walked along the balcony, the frozen wooden boards crunched under our feet, in the frosty air our breath lingered behind us like puffs of steam. Down the stairs and into the deserted, snow-covered courtyard, we searched for the first evening star twinkling in the inky-blue sky. *"See, see,"* Aunt Hania pointed it out to me. We walked back upstairs, but as we reached our door, we heard the tinkling of a silver bell inside. I stood spellbound in the doorway transfixed by our tiny flat transformed into a fairy-tale. A Christmas tree took up half the space, a silver star with the white Polish eagle sat on its tip. On the tree candles in small metal cups flickered, as the draft from the open doorway tilted the flames and gently swung the red and silver ornaments, and the colourful garlands strung over the branches. *"A little angel brought it while you were out,"* Uncle Zbyszek said quietly, smiling. The scent of pine permeated the air, silver knives and spoons glistened on the snow-white tablecloth. For one short hour the awful reality, fear, separation, and longing, were forgotten in the magic glow of Christmas.

Chapter XIII

1945 – But Auntie, I Thought the War Is Over!

I started going to school in Jarosław, straight into second grade. Up to now, there had been no school, but I learnt my three Rs under uncle's watchful eye and, luckily, I loved to read.[96] I owned two books: one of dwarfs and the other Hans Christian Andersen's fairy tales. When my uncle read them with me, he would occasionally mutter under his breath that Andersen's tales were hardly the stuff for children. I demanded to know why then were they called fairy tales since in my mind fairy tales were only for kids. *"Not always,"* Uncle Zbyszek would reply. Anderson's are too dark he would explain, children should read the sunny stuff. No doubt he had us, the wartime children in mind.

Still, sad or not, I never got enough of them. I cried over the little match seller's fate and over the nightingale in the ungrateful emperor's garden; I rejoiced with Thumbelina who was saved by a swallow and escaped living with the mole underground forever; I suffered through the drama of Kai and Gerda and the wicked Snow Queen. As for school, it was not my happiest time. Each day all the teachers checked the pupils' heads for lice, not surprisingly, since lice were ubiquitous. At the age of seven, I was a platinum blonde, so any bug making its home in my hair would have been easily noticed. Yet one day my teacher imagined that she had spotted something and just in case I was sent home with a humiliating note, putting in doubt the state of my hair. I brought home the offensive instructions to have my head rubbed with naphtha and Aunt Hania exploded at this unwarranted insult. Of course, there was nothing in my hair, which was washed daily with a horrid coarse soap that got into my eyes and stung

---

[96] *Abbreviation for reading, writing and arithmetic* The three R's appeared in print as a space-filler in "The Lady's Magazine" for 1818, although it is also sometimes credited as arising from a phrase coined in a toast given by Sir William Curtis, Member of Parliament, in about 1795. Wikipedia.

and often rinsed with a brew from dried chamomile flowers collected during the summer.[97] In our family, hygiene was deemed of paramount importance and strictly observed. So, auntie categorically refused to perform the naphtha cure and demanded an apology from the overzealous teacher. Back when I was two years old, Aunt Hania had cut my hair almost to the skin, after which it grew back very thick and soft. Now she collected rainwater to wash it because it was softer than the water from the faucet. There could be no question of any bug nestling in my hair, Aunt Hania firmly stated with holy indignation.

Teachers also checked our hands daily for fear of a measles epidemic. Ever since I was little, I had a tiny wart on my wrist which now suddenly attracted attention and became suspect of an early symptom of measles or some other childhood disease. Again, I was dispatched home with a note. This time it took uncle's personal intervention with the schoolmaster to clear up the matter. My final unhappy run-in was over the choir. The school was preparing a concert, we started to practice, I sang hopelessly out of tune, and the music master had no choice but to remove me, and in doing so, he excluded me from the year-end performance. No chance for me to sing about the princess who wove white roses into her golden hair. Crushed, I refused to go back to school.

The war ended officially on 8 May 1945 and even though Russian troops remained on our streets, people were hungry for normality and wanted to celebrate. Uncle Zbyszek was asked to give two concerts. Posters were pinned up announcing that on 1 September 1945 at 19:00 hours in the hall of the athletic association in Przeworsk, *"Dr Zbigniew Neuhoff, pianist, and Franciszek Brania, violinist will perform music by Beethoven, Chopin, Mozart, Paganini, and Rimsky Korsakov."* Tickets cost 20 and 40 zlotys and a note warned that late-comers would not be admitted once the concert starts.

An earlier concert had taken place the week before in Jarosław on Sunday, 26 August, at 19:00 hours in the House of Culture. This one had been announced on an enormous yellow placard and was dubbed *An Evening of Song and Music.* Tickets sold out in one day. A tenor, Kazimierz Czarnecki, joined my uncle and Mr Brania, and the repertoire was broader, including compositions by Moniuszko, Bach, and Mozart in the first half of the programme, and works by Niewiadomski, Puccini, Tosti, Noskowski, Chopin, Różycki, and Kreisler in the second. I had never been to a concert; this one was to be my first. We sat, Aunt

---

[97] Carbolic soap used during the war, mildly antiseptic containing carbolic and/or cresylic acids.

Hania and I, in the front row, as befit the family of one of the performers. Mr Brania, a good violinist, played with great emotion and as he did so he closed his eyes and inhaled so deeply that his nostrils quivered. I noticed this and the silly kid that I was, instead of listening to the music I watched for the vibrations of Mr Brania's nose. Soon I began to giggle. Auntie noticed it too, the corners of her mouth began to twitch, but she controlled herself and threw me a withering glance.

My first encounter with live theatre came about that time as well, when I was taken to see Fredro's play, *The Maidens' Vow,*[98] performed by a group of amateurs. It was around my seventh birthday and I was undergoing a metamorphosis from childhood to girlhood and while I didn't fully understand the play, it began my lifelong love affair with the theatre. Ladies in diaphanous pink and pale-blue gowns floated across the stage, gracefully curtseying left and right. I was mesmerised by the costumes and gestures and at home I began to perform little stories of my own invention in front of the mirror, that included deep curtseys and graceful twists and turns. That first contact with the stage opened the doors to a childish fantasy world. Earlier I had been picked to walk in the Corpus Christi procession. Girls in summer dresses carried baskets of flowers and scattered petals as they preceded the monstrance carried under a baldachin. I too wore a frilly dress for that occasion, but while I hoped to be picked as a flower girl, to my disappointment I was only given a ribbon from one of the banners to hold. Now was the time for such major preoccupations.

A vintage pre-war comedy was being shown in the local cinema and my aunt took me along to an afternoon show, probably because she herself wanted to see it. The lead character was played by the remarkable Actor Adolf Dymsza and Mieczysława Ćwiklińska, one of the most talented actresses of her time, was his partner.[99] We had seats in the balcony and I was mesmerised by the story of *a thief in love who stole the sun's rays,* as the song went. At the peak of romantic tension, I began to cry and asked loudly between sobs: *"Auntie, but will they make up?"* The whole cinema burst out laughing.

Summer brought us some lovely weather. We went out of town for long walks in the surrounding countryside, along trails and down country lanes, I romped through fields of wheat picking red poppies and blue cornflowers, while Uncle Zbyszek took photographs.

---

[98] Śluby Panieńskie, comedy in verse by Aleksander Fredro written in 1832.
[99] The title of the film was *Zakochany Złodziej – A Thief in Love.*

Poppies and cornflowers

It was beautiful and peaceful, but in spite of that, he and Aunt Hania didn't want to stay in Jarosław and in August my uncle went to Silesia in search of work opportunities. He was well aware that as things stood, with Russian troops still in the country and a communist government installed by Russia, practicing law was off-limits for him. While he was to be away, auntie and I were to spend some time out in the countryside.

We stayed in a village, in a room rented from a farmer, it was quiet and restful. We walked in the woods, picked berries and mushrooms, bird songs and crowing of roosters woke us up in the morning, at night we were rocked to sleep by the gentle whisper of the wind in the pine trees. Finally, it was time to go home. On our way to the train station, we walked along desolate railroad tracks, we passed a long line of freight cars, and suddenly out of nowhere, we were startled by a burst of yelling. Then we saw the armed Soviet soldier standing guard by the tracks. He was screaming at us at the top of his voice, swearing in

Russian, threatening us with his machine gun. We broke into a run and when we finally reached the station I couldn't stop shaking. *"But auntie,"* I blurted out after a while, *"hasn't the war ended?"* Aunt Hania remained silent. How could she explain to a child that the war had ended, but not for everyone?

One day we were surprised by unexpected visitors, two old friends from uncle's Pol.K.O. days in Lwów, Jadwiga Sawracka and Jasia Milczanowska who still carried the scars from the hot irons that were pressed to her arms by the Gestapo. They lived in Kraków now and brought me a gift of a miniature doll's tea service, painted black with pretty coloured flowers in the traditional Cracovian pattern. A luxury unseen during the war that thrilled me beyond words.

In October uncle was offered a position at the Bytom conservatory in Silesia, as professor of concert level piano. As yet there had been no contact with my mother and granny, but before leaving Jarosław Uncle Zbyszek wrote a letter dated 23.9.1945. *"My dearest, I'm taking advantage of an occasion that presented itself and sending this letter out into the world – hoping it will somehow reach you. In May 1944 we left Lwów and moved temporarily to Jarosław. We now plan to move again, further west – to Bytom. We survived the devastation – we are alive and healthy and holding up. Ewa started school, second grade, she is very intelligent, tall, and slim. She mainly resembles Zosia, but some traits remind me of her father.*

Her face is lovely (anyway I can't be objective because for me she is the most beautiful little girl). Particularly her hair attracts people's attention, it is perfectly platinum. She knows about her mummy and granny, until now unfortunately only from photographs, and she speaks of them often. I have just accepted the post of professor of concert level class at the Bytom Conservatory. This season I gave very successful concerts in a number of towns which resulted in this prestigious offer. Materially we have nothing, since the houses in Tarn. are destroyed, the villa was bombed last year. All the furniture, paintings, antiques and clocks turned to dust. We thank God that we got out of this horrible experience alive, with only some lingering remnant of fear. We miss you very much and trust that soon we will be able to swap stories face to face...

Here is my address: Bytom conservatory, Moniuszko Street number 7, and when you get this letter please send us a few words with news of yourselves..." Writing about the family, uncle listed those who died during the war, others he mentioned discretely just that *"they will probably not return."*

There is no indication of how my uncle sent this letter and who the mysterious "opportunity" he mentioned may have been. In all probability, it was someone from the Polish army in the West who would have been presented to him as a reliable go-between, somebody who could be trusted with a letter. In those early post-war days, contacts were not divulged and names were not mentioned. In the event the message did reach my mother in London and contact between her and us was re-established. Shortly after dispatching his letter, Uncle Zbyszek left for Bytom and rented a flat on Fałat Street at nr 8, while Aunt Hania and I remained in Jarosław for the time being.

It was a dismally cold winter and a lonely one for us. Contact with Uncle Zbyszek was by mail only or at best by telegram, telephones were not available. Finally, before Christmas, we too set off for Bytom leaving most of our belongings behind in the flat. We got to the station at dawn on a very cold day, it was still dark and the streets were deserted. Aunt Hania carried a large suitcase with those bits of our earthly possessions that were to be salvaged. Deep snow lay on the ground. We crawled over railroad tracks to reach the station, only to find out that the train was not there and nobody knew when it might come. Rail service was still a very iffy affair. We found a bench in the dilapidated waiting room and settled for a long wait. Soon we started on the sandwiches and hard-boiled eggs that Aunt Hania had prepared for the journey, almost depleting our supplies by the time the train came four hours late.

The delays continued at various stations throughout the journey and we arrived in Bytom at night, exhausted. We were eight hours late. To our despair uncle was not at the station. An unfriendly station master told my aunt that our train had not been expected that day. We started wandering around the city, on this very cold and dreary night, where the streets were empty and there was not a soul to ask for directions. Taxis were unheard of, so dragging the heavy suitcase my aunt could barely walk. In the end by some miracle, we met a man who pointed us in the right direction and we finally reached Fałat street well after midnight. Uncle Zbyszek was overjoyed and tried to explain that he waited all day at the station until he was told there would be no more trains that night, but Aunt Hania wouldn't even listen. She was stressed out, crying from sheer exhaustion, the atmosphere turned leaden, we went to bed without supper, just a glass of warm milk for me.

Our second-floor flat had no balcony; there was no tree in front of the window, although in the winter that wouldn't have done much good anyway. But the apartment was cosy, two rooms, kitchen, and bathroom – a welcome improvement over our recent primitive lodgings. The few pieces of my mother's furniture that survived the bombing of our house remained in Jarosław to be brought over later on at some unspecified time, although we could have used them in Bytom.

As soon as mother received uncle's letter which he had sent from Jarosław she tracked us down through the International Red Cross and we received our first care package through UNRRA,[100] with all sort of delicacies, for me hitherto unknown exotic luxuries. And so, we celebrated our first post-war Christmas with a tree topped by the silver star with the Polish eagle, and with Swiss chocolate, raisins, and Portuguese sardines in oil. We were settling in.

Shortly after Christmas, a mysterious visitor showed up, who spent a couple of hours talking to my uncle, while auntie and I remained secluded in the bedroom. It was highly unusual that Aunt Hania should not take part in the conversation. With my wits sharpened by the war, I began to sniff a secret, wondering if the visitor had news of my mother. Perhaps she and granny were on their way to join us? I tried to listen through the door, but auntie grew angry. *"What a silly idea,"* she said, *"the man has a business proposition for your uncle. Get back to your reading, and stop snooping. It's not nice."* The man left and did not return, but as I found out much later this visit indeed had something to do with my mother. The man was a guide, one of several who brought people out of Poland to Germany across the so-called *green border*. Many like my mother, who could not return to communist Poland themselves, were desperate for ways to reunite with their families. Smuggling people out of Poland became a flourishing business. She, like many others, began to search for ways of organising our escape. That visitor was a first of several, but each time one of these guides showed up, Uncle Zbyszek would turn down the offer. He felt the risk was too great.

In a letter dated just after New Year's, he wrote to my mother: *"My dearest, I happen to be in Warsaw and I'm taking advantage of an opportunity to send this letter. I will start with the obviously most important subject – Ayka. My dear, have no concern about her. We are trying to create the best possible conditions for her physical development, which leaves nothing to be desired. She is tall, slim (in that sense she resembles you at that age) and extremely lively. That indicates good health and resistance. Amazing intelligence, she was prepared privately at*

---

[100] United Nations Relief and Rehabilitation Agency.

*home by Hania and got straight into second grade; she reads for hours on end,
fairy tales and stories, and asks for the meaning of unfamiliar words, something
that expands her lexicon daily. She draws and paints with a passion, primitive
things, of course, and every evening she plays a game of domino with me. I must
confess that Hania's system of upbringing produces outstanding results,
assuring the child's intellectual development. She dresses her beautifully, since
as you may remember, Hania has an excellent taste in clothes, and makes all
Ayka's coats, dresses, and berets herself. My only great disappointment is a lack
of musical talent. She loves music, but I have scant hopes that she will ever
perform. On the other hand, she has a great sense of rhythm, so also a good feel
for dance. I need to point out that the child has an exceptional facility for
mathematics and ability for figuring things out, and she is decidedly inclined that
way, which she probably inherited from her grandfather. Apart from these traits
she has a striking lack of fear of strangers and feels quite at ease everywhere.*

*Undoubtedly, it would be better if her upbringing took place on different
terrain, but this is hard to achieve. It would also be better for us if we could be
together with you, there were even some attempts in that direction, but
unfortunately, they came to nothing. Still, we should continue to think about it.*

*Right now, we are living in Bytom, but eventually we intend to move to
Kraków. The difficulty lies in the huge over-population of Kraków with people
from all parts of Poland moving in and creating a shortage of housing and
making it hard to find a job. I'm staying in Bytom only because I have a good
position and decent lodgings. I already told you that I'm working at the
conservatory where I'm giving advanced courses in piano and a concert level
course. The director was planning my concert in Bytom and Katowice –
Beethoven piano concerto with orchestra, which he was going to conduct
himself, but he died unexpectedly. I've not had much experience with another
conductor, so I asked for a later date. Several members of the conservatory
proposed me for the post of director, but I declined since I can't see us staying
in Bytom for a very long time. Bearing in mind that my official profession will
not provide a reasonable income to shore up our finances, I signed a partnership
in Katowice with an individual who is in the business of manufacturing leather
articles. All this cannot dispel a deep depression and an urge to fly away
somewhere far. Our family is dispersed. Hela with her children live in Kraków,
Toldzio and Czesio got married, Janka Holl. also lives there, her husband and
youngest son were killed. Misio's family is decimated. He, Tadzio, Mieczek and*

Dzidek are all dead. Only Bolek is still alive. Uncle Maks and Jasio are dead. We know nothing of Władek's whereabouts. Paulina lives by herself in Tarnów, Ala and her husband are who knows where. Jasio's wife, son and daughter are in Bielsk. Our fortune is gone, the houses in Tarn, the villa in Lwów destroyed with all other belongings. This does not bother me greatly; it makes things easier. Now that you have this handful of news, I will end here and send you my love, Zbyszek 10 January 1946."

This letter described well the post-war drama that was not ours alone. Thousands of families from the *Kresy*, the Marches of Poland, the Eastern Borderlands ceded to the USSR by the Allies' Yalta agreement, had been similarly decimated and scattered across the country and beyond, and left without means. My uncle's business venture that he mentioned in his letter was paid for with the sale of my grandmother's large diamond brooch. Most of her beautiful jewellery that was left behind after she and mummy were arrested by the Soviets, had been hidden in a deep armchair, which was destroyed when our house was bombed. But that one gorgeous brooch in a velvet box remained in an attaché case in the basement where uncle kept all our documents and so it survived. My uncle, an aesthete and an erudite was no businessman and the money quickly evaporated in the hands of the supposed partner. Writing about his *profession* Uncle Zbyszek referred of course to his work as an attorney. In a country where the judiciary was now controlled by the communists, practicing law was not a viable option for him since there could have been no question of an independent judiciary. And yes, he would have preferred to live in Kraków, a town culturally and historically so closely linked to Lwów and to his youth, where the surviving members of our family had settled.

One week after my uncle's letter, my aunt wrote to my mother on 17 January, also through the mysterious courier. Auntie was a good deal more objective about me than my infatuated uncle. *"Zbyszek wrote about Ewunia in his letter sent early in January. For my part, I should only add that she is the sweetest creature, totally spoiled by Zbyszek for whom she is the whole world. He lets her get away with everything. My attempts to impose some discipline are useless. Incredible vitality and life energy. She looks forward to mummy's parcels, hoping that they will contain chocolates, oranges, and bananas. I tried to explain that these items can't be sent, but she insists that mummy could send them in a pocket of a coat."* The rest of the letter was devoted to the issue of what should be done next: our escape from Poland or my mother's return. *"A decision* *concerning Bożena's arrival [*mother's third name was Bożena*] is tough. Zbyszek and I differ on the subject. I feel decisively that we should stay put and that she should come here. Zbyszek is undecided, but leaning towards our leaving. The rest of the space on this sheet is for Ewunia who wants to show off her crooked handwriting. She is an extremely quick learner but writes like a chicken scratching in the sand.*" There were a few lines from me scribbled at the end of the letter in my bad handwriting: "*Dearest mummy, I received your letter for which I thank you very much. I'm waiting for the parcels you send us with so many wonderful things which you mention. I would like you and granny to come here. Kisses for you and granny, Ewa.*"

The dilemma posed in my aunt's letter – to remain abroad or return to Poland – was a drama faced by most Polish soldiers who fought in the Allied forces. By 1946 the army had not been demobilised yet, but it was expected that sooner or later it would be. On the one hand, there was the fear of persecution by the communist regime, arrests, deportations, and executions of members of the Home Army, the disbanded resistance force, which had already begun in earnest, and would also undoubtedly threaten the soldiers of the western army upon returning home. On the other hand, the fate of separated families and the lack of adequate professional preparation to function on foreign soil were significant factors. These considerations for and against weighed heavily on personal decisions taken and resulted in many tragedies that followed.

As for professional preparation, it would be another three years before the Polish University Abroad[101] would be created in London allowing countless men and women from the Polish armed forces to obtain their university degrees. One exception to this was the medical profession. Among the Polish military arriving in the United Kingdom from 1940 onwards, there was a significant number of doctors, professors, and students of medicine. While Poland's universities were being destroyed by the Nazis and the Russians and its intellectual elite decimated in concentration camps and the gulag, the Scots stepped in to help Polish soldiers to continue their studies, and the Polish School of Medicine at the University of Edinburgh was born. It operated from 1941 to 1949 and was the only official Polish institution of higher education in the world during the war years and beyond.

So, it was decided that for the time being, we would remain in Bytom. But because of the planned move to Kraków, it made little sense to enrol me in school

---

[101] PUC – *Polski Uniwersytet na Obczyznie* – started in 1949.

there. I spent my time playing with the single raggedy doll salvaged from our bombed house, reading fairy tales, and doing my lessons under my uncle's supervision. When the weather permitted, he and I would also take long strolls along Fałat Street, watching the carts roll by, filled with coal and hauled by Percherons, powerful horses with hairy legs. They looked enormous and I often dreamt that I was standing at the end of a long corridor and two Percherons were walking towards me. There was a wall behind me, I pressed my back against it, I had nowhere to escape, and the horses kept coming ever closer, filling the entire width of the narrow passage. Yet they always stopped a few paces away. I told my uncle about my dream. *"Those are very tame horses,"* he said, *"look how hard they work. For sure they would not hurt you."*

On our walks, we often passed a small patisserie, a little hole in the wall, where somehow, I always I managed to slow down. With a well-practiced manoeuvre, I would swing my uncle around so that we faced the display window. Uncle Zbyszek would weakly defend himself, but in the end, he always gave in: *"Alright,"* he would say, *"I'll buy you a pastry, but will you promise to finish your soup at home? Because if you don't auntie will be very mad at me."* Invariably I promised to eat my soup, and we would go in. Chocolate covered éclairs filled with cream were lined up on a tray and the elderly woman behind the counter smiled and waited, although she already knew what my choice would be. *"That one, please,"* I would point politely to the chocolate éclair. *"Well, then let's have two,"* Uncle Zbyszek would say sounding resigned, although he couldn't fool me, he was just as fond of cakes as I was. We would sit at a small round table by the window. *"You have chocolate on your nose,"* he would laugh handing me one of his large chequered handkerchiefs whenever I bit too deep into the cream. We would return home, slowly walking up the stairs, happy to share our secret misbehaviour.

The winter that year was extremely cold, our strolls became less frequent and time dragged on in expectation of nothing. Around three o'clock it was already dark. That one evening by the middle of January as we sat at supper, there was a discrete knock on our door. Uncle Zbyszek got up, walked to the door and through closed doors quietly asked who it was. *"Friends of Zofia,"* a male voice answered just as quietly. My uncle opened the door carefully before unhooking the chain. There were two people outside, a man and a woman, they had a large suitcase with them. As they entered, they turned around making sure there were no neighbours peeking out. *"We have a message from your sister,"* the woman whispered. Our flat filled with a thrill of expectation. Those were my guides, Adam Dydyński and Zofia Mścichowska. And thus began my unsuccessful escape to join my mother in London. The feverish preparations, coaching me in my new identity, the painful separation from my uncle and aunt, the train ride to Cieszyn/Těšín, the prison, the convent, the Czech family, and the return to Bytom two weeks later.

After that failed attempt, time crawled along in endless boredom and I became convinced that nothing could or would ever change. My mother's world, the bright rainbow tasting of raisins and Swiss chocolate which for a brief moment appeared to be within my grasp, dissolved into a grey funk of bitter disappointment. A week went by since my return from Cieszyn, then another, and another, without a word from my mother. I came to think that from that faraway world of hers she would never get in touch with us again. Maybe, I thought, she would find some other little girl to love and we would never meet. Daily life returned to its drab monotony, but now it was filled with a murky fear of the outside world. I was afraid of Soviet soldiers in their *chapkas* with red stars, afraid at night of steps on the street, afraid of security men with armbands called *Bezpieka.*[102] When my world was at its darkest and it seemed that fear and hopelessness would stay with us forever, my mother showed up at our door in Bytom, on Fałata Street at number 8.

"Do you know who that lady is who came here this afternoon?" My aunt had asked. *"Yes,"* I answered sullenly, *"she's an old friend of mummy."*

Aunt Hania shook her head. *"No,"* she said quietly, *"she is your mother."*

---

[102] *Bezpieka* – the abbreviation for *Urząd Bezpieczeństwa* – Office of Security, i.e. communist secret police.

Chapter XIV
Flight to Freedom

Events following my mother's unexpected appearance in our flat and my aunt's revelation remained like flashing pictures in my mind. I was eighteen months old when my mother was taken away by the Soviets, so I retained no image of her other than from the photographs my uncle showed me. For her, I was a new creation as well. After all, she wasn't with me when the caterpillar transformed into a butterfly. Yet our bonding was instantaneous from the word go and for that, I had my uncle to thank. Ever since I had the use of reason, Uncle Zbyszek kept my mother's presence alive in conversation, in passages read from her letters, in anecdotes from their shared childhood. Throughout the war, I grew aware that mother had been "taken away" by the Russians to "Siberia". And that now both she and granny were safe elsewhere.

I even knew that mother was serving in the Polish army, but that it was not the Berling army, though to me the difference wasn't clear. One was Polish but was British, the other was Polish but was Russian, whatever that meant. As soon as the war ended and the parcels marked UNRRA started arriving with cans of Portuguese sardines, tins of Swiss cocoa, raisins, almonds, things I had never tasted before, they carried my mother's imprint, lending her an exotic aura. My failed escape was followed by three long weeks of silence when it seemed that nothing could possibly change now. And suddenly mother was here.

Aunt Hania was still in shock, very pale, wiping her eyes every few minutes. She told mother about my ill-fated journey and assured her that she could safely speak in front of me. *"All that time in Czechoslovakia, Ayka never betrayed her name or any other information,"* she said tearfully over and over, and my sense of pride ballooned by the minute because I wanted mother to know how brave I was. Mother smiled. She already took off her coat and was sitting at the table in her khaki uniform. Aunt Hania stared at her in disbelief.

"Zosienko, why aren't you in civilian clothes?" She asked horrified.

"I had no time to change. Everything happened so fast." She expected Adam to bring us across the border to Germany. She was waiting for us in Meppen where the Polish First Armoured Division was stationed, the one that fought to liberate Holland. Its current commander was General Klemens Rudnicki whose wife, Wanda, was mother's schoolmate at the convent of the Sacred Heart in Lwów.

"I knew that Adam and Zofia reached you," she said. *"How did you know, mummy?"* I asked. She just smiled but did not answer.

Then suddenly the contact snapped. After two weeks she began searching for us in refugee camps for displaced persons, throughout West Germany. And then she received confusing news that something had occurred at the Czech border, but it was hard to get the details.

At that point, she found out that a group of intelligence people was going into Poland. She had twenty-four hours to make up her mind whether to join them and she decided to go. Wanda Rudnicka procured a civilian coat and cap, but there was no time to find anything else, so mother removed the insignia from her epaulettes and the "Poland" badge from her sleeves. In fact, as a staff officer, she was not allowed to take the risk of getting caught. Capture by the Russians or the Polish communist security without question would be trumpeted as an espionage affair, a show trial would follow, with either a death sentence or the Soviet gulag. General Rudnicki made it clear to her that she was on her own and that officially he knew nothing. Unofficially, mother promised him if caught not get taken alive, so at all times she carried a vial of potassium cyanide pills. Cruising through the army offices she found a fake identity card made out to one Krystyna Kobyłecka and took it as her only document with which she intended to cross the *green* border. Since she didn't want granny to worry needlessly through lack of news, she spent the remainder of that night writing post-dated letters, which Wanda was to mail every few days.

It was still winter and her thin coat was not really adequate for the bitter cold, her brown military shoes of thin leather, appropriate for London pavements, were hardly suitable for crossing the snow-covered Carpathian Mountains. Several nights spent in hideouts and dens, the dust and the dirt, brought on acute conjunctivitis that caused her eyes to ich and water.

As soon as the group crossed into Poland, they separated. Although my mother never divulged the trajectory of the route she followed, many years later by a strange coincidence, I received a note from a friend to whom once in a casual conversation I described mother's foray into communist Poland. Richard wrote,

"Dear Eva,

After hearing about your mother's courageous escapade, I remembered an incident that took place right after the war, which on reflection seems to me could have more than passing bearing on her story. It is about an encounter I had with two ladies in the locality of Karpacz Bierutowice [103] *in the Karkonosze Mountains, in the winter of 1946.*

Right after the war, between December 1945 and June 1946, I got a job with my father's help, at a vacation place in the Sudeten in Bierutowice, in the region of Jelenia Góra. The location is close to the Czech-Polish border, and to the Śnieżka Mountain where there was a lodge, at the time used both by Poles and Czechs. That was where I worked.

One evening, towards the end of February or at the beginning of March, I am not quite sure, it was already dark when two women showed up, one quite young, the other slightly older. They were dressed in a combination of civilian clothing, overcoats, I think, but underneath they wore what was then called 'Anders-style' uniforms, typical for people returning to Poland from the Polish army in Great Britain. They spoke fluent Polish and requested a room for the night and something to eat. The manager ordered the German staff (former owners of the hotel with whom we had good relations) to prepare the food and to give the ladies a room in the attic. I exchanged only a few words with them. By the time I got up early next morning they were gone and I never saw them again.

The night before one of them addressed the staff in fluent German, but between themselves, they spoke Polish, and I overheard the younger one asking: 'How will you reach your people?' The older one answered: 'I have contacts.' The following day in the afternoon the UB[104] *showed up at the lodge. They asked if two women had spent the night here. The manager answered that indeed they did come, but did not spend the night because she had refused to lodge them. Where they went from here – she did not know."*

---

[103] Karpacz is a town situated at the foot of Śnieżka Mountain in Karkonosze Mountains, through which the Czech-Polish border runs.
[104] Communist Security Police.

The crossing into Poland took nine days. On 2 March at dawn mother reached Kraków, and was overwhelmed by memories. Still, she controlled her emotions since she did not have the luxury of letting her guard down. Utmost caution was in order. She knew the town well and moved around with ease, but carefully. She was also very hungry. At that early hour, there were few people about, the streets were deserted and most eateries were closed, except for Jama Michalikowa, a truly Cracovian institution. It was one of the oldest *cafés* in Kraków that started as a typical hole-in-the-wall patisserie originally called Cukiernia Lwowska (Lwów Confiserie), in a single windowless room back in 1895. Not for nothing it was called Michalik's Den (Jama). It was located in the heart of town on Floriańska Street close to the Academy of Fine Arts and its owner, Jan Apolinary Michalik, had a soft spot in his heart for the famished artists; he used to invite the students to eat free of charge in exchange for their small works of art. The Kraków Academy produced some of Poland's finest painters.

This time they had no fresh rolls or buns, a somnolent waiter told my mother as she settled at one of the small tables, only four cream éclairs left from the day before. Zofia ordered all four and devoured them. The waiter was either too sleepy or too familiar with eccentric *habitués* of this unique den of Cracovian bohemia, to even care.

Next, she needed transportation. Trains didn't run regularly, so mother wandered around in search of information, but prospects were not good, she realised that she would not reach Bytom that day. By late afternoon, with too many police around, she needed to find a safe haven. A hotel would have been nice, but too risky because of raids by security services; still, there was the ancient church of St. Mary where sixteen years earlier she was married at the magnificent Veit Stoss altar, which was no longer there, having been dismantled by the Nazis during the war and shipped off to Germany.[105] Slipping into a confessional, my mother waited quietly for the custodian to lock the doors for the night. In that way she spent the first night in her beloved Kraków. The next day she found a lorry going to Bytom and arrived at our flat.

All this mother told us while we were waiting for Uncle Zbyszek to return home. But it was getting late, and over my vociferous protests I was packed off to bed, so I was not there to witness when sister and brother were reunited. When I woke up in the morning, not for a single moment did I doubt that my mother's

---

[105] It had been hidden in Bavaria, in the basement of the Nuremberg Castle. Recovered in 1946 and returned to Kraków.

appearance was real. I hopped out of bed and rushed into the living room in search of her. The previous evening's wonder continued, she was still there, sitting at the table in my aunt's dressing gown. She had bathed and was arranging her wet hair on little rolls. A pleasant scent pervaded the room and I traced it to a tiny bottle of eau-de-cologne labelled *lavender*. Everything about mother was different. The dainty mirror in a red leather case propped up on the table, her brown leather travelling bag that smelled of unfamiliar toiletries, the scented soap, her brown shoes with wide square heels now polished to a high gloss with paste from a metal box that said *Kiwi*. Her cigarette holder, long and slender, half silver, half black, unlike uncle's short amber one with a gold ring around the edge, sat next to a flat box with the word *Chesterfield* across the top. Her uniform was neatly folded on the chair. She was smiling as she watched me rummage through her belongings. She looked more rested than the night before, but her eyes were still bloodshot.

To my great distress, she was gone the next day before I got up and she kept up this routine throughout her two-week stay in Poland, coming and leaving unexpectedly every few days. When she was with us, I was glued to her and listened with my mouth open to her and uncle's conversation. They spoke of friends, of colleagues, of lawyers. They talked about my father. I couldn't have known then that mother was crisscrossing the country searching for any scrap of information about him. She moved around still in her British uniform under her thin overcoat, only changing her shirt each time she came home. She had two shirts and as soon as mother arrived, Aunt Hania washed and ironed the one she took off and hung it up ready for her next disappearance.

One day, on her way back from Kraków, mother nearly ran into trouble. She was travelling by lorry converted to a bus of sorts, popularly called an *autocar*. Passengers sat in the back on benches under a tarpaulin top, the weather was foul, and it was pouring rain. The *autocar* had left Kraków early that day and all mother needed to do to get on it was to pay the driver. No questions asked, no documents required. She only carried her small travelling bag, a bit too elegant perhaps for the times and for her own modest outfit, the beige coat and peaked cap. But then those days people travelled with whatever they could lay their hands on. Once she got on this bus-truck, she felt comfortable. No matter that the passengers were crushed inside like so many proverbial sardines in a can. Nobody spoke; all seemed absorbed in their own thoughts, relieved to be on the road, even though the traffic was heavy and at times barely crept along. Only when they had to give way to convoys of Soviet military vehicles, the mood in the *autocar* grew markedly dark and tense, with curses muttered through clenched teeth, but quietly. On the other hand, when they were stuck behind a horse-drawn cart loaded with wood, crawling at a snail's pace, except for a mild expletive or two, nobody grumbled as long as the lorry kept moving.

However, when they arrived in Katowice the driver pulled over in front of the railway station and without any preamble, informed the passengers that it was getting dark, indeed night had already fallen, that the roads were dangerous, bands of gangsters were roaming the countryside and no way, no, not even for more money, would he risk his lorry by going on to Bytom that same night. Tomorrow, he said. He stood by the cabin door, his feet firmly planted, legs astride, arms crossed, chin up in the air, and looked defiantly at the group of irate passengers. Take the train, he suggested ironically, shrugging his shoulders. He slammed shut the door and walked away. One of the male riders kicked a tire in frustration and spit in the direction of the driver's receding back. It was raining, the night was chilly, and a few street lanterns shed a half-hearted light on the wet pavement beyond the station. The group started to move away reluctantly, dispersing in search of accommodation for the night.

Mother weighed her options. She could remain on the street of course, not an attractive option. There was no church in sight where she could have sat out the night; all churches were locked by now anyway. A steady hum of voices drifted from inside the station, so she walked into the waiting area. It was brimming over with people. Even though it was cold, the stuffiness of the air was overwhelming. Not a good idea, she decided and walked out. The rain had turned heavier, the chill was penetrating, her coat and peaked woollen cap were getting soaked through. Looking up and down the street, a little way off in the feeble light of a lantern, she spied a hotel signboard and headed towards it. After hours of a bumpy ride on the hard bench in the truck, the prospect of a pillow sounded irresistible. Splashing through puddles, she reached the door of the hotel and walked into a small, dingy lobby, dimly lit. After a long and pregnant pause, a sullen clerk behind the counter, clearly unhappy with this intrusion, put away his newspaper and let her know that yes, a room was available. Mother said she would take it.

"Your document," he said curtly.

She dug into her bag furiously. After a long while, she looked up at him, sucking in her cheeks in dismay. *"Bother,"* she said, *"I left it at home."*

"Then you better get the permit from the militia, just down the street," he growled.

Zofia turned on her most winsome manner, *"Look here, it's pouring rain and I'm soaked through; couldn't I just get it in the morning?"*

He glared at her. Perhaps he should invite the militia here, he suggested viciously, and then she could deal with them on the spot, without going out.

Now she in turn looked at him angrily. *"Fine, I'll go,"* she said in the haughtiest manner she could muster. *"Just remember, if that room isn't available when I return, you'll be dealing with the militia..."* She left the threat hanging in the air as she stalked out, head high, and back erect. So much for the pillow.

She cast around for a shelter. No good staying out in the street, apart from the rain there were bound to be police patrols. She decided to go back to the railroad station and melt into the crowd. That little identity card that she carried wouldn't take her far with the security service, for sure. On the other hand, it could take her further than she cared to go. She smiled at the thought, as she recounted the incident to us the following day. Mother's dry sense of humour never left her.

Hundreds of people waited for the train, but there had been no train that day, or the day before, or two days before that. They just camped all over the place, in the waiting area and on the platforms, with children, bundles, and beat-up suitcases secured with string and leather belts, hoping against hope that someday the train would come. For the second time that evening, mother walked into the crowded station. Stepping over luggage, tripping over blankets and thermos flasks strewn around the floor, she surveyed the scene resembling a refugee encampment. These people had been waiting for a long time, for days perhaps. Children scurrying through the crowd, babies crying, the hum of voices that sounded like a beehive on the outside, now inside the building ballooned into a cacophony, reminding Zofia of crowded Mid-eastern bazaars. A woman with a small tin cup of milk or water secured from some secret source, struggled across the floor trying to reach her family in the corner where a hungry baby was yelling and an older child, wrapped in a blanket, was chewing on a piece of bread. The air was thick with cigarette smoke and a persistent sound of a hacking cough.

Mother's conjunctivitis bothered her, the dust whirling in the air increased the itching, her eyes began to smart badly, but still she resisted the urge to rub them for fear of further infection. Carefully, she took stock of the location. There were several doors leading out into the street and a railway clock in the middle of the hall towered over the crowd. It was hard to move, but she inched her way along the walls, step by step checking the entire perimeter until she spotted a small open space by one of the side doors. As soon as she reached it, she slid to the floor, leaned against the wall, pulled her knees up to her chin, tucked her travelling bag under her coat, and settled for the night. Across from her, the clock's face stared down impassively on the human anthill below.

Slowly the noise began to subside as people got ready for another night of waiting. Occasional raised voices, a baby's whimper, and a muffled caress, all that was simmering down. Should not sleep, should not sleep, mother repeated her mantra, but as hours ticked away, it got harder to keep the eyes open. She lit a cigarette, then another, watched the grey smoke curl in the air; she had not eaten since the morning, her mouth felt dry and the cigarette tasted bitter, so she rummaged in her bag for some caramel candies. It was going to be a long night until dawn. Even though the floor was hard and her legs felt cramped, it was difficult to fend off drowsiness while the rain kept up its steady patter against the tin roof of the building. The clock's hands moved slowly, from midnight to one, to two, the silence was disrupted from time to time by a harsh snoring or spasmodic coughing.

Zofia propped her head against the wall, her eyes wide open, vigilant, watching the hands of the clock as they crawled along. If only the damned thing would move faster, she thought. She felt foolish keeping this night watch when she could have snatched an hour's sleep. Perhaps she could just doze off for a bit after all? With a slight jerk, the hands of the clock jumped to three when all the doors of the waiting area burst open and a woman's scream, 'łapanka',[106] pierced the air. Militiamen rushed into the hall, machine guns in hand, and pushing through the crowd they positioned themselves along the walls, next to every door, except the one where mother was sitting. She scrambled to her feet like the rest of the startled people and in a flash, clutching her bag, slipped out through that unguarded door and flattened herself against the wall. The door slammed shut behind her, as did all the other in a series of sharp explosions.

A row of police vans stood lined up in front of the building, but surprisingly there were no guards. She waited, hardly daring to breathe, listening to the commotion inside, the yelling, and the screaming. The street was empty and dark, so dark in fact, that she could barely make out the outline of the *autocar* parked on the side of the station. Gliding along the wall, Zofia crept toward the

---

[106] Slang expression meaning a police raid or round-up.

shapeless hulk and keeping well within its shadow, circled it from the back. Then waited, straining her ears for signs of movement inside the truck. All was quiet. Gently lifting the edge of the cover, she hoisted herself inside; dropping to the floor she crawled under a bench and lay flat as she pushed her travelling bag against the tarpaulin. Then she carefully felt her breast pocket for the little vial of cyanide pills. She took it out, held it in her hand and lying motionless on the floor of the truck, she prayed silently not even moving her lips that she might not have to use them. Hail Mary, Mother of God, you too are a mother... please let me, please let me... She replaced the vial and pulled out Maks's watch, feeling the slim case in her palm and the short heavy chain with the gold square pendant. With the tip of her finger, she traced the monogram MH engraved on it. Zofia knew that if she sprung open the back cover of the case, she would find a small round photograph of a nine-year-old girl in a winter coat and hat. She slipped the watch back into her breast pocket and for a moment in the pitch darkness of the lorry, she imagined because surely it was just her imagination, that the round case was throbbing against her heart.

Inside the building, the uproar continued unabated for a long time. Doors were being ripped open, harsh voices barked commands, more scuffling and screaming, people were being led outside, boots thumped on the cobblestones, shots were fired, and finally all grew quiet as the vans drove off. By morning the rain had ceased and as the day dawned, pale sun-rays glistened on the wet pavement, peeking from behind the steel-grey clouds of the night before. While she waited for the driver of the *autocar* to resume the trip to Bytom, Zofia tightly wrapped her damp coat around her stiff and aching shoulders and allowed herself one wry reflection that it had been a very long night indeed.

From conversations I overheard between my mother and Uncle Zbyszek, I had already figured out that sometime soon we would be going away. I heard Uncle Zbyszek assuring her that he and Aunt Hania were ready to come with her. As the packing commenced there was no end to wrangling over what went, what was to be left behind? Mother insisted that we must pack as little as possible, I wanted all my toys, my aunt said, *"we'll take them,"* but mother was adamant and unsentimental and categorically said *"no"*. After a tug-of-war and abundant tears, finally, she agreed to my rag doll, my teddy bear, the small bulldog, and books of which she wholeheartedly approved. A major problem arose over the family silver. Since the bombing of our house in Lwów, my grandparents' solid silver tableware had been travelling with us in a large, battered suitcase, all twenty-five kilos of it.

"We can't take it like this," mother objected. *"We need a small sturdy suitcase."*

Uncle Zbyszek said we didn't have a small sturdy suitcase. Well, we need to get one, she decreed. She was very resourceful. After a few days on a return trip from Kraków, she presented her brother with a neat little green case reinforced with wooden straps. Uncle Zbyszek was amazed. He wanted to know where she found it. She happened to be on a streetcar in Kraków when she overheard two men exchanging the address of a luggage maker. She took note of it, got off the tram, sought out the house. Crossing a dingy inner courtyard, and going up a dark staircase to the second floor, Zofia found the flat and knocked. A man opened cautiously, looking out to see if there was nobody else behind her; then he invited her in and confirmed that he made luggage and could have a small suitcase ready for the next day. *"Would madame wish to have it with a double bottom?"* He asked helpfully. Madame assured him that a single bottom suitcase was all she needed.

Throughout all this time, while in Bytom mother moved around with great caution. Each time she left our flat, Uncle Zbyszek or Aunt Hania would check the landing and the stairs to make sure all was clear, meanwhile, I was being kept away from people, above all from our inquisitive neighbour Mrs B. I overheard my aunt telling her that I was sick and had to stay indoors. Bad cold, she said and she wouldn't want Mrs B to catch it. At home the mood was tense, everyone jumped at the sound of footsteps on the staircase, and when the doorbell rang mother instantly disappeared into the other room, where our packed suitcases sat under the bed. The date of departure was set and then abruptly aborted at the last moment, which added to the stress. Then early one morning without further warning mother announced that she and I were leaving for Kraków immediately and Uncle Zbyszek and Aunt Hania were to follow the next day.

It was Saturday, 16 March 1946. Uncle took us to the station with our one suitcase, we took the train and by midday, we reached Kraków. It was not very far from the train station to our destination on Franciszkańska Street at number 3. Mother did not tell me that we were to stay in the archbishop's palace, but since I didn't know what an archbishop was, it didn't matter anyway. We entered the courtyard and were met by an elderly woman who greeted my mother warmly, as if she already knew her, and smiled and patted me on the head. She took us to a small room and returned after a while with coffee for mother, milk for me, and some rolls. We dropped off our suitcase and mother's bag and went out, heading straight for the gothic Basilica of St. Mary on Market Square. The church was dark and slightly forbidding. Mother told me that she and my father were married there.

"Not in Lwów?" I was surprised. She smiled.

"No. There were too many suitors that I turned down, so getting married in Kraków made more sense. I came with your daddy, grandpapa and granny, Uncle Zbyszek, your Aunt Lusia and Uncle Lolo, and a few other people. Fourteen in all. And we were married at the Wit Stwosz altar, the triptych," she explained as she looked wistfully down the nave towards the empty space where the altar was no more. At times mother was forgetting that at eight – well seven and a half really – I would have had no idea what a triptych was. But I was not that interested in the altar; I was thinking of Cinderella and how she was dressed for the ball.

"Did you wear a long white dress with a veil, mummy?" I asked.

Mother smiled. *"No, darling. I wore a cream-coloured suit and a hat with a birdcage veil."* That sounded disappointing.

"What's a birdcage veil?" I still wanted to know.

"It's a short veil that just covers part of your face."

I was unimpressed.

"When I get married, I want a long dress, like Cinderella's" I declared.

From the Basilica, we walked over to a large low building surrounded by a covered gallery, that took up a good chunk of the huge Market Square. Mother told me that long ago it was a hall where merchants traded cloth, which was why it was called *Drapers' Hall.*[107] Now there were little shops all around the arcade. Since the next day was uncle's names-day – Zbigniew – mother bought him a tie as a present. Then we visited a bookshop and she picked out several books in Polish, some beautifully illustrated like *Tales of a Thousand and One Nights.* Also, *Heart* by Edmondo de Amicis, *Little Lord Fauntleroy* by Frances Burnett, *In Desert and Wilderness*, the story of Staś and Nell, two children lost in Africa, by Henryk Sienkiewicz, all of them that she and uncle had read as children. And

---

[107] *Sukiennice.* Cloth Hall or Drapers' Hall. Renaissance building surrounded by arches supported by a colonnade of slim pillars, where merchants met to do business, trade spices, silks, and other exotic imports from the East and textiles, armour, tools from the West, and more particularly salt from Poland's Wieliczka salt mines.

another one that mother said would tell me all about Wit Stwosz's altar. I couldn't wait to start on them. Up to that time, the only books I read were fairy tales. This nineteenth century children's literature acquired by my mother in the Drapers' Hall on the eve of our forever exile, would shape my romantic idealism for years to come.

Loaded with our errands we returned to the archbishop's palace. In the meantime, while we were away, a huge crowd had gathered in front of the building and just as we approached a black car pulled up to the gate. The Archbishop Metropolitan of Kraków, Prince Adam Stefan Sapieha, was returning from Rome where he was made cardinal by Pope Pius XII. As he stepped out of the car, the crowd broke into applause and cheers. *"Take a good look at him,"* mother whispered, *"This is a very great man."* She didn't explain why.

We spent the rest of that day cooped up in our small room. The next day, Sunday, 17 March, Uncle Zbyszek and Aunt Hania arrived with the rest of our luggage, including the notorious small green suitcase. In the afternoon we took a short walk across town, it was mother's and uncle's farewell to Kraków, forever. Then we returned to our lair in the archbishop's palace and waited, and waited, and waited. Our guardian angel brought us tea, once, twice, three times. I grew tired of milk and cookies and of fairy tales that I was told to read. By now I knew them by heart, but the tantalising new collection was packed away and out of reach. Our suitcases stood by the door as if on the ready to sprint by themselves. Nobody told me to take a nap, which was fine by me, because I hated going to bed early. I had already decided to become an astronomer when I grew up, so that I could spend the nights watching the stars.

Few words were being spoken by the adults, Aunt Hania, very pale and drawn, sat on the edge of the bed; mother and uncle reached for cigarettes, one after another. I sensed the nervous tension between the adults, and had I been able to define it, I would surely have said that the air in the room crackled with electric discharge, or perhaps as in the expectation of rolling thunder after a flash of lightning. At my age, this translated into fidgety restlessness and a growing feeling that "something" was bound to happen at any moment. That moment was long in coming. It was already dark outside when we heard a discreet knock and a man in a leather jacket stood in the door. He turned to my mother:

"Ma'am, we are getting ready to start boarding."

"My brother, Doctor Neuhoff and my sister-in-law," mother said, introducing my uncle and aunt.

The man acknowledged them with a quick nod without shaking hands and disappeared. He was a man in a hurry. Nobody paid attention to me. We put on our overcoats, the adults picked up the suitcases, I was nudged to walk ahead of them, and we stepped out into the courtyard where two lorries were faintly visible in the dark, and a jeep beside to them.[108] People were milling about in silence like so many shades; occasionally a flashlight flickered and was turned off promptly. Somebody embraced me from behind and I recognised Zofia Mścichowska and Mr Adam, but mother placed her finger on my lips. Two men helped Aunt Hania into one of the lorries, then they hoisted me inside, my uncle and mother got in last. There were already a few indistinguishable figures under the tarpaulin. Uncle Zbyszek said to mother that I should sit close to the side: *"Ayka frequently feels sick on the tram,"* he warned her. I was shoved right into the back, against the driver's cabin. *"Just raise the edge of the tarpaulin if you feel like throwing up,"* uncle advised, matter-of-factly. It must have sounded a bit unsettling to our fellow travellers, I imagine.

Finally, we heard the motors revving up one after the other, the hinges of the portal squeaked as it swung open. *"It's eleven o'clock,"* Uncle Zbyszek noted quietly. The convoy moved out of the gate, the jeep leading the way. From the silence in our truck, it would have been hard to guess that fifteen or so people were crammed inside. Barely raising the edge of the tarpaulin, through the crack I watched the grey façades of the houses sliding by, there were still lights in the windows here and there. Several hours later we reached Prague and there were tense moments when we came upon a police patrol that gave us chase. Shots were fired, our trucks raced down the cobbled streets, wobbling as they took sharp turns. I whispered to my mother that the Czechs might recognise me if they caught us, but she said not to worry, we were on a different road. Finally, we shook the patrol off our tail, got out of town and headed for the German border.

Our escape route must have been well planned, the border crossings prepared beforehand because without delay we got through the first one and by morning we were in the mountains of East Germany. We came to our first rest stop in a wood clearing. Before I could wiggle to the edge of the platform, there were

---

[108] UNRRA lorries, returning "empty" to western Europe after delivering the relief cargo, frequently transported legitimately repatriated French or other prisoners-of-war or, as in our case, escapees from Soviet-dominated Poland.

plenty of people already on the ground, stretching their backs, bending their knees and arms. Others sat on fallen logs lighting cigarettes. For the first time, we saw each other in broad daylight. Some thirty-odd people, including a few kids.

Mother took me into the bushes for a pee. When we returned to join Uncle Zbyszek and Aunt Hania, we were approached by two ladies whom my mother introduced as the wife and daughter of Colonel Kosiba, a colleague of hers. She had promised to take them along with us, but when she met Mrs Kosiba who was quite elderly, she wasn't quite sure that it was a good idea. A risky trip could be too much for her, she worried. But she underrated the lady's spunk.

"To join my Adaś," Mrs Kosiba had cried out, *"I am ready any time!"* And here she was, true to her words, serene and smiling after the nightlong trek as if she were on a pleasure trip.

Even though it was chilly, we relished the crisp air. Our drivers milled around, doling out biscuits and pouring tea from thermos flasks into tin cups. I wandered away from our little group to the edge of the clearing and looked back on the road behind us. For the first time in my life, I saw mountains and a winding silver ribbon of the serpentine road down which we came.

Back in the trucks, we were ready to roll again, when the other lorry developed engine trouble. Two men from our crew drove off in the jeep in search of a blacksmith to fix the broken part. The rest of us stayed in the woods. It was cold but sunny and eerily quiet all around, but even so, people spoke in low voices, and children were kept hidden in the undergrowth. Every few minutes somebody sauntered over to the edge of the clearing peering down the road, checking for approaching vehicles, hoping to catch sight of our returning jeep. I overheard one worried man whispering that we were really exposed because we had no documents; the jeep took them, he said. Several hours went by, the tension was mounting, people grew increasingly fidgety and nervous wondering whether something bad may have happened. Finally, the jeep reappeared, the drivers quickly repaired the ailing truck and we were off. Another night on the road without incident, but towards the morning the ill-fated lorry broke down again. This time there was no attempt to repair. It was simply tethered to our truck with a heavy rope and we proceeded slowly, hauling it along. We arrived at the east-west German border mid-afternoon, with an eight-hour delay, which in the end proved providential. The crew found out that throughout the night a flying search patrol had been lying in wait for us at this crossing, but finally gave up and left two hours before we got there.

We drove into the Allied-occupied zone. Our last stop was a bombed, devastated Nuremberg. Mounds of debris, jagged skeletons of churches, burnt out houses; the air was saturated with a foul stench of rot. Uncle Zbyszek muttered to my mother that there must be hundreds of corpses in these ruins. We reached the outskirts and the convoy stopped at a low building. After hours in the dark, the evening light hurt my eyes. We were ushered inside and the kids were told to line up for food. There were more children already queuing up; perhaps it was a Red Cross feeding post. At the end of the corridor, a woman was dishing out rice with milk from a sizeable pot that stood on a table. She popped a spoonful straight into each child's mouth. The queue was long and by the time I got to it the pot was empty. I felt horribly cheated as I stared at it, my chin beginning to shake, my mouth bent into a little horseshoe, but before serious tears started to flow my mother rushed up and dragged me away by the arm. She really didn't want me to have milk and rice with this communal spoon. I got biscuits and a cup of warm milk instead and we spent the night on bunk beds.

The next day one more unforeseen disruption: we pulled off the road when a woman from the jinxed truck developed a panic attack. She was carried out and stretched on the grass, a crew member administered drops of Valerian. It was another chance for the rest of us to get out and stretch our legs. Finally, by mid-afternoon, we reached the base of the Polish First Armoured Division[109]. After four days and four nights, our flight to freedom was over. The convoy rolled onto the premises of the army camp and we were instantly surrounded by a crowd in uniforms. An officer in a black beret ran up to our truck just as my mother jumped off, grabbed her, and lifted her up. Captain Jazdowski, who organised her foray into Poland, was visibly moved to see her safely back. Wanda Rudnicka, my mother's childhood friend, was also on hand to greet us. She and Uncle Zbyszek had worked together in the Pol.K.O.in Lwów under the Nazi occupation.

The next day we had breakfast in the officers' mess. Mother's uniform had been cleaned and pressed during the night; she was impeccably dressed, the rank

---

[109] The Polish 1st Armoured Division of the Polish Armed Forces in the West. Created in February 1942 at Duns, Scotland, it was commanded by Major General Stanisław Maczek. The division served in the final phases of the Battle of Normandy and the Battle of Chambois, then fought throughout the campaign in Northern Europe, as part of the First Canadian Army.

insignia, two stars, and two stripes were back in place together with the badge *Poland* sewn back onto her sleeves. One of the officers snapped us a picture.

March 1946. Meppen. Our first breakfast in the officers' mess

As we were finishing our breakfast, mother took a round fruit out of a box that was standing on a chair and handed it to me. I had no idea what it was. *"It's an orange,"* she explained. *"There is a whole box of them just for you from Italy from my friend Bronka."* My first ever exotic fruit. Since I had no idea how to eat it, mother peeled it for me; inside it was raspberry coloured. While we were still at the table, Captain Jazdowski showed up with his little spaniel and wanted to know if I slept well. *"I hope you and Jeep will be great friends,"* he said introducing his dog. I noticed that the badge on his uniform was different from my mother's; it was shaped like a wing, in black and orange. He caught my roving eye. *"Our insignia are hussar wings,"* he said with a smile. I had no idea what that meant, so I just nodded knowingly.

Many years later, when I immersed myself in Henryk Sienkiewicz's historic novels, The Trilogy, [110] I would meet the hussars, the elite Polish cavalry present on every battlefield since the sixteenth century, as they charged into battle with

---

[110] Trylogia, The Trilogy, by Henryk Sienkiewicz, published 1884-1888, three novels on wars fought by Poland during the 17th century: the Cossack rebellion, the Swedish invasion of Poland, and the war between Poland and the Ottoman Empire. The author's intent behind this work was to boost the morale of Poles in their partitioned land.

immense wings attached to their helmets. The wings made of sturdy feathers gave a swooshing sound that sowed panic in enemy ranks. Reading the novel, I remembered the winged insignia on Captain Jazdowski's sleeve. Perhaps these twentieth-century Polish hussars also needed their wings as they were charging on tanks into the murderous battles liberating Ypres, Ghent, and Breda?

Emblem of the Polish 1st Armoured Division

That evening at dinner in the officers' mess, Uncle Zbyszek met another colleague, a civil court judge from Lwów. Familiar faces appeared in our new expatriate existence making this unknown world less strange and forbidding. Mother found us a room in Meppen in the house of a German family, and two days later she left for London. We were now under the care of the army. Captain Jazdowski devoted a great deal of time to us as did Wanda Rudnicka. Her husband General Klemens Rudnicki, now commander of the First Armoured Division, was another one lucky enough to have gotten out of Russia alive. After the German invasion in September 1939, as a colonel while organising underground resistance in Lwów, he was caught by the NKVD and imprisoned in Moscow. After the amnesty he joined General Anders's troops, as did Colonel Okulicki, Bronka Wysłouchowa, and my mother. This new world into which I was about to enter, was indeed a world of survivors.

In the British-occupied sector of Germany, the area assigned to the Polish troops covered almost six and a half thousand square kilometres in the valley of the River Ems and included the towns of Hummling, Lingen, and Meppen, and the counties of Bentheim, Cloppenburg, and Bersenbrück. At the time, Bersenbrück was home to the Polish Parachute Brigade where we were welcomed by Zofia Mścichowska, my erstwhile guide and fellow jailbird from Tešin. The First Armoured Division's headquarters were located in the small town of Haren, renamed Maczków by the troops, in honour of their former commander, General Stanisław Maczek, who led them into battle for the liberation of Holland.[111] In Maczków, the streets had been given Polish names and the most galling to the German population must have been the one named after the Home Army, Armia Krajowa (AK), that launched the bloody Warsaw uprising in August of 1944.

Fulfilling his promise to my mother that he would take good care of us, Captain Jazdowski frequently took us for long drives in his jeep, touring the countryside, always in the company of his spaniel, Jeep.

Ewa with Jeep the spaniel

---

[111] 101 General Stanisław Maczek led the First Armoured Division in the victorious Battle of Falaise and later was the liberator of Ypres, Oostnieuwkerke, Roeselare, Tielt, Ruislede and Ghent in Belgium and Breda in The Netherlands. After the war for the remainder of his life he lived in Edinburgh.

Among many war sites around Meppen, we visited the Krupp experimental fields. Scattered over a large area, like a fortress in ruins, huge jagged iron structures with massively thick walls, lay perforated or destroyed by cannon-balls from the howitzers that still stood there. It was a lunar landscape, an image of a shattered power. Captain Jazdowski snapped pictures of me with Jeep sitting in the barrel of the cannon and me poking my head through the hole in the iron wall blown out by that same cannon.

Peering through the wall on Krupp experimental fields.

There were several people among the military on the base, with whom we became very friendly, and among them two sisters: Marta and Monika Jeżewski, Polish ATS officers. The older Marta wore heavy black-rimmed glasses, spoke little, and was very serious. Her sister Monika was a petite, delightful person full of laughter, who spoiled me to perfection.

On Easter Sunday, our German landlords organised an Easter egg hunt for their children and as a matter of courtesy invited me to join. For obvious reasons, we did not socialise with the Germans so this created an awkward dilemma for Uncle Zbyszek, but since it was children who were involved, he reluctantly agreed. This tradition did not exist in Poland. The German kids congregated in the garden, ran around peering under bushes, it was a strange custom for me. I trailed behind them, without any clue as to what they were saying and where I was supposed to look. Since I didn't find any eggs I went off on my own. Just then I was going through a phase of collecting bits of coloured glass; now burrowing in a flowerbed under our window I found a pretty deep-blue piece. It was a small consolation. I already had a whole box of green, yellow, and red fragments, but no blue. I happily showed it to auntie and Uncle Zbyszek who examined it carefully.

"Where did you find it?" He sounded intrigued. He took out a small magnifying glass that he always carried with him and examined the prize.

"In the flower bed under the window." This was no ordinary glass, he told me. It was a sapphire with what appeared to be a Polish coat-of-arms engraved on it. How did this lovely stone from a signet ring end up in the modest garden of a small German town, buried so close to the surface too? War loot or the price of a piece of bread, perhaps?

We waited for my mother to arrange our entry into Great Britain, but it was slow. In a letter dated 11 May 1946, Uncle Zbyszek discussed the matter of our departure and the difficulties this presented: *"We received your letter dated 4 May and are glad that things concerning our departure from Meppen are moving along. Yesterday Wanda Rudnicka came to see us and said that transport by car to Belgium would be difficult at this time. According to the latest orders, only military personnel on active duty can travel, which means no P.W.X., and even that with special permission from the local British authorities. Wanda thinks that it will be possible to go by train, also with permission, though I don't know who's... We bought new shoes for Ayka; the other pair was falling apart. They cost 7 dollars. I hope the price is not too steep, they would probably cost more in London, and they are really of excellent quality... The last transport from Poland arrived safely, but Adam Dydyński's sister did not come due to illness. The poor man lost all the money."*

Correspondence between mother, uncle, and auntie spoke volumes of everyday problems that ordinary people faced in these early post-war years. From London my mother sent us pyjamas, shirts for Uncle Zbyszek, and cigarettes. In one letter Aunt Hania asked her for some fabric to make sandals for me, *"...sandals for Ewa are necessary, because her old shoes are in shreds, and I don't want her to wear the new ones for every day... Wanda Rudnicka will show me how to make them."* Bronka Wysłouchowa kept sending boxes of oranges from Italy.

It was now certain that I would be going to England, but Uncle Zbyszek and Aunt Hania were unsure what to do with themselves. They thought they might settle in Belgium perhaps. Aunt Hania wrote: *"Borysiewicz, who is presently in Meppen, made contact for us in Belgium. He talks of opportunities in watch and clock repair, as the first option, music as second, and photography as third..."* then she added, *"it is very hard for Zbyszek to practice. The room with the piano is often occupied by the owners' children who do their lessons there, besides, the piano though new is not well-tuned, so it's hard to play it."* For my uncle, an erudite and an intellectual par excellence, choices were dismal in his expatriate existence. Watch and clock repair? Music teacher? With no money, no contacts, not even a piano to call his own. On foreign soil, there would be no question of practicing law.

In the meantime, my life in Meppen was blooming. In another letter to my mother, auntie wrote: *"Ewunia is healthy, looks lovely, has a good appetite, and is in her usual excellent mood. She is all the [military] ladies' pet. They take her out in the car, to the cinema, for walks, and ply her with sweets and fruit."* Aunt Hania worried about my schooling; I should have been going to third grade by now as well as preparing for my first Communion. I, on my part, assured my mother and granny in letters that *"every day I am learning to read, write, and count and I took already two lessons of catechism with a priest to prepare me for First Holy Communion."*

Finally, by the end of May, it was settled: we would be going to Brussels by train. Uncle Zbyszek and Aunt Hania received regular military uniforms and appropriate documents. We said a tearful goodbye to our friends: Marta and Monika, Captain Jazdowski and his spaniel Jeep, Wanda Rudnicka, and so many others who showed us so much kindness during our stay in Meppen.

Goodbye to our frends. Auntie and Uncle Zbyszek in uniform

A military jeep drove us to the station with our luggage and we boarded the train. Auntie and I had a sleeping compartment with bunk beds; we had the suitcases with us, except the green case with the family silver, which my uncle took with him into a different car where he got a seat. Around midnight, we were already fast asleep when we were woken by Uncle Zbyszek. The train was standing at a station. *"Haniu,"* he whispered hoarsely, *"here is the silver. They are throwing me off the train. You go on to Brussels with Ayka."*

"Good God, what happened?" My aunt panicked, but uncle had no time for explanations. Two uniformed men, visible in the dark by their white helmets and white belts, stood in the door to our compartment, waiting to escort him out. He left, they closed the door, and after a while, the train moved on. We were going off, my aunt and I, alone into the unknown. Aunt Hania, who spoke no English and little French, was a bundle of nerves. There was no more sleeping that night.

In Brussels, a conductor helped us off the train with our luggage, and like two lost sheep we stood there not sure which way to turn when miraculously Uncle Zbyszek appeared walking towards us from the other end of the platform. He told us that during the night two American Military Police were checking documents and for some reason, they didn't like his. Perhaps his German surname made him a suspect and they took him for a German fleeing with false identity papers? Whatever it was they didn't bother to check any further, just unceremoniously threw him off the train. He barely managed to bring over the case with the silver. A German train conductor witnessed this and approached him. Uncle Zbyszek explained his dilemma. The conductor, who also probably took him for a German, assured him that he would get him back on the train and before it started to roll, quickly led my uncle to another car. It was dark inside, Uncle Zbyszek stumbled across a long hard bench, found a seat, and so spent the night. *"I even dozed off for a bit, and just imagine how I felt when at dawn I saw these two huge Yanks who threw me off the train, sprawled on a bench right across from me. They were fast asleep. I just pulled my hat down as far over my eyes as I could and pretended to be also sleeping."*

We took a taxi to the hotel in the centre of Brussels which mother had reserved for us. The next day my grandmother arrived from London. She was calm but it must have been a huge strain on her; it was hard not to shed tears after six years of separation from her son and daughter-in-law, and the granddaughter quite changed from the last time she saw her. We had two rooms, I shared granny's. It was a glorious sunny June day, the streets were crowded, flower vendors and fruit stalls everywhere, with carts brimming with cherries. Flowers sold on the street were a delightful novelty, until now there were no flowers in our drab lives. Brussels emerged as a colourful and prosperous world. An escalator in a large department store, which we took up to the restaurant, was the ultimate word in luxury. And I had never eaten in a proper restaurant before.

Each day granny went to the British consulate to get our documents processed for travel to England, but it was an uphill battle. The Brits didn't want more foreigners coming to their island. After two unsuccessful weeks, granny returned to London and my mother arrived, in uniform, or as Uncle Zbyszek jokingly noted, in full regalia. The British consul quickly inscribed me into her travel document, but an entry visa for my uncle and aunt was delayed. We had to part now, I to England with my mother, and they to Italy with the Polish Second Corps. Another tearing apart, for them and for me.

Chapter XV
It's London. June 1946

From Brussels to Calais by train, and from there by ferry to Dover. Normally a rough crossing through the English Channel, or La Manche for the French, this time it was nice and calm. I stood next to my mother at the railing and from a distance, I saw the white cliffs of Dover. Mother and granny no longer lived in a boarding house on Belgrave Road; they had a flat in Barons Court. Several other Polish officers had flats in the same building on Barons Court Road; General Bór-Komorowski lived one floor below us with his wife. To shore up her finances, mother sublet one room to Colonel Porwit and his son Christopher. They were just another one of these families torn apart by the war since Mr Porwit's wife was in Poland and he was struggling with the decision whether to return to communist Poland; every evening there were lengthy conversations with mother and granny on that score. Should he and Christopher go back? By now it was almost impossible to smuggle anyone out of Poland. Shortly after our escape, another transport was caught and people were jailed, including its principal organiser, a man known as the *White Captain.*[112]

At home, upon our arrival, I found a package from my mother's friend, Bronka Wysłouchowa: she sent me a small reproduction of a painting by Pierre Mignard, the "Virgin of the Grapes," and a beautiful doll, wrapped in tissue and cotton wool in a blue box with white daisies. The doll, epitome of luxury, wore an organdie dress, had real hair and eyelashes, and fluttered her eyelids. But my greatest treasure was a teddy bear from my mother. After she arrived in London from Cairo, mother became familiar with English children's literature, rich in humorous stories of quaint animals: bears and pigs, mice and donkeys. She

---

[112] Stefan Rybicki – Biały Kapitan. Known by that *nom de guerre* because of his light-coloured uniform of the French Foreign Legion where he served before and during WWII.

delighted in these stories, the *Wind in the Willow*, *Alice in Wonderland*, and above all in A.A. Milne's *Winnie the Pooh*. In her wallet, she carried a little cut-out from a newspaper of a skipping boy and his bear – Christopher Robin and Pooh. When chances of our ever getting together looked grim, the little picture acquired a symbolic meaning, but when our reunion became a reality, as soon as she safely returned to London from her foray into Poland, a yellow teddy bear was purchased and sat on the bed awaiting my arrival.

Mother's office in the Polish army's headquarters was located in the Rubens Hotel in the vicinity of Buckingham Palace. Eventually, she took me there to introduce me to her fellow officers and to her superior Colonel Maria Leśniak, whose deputy she was. I was delighted with the place, and I grew fascinated with the women's uniforms and insignia.

General staff headquarters in the Rubens Hotel.

Mother shared her room with Major Maria Trojanowska, who also got out of Russia thanks to the amnesty. Before the war, Mrs Trojanowska was an instructor of military reserve training for women, and when the war broke out, she joined the underground resistance movement, became a courier and emissary; in Lwów, organised the escape routes for soldiers through Romania and Hungary, who then went on to France and Britain to join the Allies. Her codename during those early months of the war was "Rysia" and it stuck, so everybody continued to call her that. Major Rysia Trojanowska. She was smuggling General Karasiewicz-Tokarzewski out of Lwów when a Soviet patrol grabbed her. The Russians accused her of spying and she was sent to the gulag. In the process she lost a finger and wore a black glove on one hand.

Over the next few months, I got to meet other officers, some were mother's particular friends: there was Kazia Jaworska – a small, energetic, very athletic and unpretentious woman – who commanded a training camp in Palestine; and Lilka Korzeniowska – a company commander and a very pretty woman – who gave me my first ever necklace of beautiful coral beads. But without a question my mother's closest friend whom she deeply admired and trusted, was Bronisława Wysłouchowa.

At the time when I met all these women at the staff headquarters, I could not have understood that these smartly uniformed ladies, like my own mother, calm, self-possessed, operating in the civilised environment of the Rubens Hotel, had suffered huge personal losses, survived the deprivations of the Russian hell, and throughout had managed to preserve their dignity and moral fibre in the face of tragedy with courage and oftentimes with superhuman willpower.

With colleagues at general headquarters

By this time in London, the mood among Poles was becoming dark. On 8 June 1946, London celebrated the end of the war over Nazi Germany with a huge victory parade. Fireworks at night, a military parade in the daytime. All the Allies of Great Britain took part: Australians, Belgians, Czechs, French, Greeks, Dutch, Luxembourgers, and of course Americans, except, shockingly, the Poles. Churchill and Roosevelt buckled under Stalin's pressure – he was still their ally – and gave in to his demand to exclude Polish troops from the triumphal march.

Stalin had already gotten hold of Poland. English public opinion was outraged and the British government trying to save face, issued the last-minute invitations to twenty-five pilots from the famous Squadron 303 that as part of RAF fought in the Battle of Britain. They were asked to march with the Royal Air Force. Also invited to take part in the parade were General Stanisław Kopański, commander of the Independent Carpathian Riflemen Brigade from Tobruk, Gazala, and Monte Cassino as well other Polish commanders of the air force, navy, and army. All the invitations were declined. All or none was the answer.

Bitterness already felt by Poles for the betrayal in the Yalta agreement between Stalin, Roosevelt, and Churchill that left Poland under Soviet control, now built up further. The war had ended for the British, the Belgians, the Dutch, and the French, but not for Poles. They had a foretaste a year earlier when on 7 May 1945 Germany capitulated, and throughout half of Europe blackout window covers dropped and lights blazed across Britain and France, Holland and Belgium, and crowds danced on plazas and squares, but the other half of Europe remained in darkness. In his poem, *Concert at Victoria Station,* Poet Jan Rostworowski captured the mood:

We became complicated,
We became cantankerous,
In the hub of the world,
On Piccadilly Circus.
I well remember that evening,
As it brushed the lamps with its hair,
I cannot recall the month,
I cannot remember the year,
But the black shrouds dropped from the windows,
And the lamps stood full of light,
And the trees rose up, like bells,
And the sky spread a velvety night.
And shop windows blazed with brightness,
And the stalls selling sweet syrups,
And the moon shed its silvery radiance
On the dancing girls and their sailors.
It was from that very moment
(and the square has long since emptied)
That we became cantankerous,
That we became complicated.[113]

These were heady post-war days in London, streets were teeming with troops of every stripe, smartly uniformed men and women saluted each other as they passed, so formally, so courteously. I was enthralled. Without realising it, I was drawing comparisons with what I had seen a mere few months earlier. That other

---

[113] Jan Rostworowski. *Poezje. 1958-1960.* p. 26. London. Publisher Wydawnictwo "Wiadomości". 1963. From *Concertt at Victoria Station.* Translated from Polish by Eva Hoffman Jedruch.

world now so far away, was fast disappearing behind the Iron Curtain.[114] But I still remembered it, the streets cordoned off, the infamous UB – *Bezpieka* – lurking everywhere, people talking in whispers, and the fear of strange steps on the landing. Though the Germans were gone and the war was over, the Russians were there, drunken Soviet soldiers in round caps with red stars harassing pedestrians, robbing watches at gunpoint, their women loud and coarse in shoddy uniforms strutting around in red socks and on high heels with messy long hair falling across their shoulders.

Mother wore her uniform every day even when she took me for a stroll in the park. London had so many beautiful parks and each was different; in Hyde Park, there were speakers who stood on orange crates, soapboxes, or whatever else and made speeches lambasting the government and ridiculing politicians. Mother told me that in England people could say whatever they wanted, out loud, as long as they didn't cause violence and respected the king. Remembering how we had to whisper our thoughts back in Poland I asked:

"Not even if they speak badly of the police?"

"Not even then." Well, that was a surprise.

And here mother quoted something she called a ruling by a judge who said that in England everybody had a right to their opinion, even those who were annoying, irritating, odd, and a general nuisance. I found it amazing.

"Then why couldn't people in Poland say whatever they wanted?" I insisted.

"Because they are not free." My first lesson on western democracy.

Over time I got to know most parks in London: Kensington, close to Hyde Park and Regent's Park with a rose garden where one could sit on a bench, or watch the swans from a small wooden bridge. But best of all was Kew Gardens, full of strange exotic plants, where mother took me in time of flowering rhododendrons. Pink, purple, white – a cacophony of colour – such were the rhododendrons at Kew that I saw for the first time in my life. A dazzling palette of exuberant hues. It was magic.

"Rhododendrons come from the Himalayas," mother told me.

"Where is that?" I wanted to know, *"Is it far?"*

"Yes, very," she answered, *"close to China."*

"Have you been to China, mummy?"

---

[114] Winston Churchill in his *Sinews of Peace* address of 5 March 1946, at Westminster College, used the term "iron curtain" referring to the Soviet-dominated Eastern Europe.

She was silent for a moment as if she had not heard me. Then said, *"I have been as close to China and I ever want to be. And I never want to go there again."*

I didn't understand, but I was too excited to care. I squeaked with delight skipping from shrub to shrub, sticking my nose into slender cups of delicate blooms. Mother tried to restrain my enthusiasm. She steered me gently away from an elderly couple strolling along the path and smiled at them apologetically. They smiled back, tolerantly accepting my ebullience. Perhaps they saw me as one more child-survivor from the Blitz? Or was it mummy's uniform? Her smartly fitted jacket, small red labels on her sleeves with "Poland" in white letters, indicated that she was an officer in the Polish corps. Two stars and two bars on her epaulettes, a lieutenant colonel. Memories of the Battle of Britain, of Polish squadrons 302 and 303, were still fresh in people's minds. I was not a child-survivor from the London Blitz, but these people would not have known that nonetheless, I was a survivor of sorts.

Merry-go-rounds in parks were my mother's perpetual nightmare. When I spotted one, adult resistance was futile. Big grinning wooden horses went up and down, up and down and around; she protested feebly that it was unbecoming for her to sit on a wooden horse in uniform, yet she had no choice but to join me, fervently hoping all the time that no one she knew would see her. On a wooden horse or off, she looked splendidly in uniform. As she walked down the street with her long stride, she saluted passing servicemen and women, lightly touching the rim of her cap. In the morning I watched her dress, carefully knot her tie, brush the skirt, and polish her brown shoes to a shine. I had already decided to be an officer and work in a place like mother's, at the general staff headquarters in Rubens Hotel, rather than become an astronomer working in the night.

Occasionally, when mother dressed in civilian clothes, she wore a tweed suit in several shades of brown. The label on the jacket read Harvey Nichols.

"Who is Harvey Nichols?" I asked.

She laughed, *"It's a shop."* Funny, for a shop to be called like a person.

"Why do you always wear this one suit?" I wanted to know. *"It's the only one I have."*

The only shop I knew was called Woolworth's and I loved to go there with granny. It smelled of floor polish and paint, candle wax, and soap. I sniffed the air right from the door. At Woolworth's, granny bought buttons, darning thread for my socks, shoe polish, and hairpins for herself because she rolled her hair in the back of her neck and secured it with hairpins. I could always pester her into buying me one more yellow rubber ducky or tiny fluted candles for the tree, for which I had a passion, even though Christmas was still far off. Mother wanted to know why I was so fond of these candles. I had no idea. Perhaps they reminded me of the one in our cellar in Lwów during blackouts, or those in metal holders snapped onto the branches of the Christmas tree in Jarosław? Where I came from there were no fluted candles. I asked granny once if there was a Mr Woolworth, but she didn't know.

London. 1946. Polish Red Cross. Granny third from the left.

When granny went to the Red Cross, where she wrapped and addressed care packages, she also wore her uniform and at first, she took me along. There were mostly ladies working in that office, and the queen-bee was old Mrs Wierzejska, a dignified matronly person, rather daunting too. She didn't like me. When she heard how one day I jumped alone into the underground car and left granny standing on the platform at Hammersmith, she said I was bound to grow up into a little monster. That time granny got very upset and nervous, although I couldn't see why. After all, I got off at our Baron's Court station and waited for her to come by the next train, which was logical to me. But Mrs W. was not impressed and after granny told mother what she said about me, I was taken to the Red Cross less often.

Mother preferred to leave me for the day with her good friend Mrs Irene Bochwic, who started teaching me English before I went to school in the autumn. Mrs Bochwic was not Polish, she was English and a widow; her husband was Polish and she loved him very much, which was why she liked Poles. She herself knew little Polish, so at first, we communicated in sign language until I caught on. At least she didn't think I was a monster. We sang *"here we go round the mulberry bush,"* and we read nursery rhymes about little Miss Muffet who sat on a tuffet and had her breakfast of curds and whey until a big spider scared her away.[115] Or the other one about a cow that jumped over the moon. In truth English nursery rhymes made little sense to me, I preferred my Polish rhymes. Who has ever heard of having whey and for breakfast?

In September I started school at the Convent of Sacred Heart in Putney, only because it was mummy's first school in Lwów, which didn't mean that the good sisters reduced the tuition fee out of sentiment for our expatriate status. Mother took me there every day on her way to the office, so in the morning she nudged me to get ready. I soon discovered punctuality was a big thing with her. We took the train to Hammersmith, then a bus to Putney Bridge. London double-decker buses were a revelation, I could have ridden them all day long, they offered such glorious entertainment. English housewives in morning slippers and housecoats, with their hair set in rollers, swept their front steps, picked up bottles of milk, and chatted across the fence with neighbours, while a dog sat on the doorstep, or a cat brushed against its mistress's legs. From the upper deck, I saw lovely small gardens filled with blooming roses and evenly clipped hedges.

Our bus rides to school on the stretch Hammersmith to Putney Bridge often turned into story-telling time. Mother knew so many of them and each trip she chose a different one. Oscar Wilde's the happy prince, the selfish giant, and the remarkable rocket were frequent picks; or Rudyard Kipling's *"the cat that walked by himself and all the places were alike to him,"* my all-time favourite. I always liked cats. At other times mother told me about Lady Portia who defended a Venetian merchant from death. I often wondered in later years whether she liked the story so much because of Portia, the-lawyer.

Soon I discovered that mother had a handy Latin quotation for most of life's vicissitudes, preferably but not necessarily, from Cicero. One day I wrote in my exercise book: *"Sheila is a thief,"* about a girl in my class who, I was convinced, swiped my pencil. Mother read this and kicked up a storm. She was not yet

---

[115] "Little Miss Muffet" English nursery rhyme, first recorded in 1805. Wikipedia.

attuned to dealing with an eight-year-old. *"How could you? This could be slander. You could hurt this girl's reputation. Never ever, say things like this about people."* She paused, then added: *"Unless you have proof beyond any reasonable doubt."* I said I was sorry, I meant no harm, I had no idea what was this reputation, even less what was reasonable doubt, but I preferred not to ask. Then my mother-the-lawyer ended with, *"Remember, verba volant, scripta manent."* I may have been only eight years old, but after she explained the meaning, the lesson stuck with me for life and served me well on more than one occasion: Words fly, writing stays, watch what you put down on paper, kid.

At first, my grandmother picked me up from school in the afternoons. Hammersmith was a busy bus terminal and in a kiosk by the bus stop, drivers bought tea and pastries, which were not very good but colourful. In spite of granny's strenuous objections, if we were not in a hurry, I would dash off and stand in line with the drivers for one particular little cake sprinkled a virulent green. When my uncle and aunt joined us in London, it was Uncle Zbyszek who took over from granny fetching me home from school most of the time. After examining the sprinkles on the little cakes, he solemnly declared that the green stuff had to be Verdigris. *"Why do you eat this poison?"* he would ask, making a funny face; *"the English don't know how to make cakes."* Indeed, compared to the cream puffs and éclairs from the tiny pastry shop in Bytom, the bus-drivers' pastry didn't stand a chance. Uncle Zbyszek did not speak English, but he looked so distinguished that on the street elderly ladies would stop him to ask for directions. To avoid the embarrassment, he had a ready answer: *"Sorry,"* he would say, *"I am deaf."* Uncle Zbyszek and Aunt Hania finally arrived from Italy by Christmas, but even after they had landed in England, they still spent time in a transit camp in a barrack of corrugated metal sheet. In Polish, these barracks were ironically referred to as *"barrels of laughter,"* although auntie said they didn't feel much like laughing while they were there.

At school teachers drummed into us the notion that if we ever got lost anywhere, we should look right away for a bobby in his tall hat. I would have never approached a policeman in Poland or any other uniformed individual. But England was different. At first, I hated school. On some days I ran to the bathroom and vomited. I couldn't speak English, other children made fun of me because I was different, and children don't take kindly to *different*.

One boy was nastier to me than the rest. Sean, his hair the colour of a carrot, freckles all over his small pointed face, whenever he had a chance, he would pinch me, push me, try to trip me, always behind the nuns' back. Once, just as we were leaving the building, he stepped on my heel and shoved me so hard against the door-frame that I literally bounced off it. Then he giggled. There were many adults in the courtyard waiting for the children, including Uncle Zbyszek who that day came to pick me up, but that did not stop me. I had had enough. I carefully hung up my coat on the railing and like a fury ran after Sean with clenched fists. Blows rained on his shoulders and neck. Stunned by the surprise attack, he shielded his head with his arms, then rushed back into the building yelling and whining. I was faced by an irate nun, but my English was too poor to explain why I hit him, or to understand the undeserved dressing-down. Uncle Zbyszek was full of praise for my performance. After we got back home, he told mother that *"she really did a job on that Scottish kid."* Even though Sean was clearly Irish, the fact that he had red hair made him Scottish in my uncle's eyes. Next day mother felt compelled to see the mother superior and explain the incident. After my outburst of rage, redhead Sean left me alone for good, giving me a wide berth whenever our paths crossed. In time I acquired my own bosom buddy at school, an Irish girl Aileen O'Connor who became my best friend. Everybody seemed to have one. Aileen was one year older than me, she came from a working-class family. We visited each other's homes, played games, and to seal our bonds of friendship I took it upon myself to rewrite the history of Poland, marrying off Polish kings to Irish princesses in my invented stories.

At Christmas, the school put on a play and I was given the part of the angel in the Old Testament who visited Egypt before the Exodus; I walked on the narrow plank above the stage with a silver sword in hand, and when passing the houses of Israelites, with some difficulty I slid the sword back into the scabbard and made a sign of the cross instead. That small anachronism seemed to bother no one. Another time we performed the *Song of Hiawatha* and I got the part of an Indian in leather moccasins with a feather in my hair. I was quite active on the stage until a nun rebuked me for running around too much among the wigwams. Of course, she couldn't know how deeply disappointed I was since I badly wanted to play the lovely dark-haired Minnehaha, Laughing Water, with her long black plaits, who in the end died of hunger because the winter was harsh and her husband, Hiawatha, could not find any food. It was no consolation to me when my mother explained that my platinum-coloured blond hair hardly fit Minnehaha's image. These romantic stories excited my imagination and I made up for my disappointments by performing at home in front of the dresser mirror until one day I knocked down mother's beautiful crystal flower vase that was a names-day gift from the women of her company.

The school celebrated mother superior's birthday with great fanfare and – as would have been customary in Poland – on the way to school we stopped at a florist's and my mother bought beautiful chrysanthemums. While she was talking to the florist, I spied a bunch of pretty metal bells and asked the shop assistant who was wrapping the flowers to attach a few of them to the stems. They were cute, I thought. It was a wild idea that escaped my mother's notice; else she would have had them instantly removed. She paid and we left. When I handed the bouquet to the mother superior, the nun accompanying me solemnly explained that attaching bells to flowers was a Polish custom. It was just as well mother did not hear this or she would have freaked out. Mine was the only floral offering, but then I was *different*, bells notwithstanding.

After my early childhood of freedom, when we camped and decamped throughout the war, I now had to adjust to strict English school discipline. Each day we had spelling and multiplication tables drilled into us, and writing précis from the texts we read, a marvellous way of teaching kids to analyse, summarise, and condense in proper English. Geography mostly covered the British Commonwealth and history had a long list of English kings and queens, the great and the not-so-great, with quaint anecdotes thrown in for good measure. Classes of religion were taught for those who would shortly receive their first Holy Communion and that consisted mostly of Catholic catechism learned by rote. As soon as the weather turned warm, we played outdoor games led by Mother Hayward, a tall, lanky nun with dark piercing eyes. There were two competing teams at something called *flags* which involved Machiavellian strategies.

We ate lunch in the refectory and I dreaded the meals on Fridays because we had fish. Even worse, more often than not it was of a small slimy variety, probably baby eel. I never liked fish anyway, but this one I found frankly disgusting. It made me gag and I refused to eat it, which was not an acceptable behaviour in a convent school. In the end, a nun would stuff it into my mouth, although once I had vomited all over the table.

Food in England was rationed, even for children and I had my own ration book. Small square coupons for each product, everything meticulously calculated, each customer registered with a grocer; so many coupons for powdered eggs, meat, bread, Lyle's Golden Syrup in a green-and-gold tin in lieu of honey, and margarine instead of butter. Milk was sold in pint bottles and could be bought in a shop or delivered by a milkman who left it on the doorstep; it was also rationed. In spite of that, granny in some mysterious way got an extra bottle of milk once in a while. Nobody knew how she did it, she would not tell and my mother preferred not to ask, although she did shake her head with disapproval throwing granny reproachful glances. My mother received extra military rations for certain foods which she bought at a NAAFI store.[116] Once a month she brought home chocolates in a silver box with a wiggly name of *Lidka* on the cover. I found certain English foods strange, like porridge for breakfast which eventually I learnt to love, or crunchy WEETABIX which I never cared for. It appeared to me like a small bird's nests, and it was so dry, although the rest of the family enjoyed it.

My love affair with Polish literature began with Henryk Sienkiewicz's *"In the Desert and the Wilderness"* and *"The Yellow Poulaine,"* both bought in Kraków the day before we left. Mother bought more Polish books in London since the army published quite a few titles for the cadets' schools during the war and now continued to publish; they were available in Polish bookstores. I devoured everything she brought home, and she brought everything she could find that was deemed suitable for me, out of fear that I would become totally *anglicised* and would lose my Polish identity. She also bought schoolbooks that were too advanced for my age and these were set aside for future use. But no matter. Once I discovered them, I started reading them on the sly, without mother's knowledge. The texts were pulled from pre-war literature, some deeply patriotic and as such often tragic. The first one I ever read was the story of a group of 330 young men facing Siemion Budienny's cavalry charge during the 1920 Polish-Bolshevik war; the defenders' aim was to delay the approaching Bolshevik army, at any cost. The battle took place in Zadwórze, on the outskirts of Lwów. The Poles were outnumbered by the Russians; the Polish contingent was surrounded and massacred, fighting to the last man. In the end, Budienny's cavalry did retreat, but when the bodies of the defenders were recovered, they had been so savagely hacked to pieces that only some could be identified. Resistance provoked a Bolshevik response far beyond all rules of civilised military engagement and exposed the Russian *modus operandi* that would be repeated twenty years later. In the story, one of the young defenders, paraphrasing the words of King Leonidas at the Battle of Thermopylae, scribbled on a wall: *"Passer-by go and tell Poland that here we all died faithful to her*

---

[116] NAAFI – Navy, Army, and Air Force Institutes, running canteens for soldiers.

laws." I might not have quite understood it, but I was shaken enough to cry, stay awake that night and run a low-grade fever. The story marked my sense of romantic patriotism for life. On foreign soil and in spite of the awesome imperial British history in which I was immersed, my Polish self-awareness began to germinate.

The Polish community in London expanded upon the arrival from Italy of the Polish Second Corps that in February 1944 became an independent part of the British Eighth Army and took part in the Italian campaign. During the fourth and last battle for Monte Cassino in May 1944, the Poles succeeded in dislodging the Germans from their stronghold in the ancient Benedictine monastery after numerous earlier attempts by other allied units had failed. On reaching the mountain top, the Poles planted their white and red flag on the ruins. The mountain slope was covered by masses of flowering red poppies giving birth to the best known Polish military song of the Second World War: "The Red Poppies on Monte Cassino". The music was composed during the night of the battle by Alfred Schütz, a composer and actor; the lyrics were written at the same time by Feliks Konarski, (known as Ref-Ren), a poet and songwriter; both men were soldiers of the Polish II Corps, actors and members of the Polish Soldiers' Theater garrisoned at Campobasso in the shadow of the mountain. Monte Cassino was considered one of the toughest and bloodiest battles of WWII. In all, the siege had lasted five months with enormous losses by all Allied troops, but the final assault by the Poles opened the way to Rome for the Allies.

A prominent participant in the Battle of Monte Cassino was Wojtek the bear that had been picked up as an orphaned cub three years earlier by Polish soldiers on their way from Kazakhstan to Iraq. Since then, he had become the soldiers' companion, drinking beer and munching on lit cigarettes. As the troops were being deployed from Egypt to Italy, to get Wojtek onto the ship he was given a paybook, rank of private, and a serial number which made him officially a member of the Polish Second Corps. When the roster was checked by a British officer assigned to processing the Polish troops disembarking in Naples, the number of Private Wojtek was called out, but nobody appeared. Asked about his missing comrade, one of the Polish soldiers smiled, saying that Private Wojtek only spoke Polish and Farsi. He then led the Englishman to a cage and introduced him to a 400-lb bear.

Wojtek the Bear on trucks

...flags and uniforms

In the midst of raging gunfire at Monte Cassino, Wojtek did his share of work during the battle, carrying heavy crates of ammunition from the supply trucks to the large front-line guns. Without question, Wojtek turned out to be truly a "soldier bear". After the battle, Wojtek was promoted to corporal, and a badge was produced of him holding an ammunition shell, which became the official emblem of the 22nd Artillery Supply Company, and was put on trucks, flags, and uniforms. After Monte Cassino, the Corps took part in the rest of the Italian campaign: the Battle of Ancona in September 1944 and the Battle of Bologna during the final offensive in Italy in March 1945. At the end of the war, when the time came to transfer the troops to Great Britain, a complicated legal procedure to by-pass the restrictions on bringing animals into the country was created. Wojtek the Soldier Bear made his home in Scotland.

Now with such a large inflow of military personnel, it was easy to maintain a national identity in London, Polish bookstores, newspapers, coffee houses, and a theatre where well-known actors and satirists performed. A leading literary journal called *Wiadomości Literackie* (Literary News) from before the war was resuscitated by Mieczysław Grydzewski, its pre-war editor, who launched a similar weekly publication in London as simply *Wiadomości*. There was no shortage of outstanding journalists and eminent authors he could call upon, expatriates in need of a forum for their writings and of a public eager to read good literary stuff. For lack of better accommodation, Grydzewski secured a corner desk in the British Library where day in, day out, he worked on his publication. On her way home from the office, every day mummy bought the newspaper *Polish Daily and Soldier's Daily* and once a week *Wiadomości* and a satirical journal called *Pokrzywy – The Nettles*. The Roman Catholic church of Brompton Oratory became the *Polish* church where we went to Mass on Sundays.

Lt Col Zofia Hoffman...

Demobilisation was fast approaching and my mother faced the stark dilemma of an uncertain future. She had no profession, her law degree from Poland being useless in England, she had no financial security, and no contacts that would make a fresh start in a foreign land easier.

She had me to provide for, my grandmother, and for the time being my uncle and aunt. Above all she was struggling to secure a future for me. *"I can't give you anything except education. Remember, furnish your brain,"* she kept repeating. But furnishing the brain was the last thing on Ewa's mind. Ever since I discovered the game of *flags* at school, with its Byzantine strategies, loyalties and betrayals, I gave myself up to it with boundless enthusiasm, becoming totally consumed by it and abandoning my multiplication tables, spelling exercises, and the British colonies where the sun never set. My first report from school was dismal and brought on mother's explosive reaction. From that point on, every evening after work she sat down with me to oversee my homework.

… and daughter, a serious student of English history

And so, each night I recited endless lists of English kings and queens, read chapters of Dickens's *"Child's History of England"*, learnt about *"Magna Carta Libertatum"* signed by King John, and practiced spelling long words to the point where I could spell them in my sleep. I was told that in England everybody spelled, and that it was especially important to know how to spell one's surname. I was also told to forget multiplying by ten since nothing in England was multiplied by ten. So, I divided and multiplied by twelve because a shilling had twelve pence, although a pound had twenty shillings, provided it wasn't a guinea which had twenty-one shillings; but then a pound of sugar had sixteen ounces because here nobody ever heard of kilos. I travelled all over the map wherever English was spoken and memorised all the bits that made up the British Empire. And mother kept repeating her mantra, *"to be independent you must have a profession, darling, and a skill. Even if it is shoe-making, as long as you are very*

294

good at it." These shoes kept popping up like a refrain into our conversations until I began to dislike them heartily.

It was no easy matter to impose strict discipline on me. In our gypsy life during the war, discipline was a non-issue. And when it came to me, my aunt's and uncle's indulgence had known no bounds. Now in these new surroundings, I swayed between deeply rooted family traditions and the daily pressures of a foreign way of life. This brought on stresses and a longing for a mysterious something that I tried to grasp, but that every time turned into a soap bubble in my hands. There was resentment, there was rebellion. And yet, though I quickly absorbed novel ideas and manners, a new language and new values, in a puzzling way in my innermost self I retained a hard core of the culture of my parents' home town that was no more.